Dressed for
FREEDOM

WOMEN, GENDER, AND SEXUALITY
IN AMERICAN HISTORY

Editorial Advisors:
Susan K. Cahn
Wanda A. Hendricks
Deborah Gray White
Anne Firor Scott, Founding Editor Emerita

*A list of books in the series appears
at the end of this book.*

Dressed for FREEDOM

The Fashionable Politics of American Feminism

EINAV RABINOVITCH-FOX

UNIVERSITY OF
ILLINOIS PRESS
Urbana, Chicago, and Springfield

© 2021 by Einav Rabinovitch-Fox
All rights reserved
1 2 3 4 5 C P 5 4 3 2 1
♾ This book is printed on acid-free paper.

Research funded, in part, under the auspices
of the Baker-Nord Center for the Humanities,
Case Western Reserve University

Library of Congress Cataloging-in-Publication Data
Names: Rabinovitch-Fox, Einav, 1981– author.
Title: Dressed for freedom : the fashionable politics of
   American feminism / Einav Rabinovitch-Fox.
Description: Urbana : University of Illinois Press, [2021]
   | Includes
bibliographical references and index.
Identifiers: LCCN 2021010534 (print) | LCCN 2021010535
   (ebook) | ISBN 9780252044014 (cloth ; alk. paper) |
   ISBN 9780252086069 (paperback ; alk. paper) | ISBN
   9780252052941 (ebook)
Subjects: LCSH: Women's clothing—Political aspects—
   United States. | Fashion—Political aspects—United
   States. | Feminists—Clothing—United States. |
   Feminism—United States.
Classification: LCC GT605 .R33 2021 (print) | LCC GT605
   (ebook) | DDC 391/.2—dc23
LC record available at https://lccn.loc.gov/2021010534
LC ebook record available at https://lccn.loc.gov/
   2021010535

To Gal,
Adam and Alma

Contents

Acknowledgments   ix

Introduction. Beyond Bloomers: The Feminist Politics of Women's Fashion in the Twentieth Century   1

1. Fashioning the New Woman: Gibson Girls, Shirtwaist Makers, and Rainy Daisies   13
2. Styling Women's Rights: Fashion and Feminist Ideology   48
3. Dressing the Modern Girl: Flapper Styles and the Politics of Women's Freedom   81
4. Designing Power: The Fashion Industry and the Politics of Style   117
5. This Is What a Feminist Looks Like: Fashion in the Era of Women's Liberation   154

Epilogue. The Fashionable Legacies of American Feminism   189

Notes   195

Index   241

Acknowledgments

Writing a book is very much like making a garment. Although many people are involved in turning an idea or a sketch into a tangible piece of clothing, it is usually the designer who gets all the credit. Yet, one needs to take into consideration all the work that is being invested into making an outfit a success, whether by weavers who manufacture the fabric, the designer who draws the pattern, the sewers who construct the garment, as well as the consumer and the wearer who make the costume their own. Indeed, like books, clothes are the product of collaboration, inspiration, and yes, also long, tedious, and hard work.

This book began at New York University, where I was fortunate to find a stimulating community of scholars and colleagues. I am thankful for the advice and support I received from Michele Mitchell, Andrew Needham, Rebecca Karl, Molly Nolan, Daniel Walkowitz, and Jennifer Morgan, whose work was not only an inspiration but a model for rigorous history research. In particular, Linda Gordon, whose intellectual curiosity and acute advice helped me in charting my own path of inquiry and research, was an inspiration and a source of support to me and I can't thank her enough for that. I truly appreciate her encouragement to keep reworking and rethinking my arguments, as well as not to be afraid to take risks. Alice Kessler-Harris has been an incredible source of guidance and encouragement to me, both during my doctoral work and after my graduation, and I could never repay the kind-

Acknowledgments

ness and generosity she showed me. Alice's healthy skepticism pushed me to make my arguments stronger, clearer, and more nuanced, and to reformulate my jumbled ideas into eloquent prose. Her caring attention and invaluable advice have been a remarkable gift and for that I will always be grateful. I also want to thank Jennifer Scanlon, Carol Turbin, Tamar Carroll, Christine A. Kray, Barbara Winslow, Cori Field, Stacy Cordery, and Julie de Chantal for their advice and intellectual camaraderie.

I met wonderful people at NYU and beyond, and I am thankful for the moments we shared together. I am especially thankful to Cookie Woolner, Lauren Jae Gutterman, Bekah Friedman, Philippa Heatherington, Lana Povitz, Sarah Zarrow, Anelise Hanson Shrout, Beatrice Wayne, Laura J. Ping, Jonathan Michael Square, Rachel Kantrowitz, Yael Merkin, and Shayna Weiss, whose friendship and support I will always cherish. Academia is a much less lonely place because of you.

Dawn Durante believed in this manuscript from the beginning and saw its potential before I could even imagine it in a book form. I am very happy that I could have her as my editor at the University of Illinois Press, and am thankful for her continuous support, advice, and encouragement throughout the process. Dawn was a true advocate for this project, and I am sorry she could not see it come to an end, but I'm thankful for Alison Syring Bassford, who did a wonderful job in filling Dawn's big shoes. I am also grateful for my anonymous reviewers, whose thoughtful suggestions and comments helped make this book much stronger. The staff at the Press did a remarkable job in making this book a reality, and I especially want to thank Tad Ringo, Jennifer Fisher, and Deborah Oliver for all their work.

I was lucky to become the inaugural Wade Postdoctoral Fellow at the Western Reserve Historical Society, where I gained invaluable experience in museum work and access to a wonderful costume collection. Yet, the best thing was the chance to meet the fabulous Holly Witchey, Sean Martin, Margaret Burzynski-Bays, Dannielle Peck, and Patty Edmondson. I was even luckier when I joined the history department at Case Western Reserve University. There isn't really a better place I could have landed in. Kenneth Ledford has been a champion of my work and a wonderful supporter of my career, and I thank him for all that he has done for me in the department and beyond. I am also thankful for the friendship and intellectual community I found with Gillian Weiss, John Broich, Ananya Dasgupta, John Flores, Ted Steinberg, Jay Geller, David Hammack, Miriam Levin, Aviva Rothman, Daniel Cohen, Maddalena Rumor, and Noel Voltz. John Grabowski and Jonathan Sadowsky were very kind to read earlier versions of some of the chapters, and I am very

Acknowledgments

grateful for their comments and friendship during my time at the department. One of the best things about this department is Renee Sentilles. Renée has been an incredible supporter of this project, reading multiple versions of multiple chapters. I am thankful for her smart advice and friendship, as well as her kindness and generosity. Peter Shulman, my third-floor comrade from across the hall, has been a tremendous help in turning the manuscript into a book. I am grateful for his advice, insights, conversations, and friendship. This book is far better written because of him. I also benefited from my students in the various reiterations of my "Fashion and Power" course, who helped me rethink some of the concepts and ideas that appear in this book.

I have benefited from the support of wonderful women and mentors I found through the Coordinating Council for Women in History (CCWH) and the Berks. Thanks to Sandra Dawson, Ilaria Scaglia, Jacqueline-Bethel Mougoué, Rikki Bettinger, Kathy Feeley, Eileen Boris, Deirdre Cooper Owens, Liz Everton, Stephanie Richmond, and Jennie Brier for your friendship, wisdom, and encouragement. All of you showed me that the creation of a feminist community and network is not only possible but indispensable.

I was privileged to receive financial support for my research from various institutions and archives. I especially want to thank the Baker Nord Center of the Humanities at Case Western Reserve University, which provided crucial financial aid for this project at various stages. The Schlesinger Library at Harvard University, the Sophia Smith Collection at Smith College, the Hartman Center at Duke University, and Winterthur Library and Museum all offered generous grants that furthered my research. I also benefited from the generosity and knowledge of archivists, librarians, and staff. In particular I want to thank Emily Guthrie from Winterthur, Tal Nadan from the New York Public Library, Kenneth Chandler from the National Archives for Black Women's History, and Sara Hume from the Kent State University Museum for all their help. Thanks also to Bev Grant and the Dan Wynn Archive with their assistance in securing images for this book.

Parts of chapter 2 appeared earlier in print in "[Re]fashioning the New Woman: Women's Dress, the Oriental Style, and the Construction of American Feminist Imagery in the 1910s," *Journal of Women's History* 27, no. 2 (Summer 2015): 14–36, and in "Dressing Up for a Campaign: Hillary Clinton, Suffragists, and the Politics of Fashion," in *Nasty Women and Bad Hombres: Gender and Race in the 2016 US Presidential Election*, ed. Christine A. Kray, Tamar Carroll, and Hinda Mandell (Rochester, NY: University of Rochester Press, 2018).

Writing a book is never easy, but it is even harder when writing in something other than your native language. I want to thank friends and family who agreed over the years to read drafts, help with wording, sentence structure, and style. Laura Portwood-Stacer provided significant help in conceptualizing and reorganizing the chapters and argument that made the book much stronger.

I am grateful for family and friends who supported me and sustained me throughout the years: Julia Kraut, Tali and Sagi Schaefer, Galit Shaham, Edie Wolf, Ilana Grossman and Avi Rosenbluth, Erez and Yael Maggor, Dana Lev, Shanie Korabelnik and Naftali Cohen, Paul and Deborah Hill, and Moran Yassour and Liron Shani. All provide good conversation, good meals, and good laughs when I needed them the most. My parents, Chaia and Yuval Rabinovitch, were always there for me when I chased my dreams, even if that meant having an ocean between us. I am so grateful for everything they did and continue to do for me.

Adam and Alma do not know a life without this book, and I really admire their patience and understanding every time I gave it much more attention and time than I gave to them. I'm grateful that they were willing to "share" their mom with what oftentimes felt like a particularly needy third child, and I hope that they will forgive all the times I missed soccer practices, playdates, or just hanging out with them, and be proud of their mom. Lastly, this book could not have happened without the utmost support and encouragement of Gal Fox. I can't imagine a better and loving person to share my life with, and I am thankful for every day we spend together. Learning about fashion and women's history more than he ever wished for, Gal was a true partner in this endeavor and continues to be my rock and inspiration. You and the kids keep reminding me what are the most important things in life and I am so grateful I can call you my family. This book belongs to you as much as it is to me.

Dressed for
FREEDOM

INTRODUCTION

Beyond Bloomers

The Feminist Politics of Women's Fashion in the Twentieth Century

Feminism has a long and complex relationship with fashion. Perhaps the most known example, and the one that marked the beginning of this fraught relationship occurred in 1851, when the fashion choices of Amelia Bloomer, Elizabeth Smith Miller, and Elizabeth Cady Stanton became a public sensation. At the center of the controversy was their outfit: short skirt reaching mid-calf worn over baggy pants known as Turkish trousers (figure 0.1). "The new costume appeals... to our common sense," Bloomer argued in her reform journal the *Lily*, justifying the choice to wear a "rational dress" by pointing to its health and comfort benefits.[1] Yet, as avid supporters of women's rights who believed that women's bodies should be as free as their minds, the three women also employed the dress to promote their political agenda. "The object of those who donned the new attire was primarily health and freedom," Stanton recalled years later, alluding to the political purpose behind the decision to adopt the costume. "It was supposed to be an inherent element in the demand for political equality."[2] For Stanton and her fellow woman's rights advocates, fashion and dress were intrinsically enmeshed with questions of power and gender expectations, and thus change in dress was a critical component of their broader demand for gender and economic equality.[3] They cleverly used the gendered association of dress and appearance with women to claim access to the public sphere, applying the costume as a rhetorical tool.[4]

Introduction

FIGURE 0.1: Amelia Bloomer wears her own design. While the bloomer began as a dress reform initiative, the outfit quickly became a marker of feminists in popular discourse. (*Lily*, September 1851)

However, since the outfit included visible trousers that revealed women's calves and ankles, most commentators of the day depicted it as an attack on male status and a threat to gender hierarchies. Both the local and the national press derided the women who wore it as ugly, masculine, and dangerous.[5] "No sooner did a few brave conscientious women adopt the bifurcated costume, an imitation in part of the Turkish style," Stanton observed, "than the press at once turned its guns on 'The Bloomer' and the same fathers, husbands, and brothers, with streaming eyes and pathetic tones, conjured the women of their households to cling to the prevailing fashions."[6] Identifying the new style with its adopters, naming it the Bloomer Costume after Amelia Bloomer, the press also associated it with the feminist ideas its wearers promoted, making their appearance synonymous with their politics.[7]

Although at the time only few hundred women were known to adopt the bloomer as the expression of their political views, the costume and the debate it ignited profoundly shaped both public views and scholarly understandings of feminism for generations to come. Those who adopted the bloomer positioned themselves against the prevalent fashions of long and full skirts, constructing the outfit as an oppositional dress and a form of political resistance. As a result, contemporaries also framed the relationship between feminism and fashion as oppositional, casting all feminists as antifashionable and hostile to adornment. Indeed, the image of the unfashionable, masculine-looking, dressed-in-bloomers woman remained a potent visual trope of feminists in popular culture well into the twentieth century.[8] However, as this book reveals, the bloomer was not the only fashion image that defined women's relationship with feminism. By the late nineteenth century, mass consumer culture and the ready-made industry brought with them new fashion-related images that expanded the visual vocabulary of feminism in the popular media. The images of the Gibson Girl, the suffragist, the flapper, the Hollywood star, and even the radical feminist of the 1970s offered women the opportunity to participate in the construction of fashionable identities that popularize ideas of freedom, independence, and equality, contriving a more positive relationship of feminism with fashion.

Dressed for Freedom examines the multiple ways that women engaged with fashion during the long twentieth century, in order to challenge the enduring myth that a commitment to women's freedom and rights was incompatible with adornment practices and adherence to fashion. It traces the sartorial practices of both well-known activists and ordinary women from various backgrounds and experiences: working class and middle class, Black and White, urban and suburban, those who defined themselves as feminists and those who did not. Unlike the 1850s bloomer adopters, these women did not reject mainstream fashions for their objectifying and oppressive elements, but they carved spaces of freedom and power within the boundaries of consumerism and conventional feminine appearance. Their goal was not just to seek clothes that would allow greater comfort and freedom of movement. They wanted to make these styles popular and mainstream—in other words, fashionable. In their efforts, these women reshaped the popular image of "the feminist," and in turn also of feminism, claiming fashion as a realm of freedom, pleasure, and protest.

Challenging the myth of the antifashionable feminist opens avenues to ask new questions about the role of fashion in feminist politics. How did an emphasis on fashionability further feminist goals? What sort of liberation was possible via fashion? What were the possibilities and limitations that fashionability provided? How should we assess the importance of this consumerist feminist ideology to the popularization of feminism in mainstream culture? By exploring these questions, I assert that fashion served as a critical site of shaping public attitudes toward feminism. As women employed mainstream styles to make claims over their bodies, femininity, and social roles, they demonstrated that being fashionable did not oppose feminism or hinder their efforts to promote gender equality and social justice. To the contrary, fashion became a useful cultural arena for expressing and promoting feminist ideas, just like the workplace, the courthouse, and the voting booth. Especially for Black women, the ability to claim "fashionability" was sometimes more important than the freedom of movement clothing styles provided their bodies. These women appropriated fashion—and more importantly fashionability—as a tool to challenge and expand meanings of freedom and equality.

In addition, the focus on women's fashionable practices enables us to revise our understanding of feminism, shifting the attention to its cultural manifestations. Indeed, as fashion scholars Cheryl Buckley and Hilary Fawcett argue, the material and visual nature of fashion adds "new ways of seeing" feminist politics.[9] Scholars of feminism have long neglected popular and consumer culture as a realm of feminist activity, pointing to the shortcomings of consumer culture to deliver on promises of freedom or to significantly advance women's rights. Concerning fashion as an aspect of consumer culture, scholars have until recently viewed it as either a frivolous form of consumption meant to depoliticize and coopt radicalism, or worse yet, as a means of oppression.[10] However, as this book demonstrates, if fashion can be a mechanism of social control and repression, it also offers a means of transgression and empowerment. Consumer culture, and fashion in particular, proved to be fertile ground to challenge and redefine gender notions of femininity and to promote feminist agendas. By using their position as makers, consumers, and wearers of fashion to negotiate positions of agency and influence, women harnessed fashion into a dynamic cultural language and a political strategy to claim freedom. They found pleasure in fashion and pride in beauty, reminding us that these aspects were not foreign to the feminist struggle but an important part of it. Although the pursuit of fashionability might have precluded some of the radical gendered critique that feminists made through clothing, it also allowed for feminist ideas to thrive within the market and to be adopted by women who did not necessarily identify with or join the movement.

Women's clothes have undergone major transformations between 1890 to 1980, the period that this book examines. These transformations include moving from custom or homemade clothing to mass-produced ready-made ones; from complicated constructions tailored to a specific body to simple silhouettes manufactured according to standardized sizes; from formal wear designated to specific settings and occasions to a more casual, multipurpose wear; and from an emphasis on form to an emphasis on functionality. These developments made fashion—and fashionability—increasingly accessible to multiple groups, functioning as the "primary language in which the majority of women [could] converse in a variety of ways."[11] Some of these fashion changes corresponded with feminist initiatives of shortening skirts, discarding corsets, reducing the weight of clothes, and adopting both affordable and durable clothing that allow for comfort and movement. Yet, it would be impossible to define a single or coherent style that characterized these developments.

Indeed, my goal is not to trace the formation of a feminist fashion subculture or to define a feminist style, radical or otherwise.[12] Instead, my focus is on how fashion became a vehicle for the mainstreaming of feminism in public discourse. I argue that the feminist significance of clothes was not inherent to the designs themselves, and oftentimes there was not much stylistic difference between proponents of women's freedom and their opponents. What made fashion instrumental to the redefinition of femininity and gender roles was the meanings that women gave their clothes and the ways they utilized them to convey their feminist messages. And while some of the clothes I examine in this book started as alternative styles, women's success in turning them into common popular fashion was what made them politically relevant. The women who appear in this book did not seek to oppose the fashion world, but to turn it into a realm of everyday feminist practice. As such, the fashions they adopted and adapted did not challenge the mainstream, but more often were part of it.

As a medium that is both material and symbolic, public and private, individual and conformist, fashion has been central to the shaping of social ideas and the expression of individual identities. Particularly in the context of social movements, scholars demonstrate how fashion is an important tool of political and cultural expression. For women in particular, the clothed body became a vehicle for challenging ideas of femininity and sexuality, for asserting agency and access to power, and for conveying political messages.[13] Precisely because of the close association of clothing and adornment with the feminine in the modern period, fashion offered women a useful avenue to negotiate new identities and roles for themselves.[14] For some, fashion was the material expression of their feminist ideology and inseparable from their activism. But for many others, who did not belong to feminist organizations or necessarily claim the label, fashion offered a route to engage with feminism as a cultural style, not as a political movement.

I use deliberately the term "fashion" rather than "clothing" or "dress," to signify more than just the construction of fabrics into clothes. "Fashion" refers to a set of practices—sewing, designing, manufacturing, consuming, selling, and wearing—that have specific temporal, social, and political contexts. As Roland Barthes has noted in *The Fashion System*, fashion goes beyond the mere appearance of clothing and creates intricate systems of signs and meanings that reproduce hierarchies of value and power.[15] Yet, fashion not only reproduces and reflects meaning. It is also a constitutive force of social and cultural attitudes, and as such is a useful heuristic tool to understand these attitudes.[16] "Fashion" does not mean "style," either, although these terms overlap. A style of clothing refers to a more constant, unchangeable quality of dress, while fashion connotes a more fluid and transient characteristics defined by change. A style can fall in or out of fashion, or be fashionable in a certain space and time, and for certain people, yet not others.[17] Fashion, on the other hand, alludes to the public acceptance of certain styles, and thus is not only an expression of individual identity but is tangled in a broad social context.[18]

This book considers both the symbolic aspects of fashion, seeing it as a form of communication, and the material aspects of clothing, examining how they have shaped women's experience in the public sphere. The weight of clothes, the tightness of the corset, the length of the skirt, as well as the sensation of clothes over one's body, were all major factors in determining women's physical movement in public spaces and the activities they could perform. In the 1890s, the relatively short hemline of the "rainy-day costume" enabled women to evade the health hazards of walking in long trailing skirts on wet and dirty city streets. The narrow circumference of dresses and the decrease in the number of undergarments in the 1910s made suffrage parades a much more feasible and tolerable experience. The knee-length hemline of the flapper skirt freed her legs for dancing and driving, while sportswear styles in the 1930s and 1940s offered women practical sartorial solutions for work and home. The popularization of pants for women in the 1960s and 1970s provided comfortable yet modest attire for activities beyond leisure.

These material experiences enabled women to articulate claims of freedom and modernity, turning fashion into a political assertion of rights. By pointing to the ways in which these women not only imagined themselves as liberated, but also experienced these freedoms, I reveal how feminism was both an ideology and an everyday practice manifested through clothes.

Privileging culture and fashion as sites of feminist practices also contributes to scholarship that challenges the "waves" metaphor, which has shaped histories of feminism in the United States since the late 1960s.[19] This conceptual framework explains the development of feminism as a series of surges and ebbs in activity, similar to oceanic waves. The "first wave" refers to the period of women's suffrage and social reform activism that began in 1848 and reached its culmination with the ratification of the Nineteenth Amendment in 1920.[20] Following this swell of feminist activity, the post-suffrage years and the mid-twentieth century mark a period of decline until the resurgence of the "second wave" of the movement in the 1960s.[21] In recent years, however, scholars have been trying to find alternatives to this model, arguing it presents a narrow interpretation that obscures the complexities and wide range of issues as well as activists involved.[22] Additionally, new work has helped in revising the waves periodization by emphasizing the continuities in feminist activism during the doldrums, and the importance of non-White or nonelite activists. These studies expand our understanding of feminism as a movement and ideology, by pointing to the broad range of actors, locations, agendas, and techniques.[23] Yet, despite these important contributions, scholars' main focus is on political and social activism, thus overlooking the importance of culture as a site where women sought to advance their freedom or fight for gender equality. This book shifts attention to the consumer market and its role in diffusing feminist ideas, and thus historicizes the connection between feminism and popular culture.

Moving beyond formal organizations and politics to examine fashion, I highlight the continuities behind women's sartorial practices to express feminist ideas and identities. Indeed, the use of clothes as a form of political expression, as well as debates over the role of fashion in feminist politics, were not isolated episodes of the mid-nineteenth or the late twentieth centuries.[24] Rather, fashion was an ongoing tenet of feminism that transcended a clear division into discrete waves. Feminists throughout the period this book examines grappled with questions of whether and how fashion and women's rights can be compatible, and whether and how a feminist can embrace femininity without losing her political edge. Others have questioned the relationship between individual choice and the dictates of the market, asking what the possibilities and limits are that consumer culture and the fashion industry offered them. Yet these questions were not only on the mind of feminists but also resonated in public discourse, shaping understandings of feminism throughout the long twentieth century. By examining the fashionable politics of the Rainy Day Club of the 1890s, early twentieth-century suffragists, the modernist avant-garde, flappers, mid-twentieth-century fashion designers, and women's liberationists, I argue that fashion was more pivotal to the development of feminism than previously recognized. These women used clothes and appearance as an everyday feminist practice, adding an important cultural facet to feminism and its influence in public discourse.

Whereas critics oftentimes position women's fascination with fashion as a testament to their submissive character, women were not gullible creatures who followed designers' decrees without protest.[25] They understood the power of clothes and cleverly used fashion as a political tool. When these women fashioned their own identities and appropriated popular images and styles, they did so on their own terms. As this book delineates, women fought to keep their skirts short and their outfits comfortable even when the fashion industry pushed for styles at odds with those characteristics. However, the intersections between gender, race, and class influenced the extent to which one could participate in the fashion world or in shaping one's image. The accessibility of fashion to an increasingly diverse number of people provided an arena in which women could shape their identity as modern, liberated, and independent. But consumer culture also brought new requirements and limits that set the boundaries of these freedoms, and at times even narrowed them.

Women had to navigate between the possibilities that the new consumer culture enabled them and the limits that their class or race posed on their ability to partake in such culture. They had to determine how to engage with the liberating messages clothes conveyed and how much to embrace them. Some used fashion as a strategy to gain public support for feminist ideas, or to promote their political agendas, while others donned these fashions because they made them feel good or because they suited their active lifestyles. Certainly, not every woman who wore a shirtwaist, a short skirt, or slacks was a feminist.[26] And not all efforts to promote comfortable fashions were translated into tangible political achievements. Yet, when they adopted and adapted mainstream styles to assert their independence, freedom, and rights, the women this book examines helped to popularize the feminist ideas that these clothes carried. My goal, however, is not to claim these women as feminists but to understand how feminist ideas circulated beyond formal politics. In other words, I explore how the mainstreaming of certain styles enabled

Introduction

feminism to become fashionable as an idea. In examining the mainstreaming of feminism through fashion, I expand the spaces of feminism, arguing that as an ideology it maintained its relevancy and power to influence women's lives even during ebbs in activism.

Fashion is a form of nonverbal communication, yet accessing the message that clothes convey is not always easy. One does not usually write a manifesto to justify their fashion choices. And for many, especially those excluded from positions of influence, clothing often contains conflicted meanings which cannot always be resisted or be fully transformed. Moreover, when fashion is used to convey cultural values and attitudes, the wearer is not the only one formulating the message. The designer, the manufacturer of the garment, as well as the audience who decipher it, all take part in the process, making the message more complicated to understand.[27] In order to access how women understood their appearance and the role of clothes in shaping their experiences, I look at the discourses by and about women's fashion as they appeared in magazines, as well as in private and public writings of self-identified feminists. I also examine the visual and material evidence found in illustrations, sewing patterns, and actual dresses found in museum collections.

Although these sources undoubtedly present class and racial biases, I have tried to counter those by expanding my archival base beyond mainstream women's and fashion magazines and beyond the realm of high fashion. I trace the fashionable practices of well-known figures and self-identified feminists such as Clara Lemlich, Charlotte Perkins Gilman, Inez Milholland, Mary Church Terrell, Claire McCardell, Katherine Hepburn, Marlene Dietrich, Angela Davis, and Gloria Steinem. I also pay attention to lesser-known figures and anonymous women who might not have participated formally in feminist organizations, but who nevertheless used fashion to define and redefine notions of femininity, beauty, and gender roles. By integrating these textual, visual, and material sources, this book offers a unique lens into understanding the role of fashion in these women's lives and its relationship to feminism.

The chapters in *Dressed for Freedom*, despite being organized chronologically from the 1890s to the 1970s, do not have a strict periodical framing and at times overlap. Each chapter focuses on a specific fashionable moment that highlights a different aspect of how women used fashion to express their gender, racial, and class identities, and to promote feminist ideas. Chapter 1 analyses the image of the New Woman at the turn of the twentieth century and its feminist meanings by looking at the outfits that became most identified with her: the shirtwaist and the bicycle skirt. These fashion styles were crucial in shaping the meanings of the New Woman, forging a connection between the burgeoning mass consumer culture and media, and new understandings and experiences of womanhood. Specifically, I examine how the availability of the ready-made shirtwaist enabled college students, White immigrant garment workers, and middle-class African American women to appropriate its fashionability as a symbol of freedom and independence, and to broaden the meanings of New Woman and its most popular incarnation during that period: the Gibson Girl. In addition, the chapter analyzes the influence of the bicycle on women's fashions, emphasizing middle-class women's use of these styles to negotiate new political presence in the public sphere. This part of the chapter focuses on the members of the Rainy Day Club and its efforts in popularizing shorter bicycle skirts for everyday wear. As these women began to associate ideas of feminine beauty and utility with ideas of freedom, they moved away from the Victorian reasoning of the nineteenth-century dress reform movement to cultivate a modern sensitivity to fashion.

Chapter 2 turns the attention to self-identified feminists in order to examine how they developed both practical and theoretical approaches to fashion that made it instrumental to feminist ideology in the early twentieth century. I look specifically at suffragists and Greenwich Village bohemians to show how they used their appearance as a political means to popularize the suffrage cause and to express feminist identities. These activists shifted the issue of fashion and fashionability to the center of their concerns, yet they engaged with fashion in slightly different ways. Suffragists generally used fashion as a visual political strategy to promote women's rights by challenging earlier derogatory stereotypes of feminists in the media. Greenwich Village bohemians, many of them also active in the suffrage movement, expanded this approach and used fashion in more subversive ways to imagine new identities for the New Woman that went beyond voting rights. As they presented themselves as stylish, fashionable, modern women, both suffragists and bohemian feminists forged a more positive relationship with fashion that in turn popularized the image of "the feminist" in the public eye.

By the 1920s, the figure of the flapper—with her short, light dresses and simple silhouettes—symbolized the political freedoms women were beginning to claim and the new moral values they promoted. Chapter 3 explores the construction of the flapper image, and how her styles became the main arena where contemporaries articulated and debated women's freedom and modernity in the post-suffrage era. It discusses how the rise of the American ready-made industry enabled women across classes, races, and geographic regions to further their claims for independence, self-fulfillment, and sexual expression in the public sphere. I give particular attention to the experiences of Black flappers and how their access to fashion and leisure culture allowed them to articulate claims for gender and racial equality vis-à-vis both Blacks and Whites. The chapter focuses on the debates over skirt hemlines, and how women framed their claims for sticking to shorter lengths in political terms. In their persistence to maintain the popularity of the short skirt and the freedoms it allowed them, these women formed a model of feminist activism outside of formal political movements and feminist organizations, which offered an opportunity to define feminism in new ways.

The popularization of the flapper styles contributed to the mainstreaming of feminism in the popular media. The fashion world not only opened new avenues for self-expression, it also offered social and economic mobility. During the interwar period, the fashion industry provided women with more possibilities to gain positions of power and influence within the fashion field, turning the professional career woman into a new role model of modern femininity. Chapter 4 focuses on female fashion designers, Black and White, and their professional organizations to show how through their designs they consolidated the association of modern femininity with feminism in popular imagination. These designers promoted sportswear as the new American Look that imagined the modern fashion consumer as economically independent, physically mobile woman seeking both feminine style and comfort. The chapter analyzes the formation of professional fashion networks as facilitators of women's empowerment, as well as the role of Hollywood stars such as Katherine Hepburn and Marlene Dietrich in popularizing sportswear. By pointing to the ways in which the commercial success of sportswear made feminist ideas fashionable, it highlights how feminism operated in the interwar period beyond formal politics, offering alternative routes through which women could claim a voice and influence. The popularity of sportswear continued well into the 1950s, allowing women to continue showing their support to feminism even in periods of social backlash. The chapter delineates how, with the design language that female designers developed in the 1930s and 1940s, women articulated their commitment to ideas of freedom and independence and resisted attempt to alter their styles after World War II.

The rise of the feminist movement in the late 1960s pushed again the issue of fashion to the forefront of the feminist struggle. Women's liberationists used fashion and beauty culture as a political means of resistance and self-expression, employing it to challenge traditional gender roles and expectations. Whether by those who sought to reject beauty culture, or by those who used it to convey their support to the movement, fashion styles became central to feminist politics in the 1960s and 1970s. Chapter 5 examines the debates among feminists over the role of fashion in the movement and in promoting feminist causes, illustrating how fashion served as a site to define the meaning of feminism and womanhood in this period. It complicates the popular narrative that all feminists were angry, antifashion, "mannish" lesbians, and delineates the different approaches among feminists to practices of adornment and beauty. Some chose to resist mainstream trends, while others adapted them to suit a message of power. Yet, in their efforts, feminists, as well as women who supported them, turned fashion into an important facet of how the "personal is political." Examining the influence of feminist icons on popular styles, as well as feminist critiques on the commercialization of women's bodies, the chapter explores the possibilities and limits that fashion and consumer culture offered feminism in the period of women's liberation.

Together, these chapters reclaim fashion as a realm of pleasure, power, and feminist consciousness. Without denying or overlooking the problematic nature of fashion and its ability to oppress and curb resistance, the book explores how women negotiated the tensions that arose from the commercialization and standardization of fashion trends to convey messages of liberation. It demonstrates the political importance of fashion and consumer culture as a site of feminist practice, arguing that, rather than serving as a hindrance to women's political engagement, fashion became a useful strategy to convey political messages and to challenge gender, race, and class notions of femininity. As it foregrounds the politics of women's fashion as integral to feminism in the twentieth century, this book revisits this complex relationship, providing us with insights not only about the past but also about the present and the future. In a period when fashion again is being rethought and repurposed for advancing feminist causes, looking at the long trajectory of the fashionable legacies of feminism can offer a framework for contemporary politics.

While fashion, no matter how empowering it might be, could never replace the impact of well-organized activism, the space it opened for women to imagine and experience their liberation should not be underestimated. Twentieth-century women's use of fashion to advance their rights, to claim their freedom, and to assert their public presence turned feminism into more than a political, social movement—it was an everyday practice in which every woman could participate in fashioning herself.

CHAPTER ONE

Fashioning the New Woman

Gibson Girls, Shirtwaist Makers, and Rainy Daisies

During the last decade of the nineteenth century, a new image of feminine beauty emerged from the pages of popular magazines such as *Collier's Weekly*, *Life*, and *Ladies' Home Journal*. Typified by the work of the illustrator Charles Dana Gibson, the young American girl was depicted as a young, White, tall, single woman, dressed in a shirtwaist and a bell-shaped skirt, with a large bosom and narrow, corseted waist. While it would take Gibson a few years to refine this image, by the mid-1890s the Gibson Girl, as the image came to be known, would become so popular that her influence exceeded the pages of magazines, and she became a cultural and a fashionable icon (figure 1.1).[1] Embodying ideas of mobility, freedom, and modernity, the Gibson Girl and her fashions symbolized the changes in women's social roles and public presence in this period. According to the feminist Charlotte Perkins Gilman, the Gibson Girl was the perfect realization of a "New Woman"—"a noble type" that represented women's progress. "Not only [does she] look differently, [she] behave[s] differently," Gilman argued in her 1898 book, *Women and Economics*. She was full of praise for this New Woman: "The false sentimentality, the false delicacy, the false modesty, the utter falseness of elaborate compliment and servile gallantry which went with the other falsehoods,—all these are disappearing. Women are growing honester [sic], braver, stronger, more healthful and skillful and able and free, more human in all ways."[2]

CHAPTER ONE

FIGURE 1.1: Embodying values of youth, movement, and modernity, the image of the Gibson Girl became associated with the period's social and cultural changes, especially women's growing opportunities in work, education, and consumer culture. (Charles Dana Gibson, "School Days," *Scribner's Magazine*, November 1899)

The New Woman emerged from the social and cultural changes in turn-of-the-century United States, especially White middle-class women's growing opportunities for work, education, and engagement with consumer culture. Representing a generation of women who came of age between 1890 and 1920, she became associated with the political agitation of women in this period, and her image was often conflated with those of the suffragist or the feminist.[3] As both an image and a cultural phenomenon, the New Woman offered a way not only to understand women's new visibility and presence in the public sphere, but also to define modern American identity in a period of unsettling change.[4] In her behavior and looks, she challenged gender norms and structures while projecting a distinctly modern appearance. The New Woman was often contrasted with the passive, frail, pale, delicate image of the Victorian "True Woman," who was usually depicted dressed in wide skirts, swathed in draperies and petticoats. Unlike the True Woman, who embodied an essential, submissive, and domestic concept of femininity, the New Woman represented a contemporary, modern understanding, one that emphasized youth, visibility, and mobility, as well as a demand for greater freedom and independence.[5]

This chapter examines how the Gibson Girl and her fashions became a tangible means through which women could imagine and define their identities as New Women. Although the Gibson Girl was a fictional figure, appearing as a black-and-white illustration, the commercialization and popularity of her fashions across class and racial lines enabled different women to shape her image and expand its liberating meaning. White college students used the Gibson Girl imagery to convey their political support for suffrage while maintaining their standing as respectable bachelorettes. African American women also adopted and adapted the Gibson Girl fashions, capitalizing on the image's respectability to demand access to privileges of White ladyhood. Working-class immigrants, who were both producers and consumers of the shirtwaist that became associated with the Gibson Girl, harnessed it as part of their identities as workers and Americans who deserve their rights. Other middle-class business professionals employed the Gibson Girl's association with athleticism, and the bicycle in particular, to advance ideas regarding women's dress, promoting comfortable clothing for everyday wear. Together, these women not only created a "new look" for the New Woman but also used fashion to shape her meanings and political message, connecting the rise of mass consumer culture and media to new ideas and experiences of freedom for women.

Indeed, fashion played a crucial role in shaping the meaning of the New Woman. The period's popular fashions that became the Gibson Girl's trademark were also the ones that turned her into an archetype of the New Woman. But more than that, they, and the activities they enabled, were what made her modern. The great novelty of the Gibson Girl outfit was in the introduction of the "ensemble": a separate shirtwaist and gored bell-shaped skirt that were mass-produced in standardized sizes. The versatility of the ensemble separates enabled women to construct different outfits by using one skirt and several shirtwaists or vice versa, all tailored to the wearer's taste and financial resources. It also brought changes to women's attitudes toward their wardrobes, allowing them to dress in one functional outfit throughout the day and still maintain respectability.[6] Perhaps more importantly, the availability of the ensemble separates also contributed to a new conception of the female body, which was much more mobile. With the increasing participation of women in sports and leisure, the ensemble—now modeled as a combination of a shirtwaist and a relatively short bicycle skirt—constructed not only a new experience but also a modern understanding of womanhood.

The functionality of the ensemble and its suitability to multiple occasions, contributed to the blurring of class distinctions, serving as a democratizing force. As women across society adopted the ensemble and capitalized on its fashionability, they established the American New Woman as a well-dressed "average woman," an image that was available to multiple groups of women to claim.[7] By focusing on the influence of the shirtwaist and the short bicycle skirt, this chapter analyzes how these ensemble items became crucial to the understanding of modern femininity at the turn of the twentieth century. Through these clothes, New Women advanced their ideas of freedom and mobility, adopting and adapting the styles according to their own resources and the particular goals they wanted to pursue. In their appropriation of the Gibson Girl style, New Women thus took an active role in redefining their place in society, turning fashion into an empowering force and a political means.

However, while the Gibson Girl and her appearance signaled a shift from previous fashions, the shirtwaist and the bicycle skirt did not represent a revolution in styles so much as an evolution. The ensemble outfit did not eliminate corseting or challenge gender conventions in overt ways. Even when these clothing were endowed with political meanings or stood for women's independence of mind and their demands for freedom, the commercialization and popularity of these fashions also shaped the boundaries of their feminist promise. Unlike the previous generation of woman's rights advocates who experimented with alternatives to the mainstream, New Women at the turn of the twentieth century sought to gain incremental advancement within the current fashion system. Their goal was to create an image that would be both liberating and fashionable, and as such they sought to harness the popular trends, not to challenge them.

In fact, the New Woman's fashions became symbolic of the transitional moment women experienced at the turn of the twentieth century. Much was clearly changing. As women entered higher education and the labor force, they increasingly demanded taking an equal part in the political sphere. They adopted new behaviors and gender norms that increased their physical movement and visibility in public. Yet women still faced significant obstacles in breaking into traditionally male-dominated professions, in balancing a marriage with a career, and in claiming political and social equality. The New Woman, with her shirtwaist and bicycle skirt, both epitomized these changes and alluded to the limitations, simultaneously sanctioning and undermining women's new social and cultural status. Her fashionableness, facilitated by the popularity of the Gibson Girl, enabled a push for greater freedoms, but it also stirred the New Woman from radicalism in favor of a more commercialized approach. Fashion thus not only facilitated women's physical movement in this period, or reflected the new roles they claimed for themselves. It also shaped the liberating meanings of the New Woman and the possibilities she had.

The Gibson Girl as a Fashionable New Woman

When she first appeared in the pages of the *Century* in 1890, it was not apparent that the Gibson Girl would become the face of an entire generation.[8] Other illustrators such as Harrison Fisher, Howard Chandler Christy, and Coles Phillips also created versions of the "American Girl." Yet, by 1900, the Gibson Girl surpassed its competitors in popularity, becoming one of the most marketed images of the time, appearing in advertising and on a myriad of consumer products, including wallpaper, silverware, and furniture.[9] In addition, magazines and pattern companies advertised "Gibson skirts" and "Gibson waists," as well as fashion accessories such as hats, ties, and collars inspired by the Gibson Girl.[10]

Gibson's success in turning his Girl into an archetype of New Womanhood rested on his ability to use her image to reflect the values of the period, and at the same time to capture the changes in them. As a product of the printed media, which catered to middle-class audience, the Gibson Girl was the epitome of the White middle-class woman.[11] She often appeared outdoors, engaged in an athletic or leisure activity such as golf or cycling, or depicted in social activities such as dances and dinner parties, all of which suggested her bourgeois origins. The Gibson Girl was never portrayed performing any kind of labor, and Gibson himself presented her not as a working-class factory girl, but rather as a lady of leisure or as a middle-class college debutante.[12]

Indeed, Gibson constructed the Gibson Girl according to his understanding of what the ideal American woman at the turn of the twentieth century should look like. He used her image to demarcate the boundaries of the social freedoms that women were beginning to enjoy in the late nineteenth century, framing them in nonthreatening commercial terms. In his quick pen-stroke style, the "type" that the Gibson Girl embodied was one that was definitely modern, but not too radical. On the one hand, she represented a confident and assertive type of woman who was a potential challenge to existing sexual hierarchies and gender roles. Gibson usually depicted her in more modern form of relationships with men—often unchaperoned and in fairly equal settings—and almost always as single, not as a married woman or a mother.[13] By presenting the Gibson Girl as flirtatious while never portraying the fulfillment of her courting endeavors, Gibson alluded to the liberating possibilities that New Womanhood entailed. Yet, on the other hand, Gibson framed the New Woman's challenge as playful romanticism in relationships with men, not as a demand for political rights. He portrayed her as an object of men's desire, not vice versa. The freedom the Gibson Girl represented was a matter of style rather than substance, intended to ultimately find a suitable match, not eschewing societal or gender expectations.[14]

The commercialized non-radical femininity of the Gibson Girl was especially evident in the fashions she was depicted in. Despite offering a new degree of comfort and mobility, and despite being more masculine in look, the clothes she wore did not pose a serious threat to prevalent gendered notions, but remained within the boundaries of acceptable feminine appearance. Whereas Gibson quickly adopted the athletic ideal of the shirtwaist and separate skirt as the Gibson Girl's signature outfit, he also depicted her wearing voluminous evening gowns that did not facilitate much movement. Moreover, she always appeared corseted, and even when depicted outdoors she usually wore the appropriate sports attire, which always meant skirts and not bloomers. Yet, precisely because the Gibson Girl's clothing did not mark a break with mainstream styles, they enabled New Women to challenge gender notions and to claim new public roles without being reprimanded as radical feminists like their foremothers.

Although she was not associated with politics, the Gibson Girl represented two other main developments that contributed to the emergence of the New Woman and her challenge to the gender system in the 1890s: women's entrance into higher education and their engagement with sports. As a young, fun-loving, single woman who engaged in popular outdoor activities, the

Fashioning the New Woman

Gibson Girl was the perfect embodiment of the college girl, or the "co-ed." In an illustration titled "School Days," the Gibson Girl almost floats above the ground, wearing a tailored shirtwaist and gored walking skirt, produced through triangular-shaped panels sewn up together. Holding a golf club, rather than books, the Gibson Girl's ensemble marked a new sense of mobility and legitimacy of women's collegiate lifestyle (figure 1.1).[15] However, the depiction of the Gibson Girl as a harmless college girl represented not so much acceptance of women's entrance into higher education, as an attempt to deflate this very social change.[16] Even the identification of the Gibson Girl with girlhood, as her name indicated, suggested high-spiritedness, not political determination, undermining the potential threat that the association of the Gibson Girl with the New Woman might have otherwise entailed.[17]

Nevertheless, young students, particularly those for whom college marked the beginning of a career in suffrage or social reform, capitalized on the popularity of the Gibson Girl to gain legitimacy for their status as educated women and reformers. Indeed, while the percentage of women in higher education would remain quite low—only 2.8 percent of American women in 1900 were enrolled in college—college graduates comprised the bulk of settlement house workers, city reformers, social workers, and suffrage activists, all occupations identified with the New Woman and her political activism.[18] By appropriating the Gibson Girl fashions and imagery, these young students could claim a progressive identity and express their political views while also conveying an image of athleticism and feminine appeal.

Doris Stevens, Maud Wood Park, Inez Haynes Irwin (Gillmore), and other suffragists, for example, adopted the Gibson Girl outfit to portray a more appealing image of the New Woman, embodying the connections between the image of the Gibson Girl, college education, and feminist ideas.[19] In a 1906 photo, taken during Stevens's studies at Oberlin College, she wears a Gibson Girl outfit, presenting herself as both a college student and a New Woman (figure 1.2). Facing the viewer, with a Gibson Girl hairdo and a shirtwaist with rolled-up sleeves, Stevens represented a determined Gibson Girl, conveying both bodily and mental freedom. Yet, by posing as a Gibson Girl, she demonstrated that these qualities did not constitute a danger to women's sexual attractiveness. Other photos in that series showed Stevens with her male peers, reading books, and fooling around—suggesting that mixed-sex intellectual activities, far from being unfeminine, were strong preparation for a life of service and political engagement.[20] As they adopted the Gibson Girl's fashions, women like Stevens created a new interpretation for the political

FIGURE 1.2: Doris Stevens at Oberlin College, circa 1906. White college students used Gibson Girl imagery to express their political views while still maintaining their respectability, challenging stereotypes regarding the masculinization of educated women. (Courtesy of Schlesinger Library, Radcliffe Institute, Harvard University)

New Woman that countered negative portrayals of the politically engaged, militant feminist in the popular press: dressed in bloomers or short skirts and pursuing masculine occupations.[21]

Moreover, given that many contemporaries saw in college graduates' tendency not to marry an evidence of the dangers of the New Woman, embracing the Gibson Girl image and fashions enabled to challenge some of these accusations.[22] Since Gibson constructed his Girl as an eternal bachelorette and a charmer, suffragists such as Stevens could also claim this identity without being blamed for being responsible for "race suicide," an accusation many White students faced as they often chose to reject male suitors and stay single. And indeed, Stevens was known in Oberlin for her romances with men as well as for her suffrage activism, and was described by her friends as beautiful, spirited, and always sought after by men.[23] As they harnessed the association of the Gibson Girl with the college girl, Stevens and other students like her were able to soften public fears regarding women's increasing presence in the public sphere. Posing as Gibson Girls, they proved that women could both gain higher education and retain their feminine traits.

Yet more importantly, as suffragists adopted the Gibson Girl outfit, they could connect fashionability and women's rights, while countering previous stereotypes that presented woman's rights advocates as mannish and unappealing. In her unpublished autobiography, "Adventures of Yesterday," feminist Inez Haynes Irwin (Gillmore) described how every woman she met in college who was "slender, delicate, often very pretty, articulate, logical, and interesting"—the attributes associated with the Gibson Girl—was also a suffragist.[24] Irwin herself adopted the Gibson Girl's fashions to popularize suffrage work among her fellow students when she and Maud Wood Park founded in 1900 the College Equal Suffrage League. In another book, Irwin attributed the sartorial freedom of the Gibson Girl's ensemble to the advancement women made in the public sphere.[25] To Irwin, as to Charlotte Perkins Gilman, the Gibson Girl and her fashions symbolized women's progress at the turn of the century, mainly in education and the opening of professions such as law and business. And like Gilman, Irwin also understood the Gibson Girl as the embodiment of the New Woman: fashionably dressed and politically determined. By claiming and using the Gibson Girl's popularity to advance her suffrage cause, Irwin and other suffragists expanded the Gibson Girl meanings to include more feminist messages regarding women's rights. Despite Gibson's apolitical depictions, these suffragists used the Gibson Girl and her fashions to normalize liberating ideas regarding women's bodies and social roles in popular culture.

African American Gibson Girls and the Fashions of Respectability

With the growing circulation of ready-made fashions and magazines, the popularity of the Gibson Girl grew and her image transcended its affiliation with White middle-class collegiate culture. Although Irwin, Stevens, and other women instilled political and feminist meanings in the image, contemporaries began to associate the Gibson Girl with a more generic understanding of modern womanhood.[26] Indeed, the image became so ubiquitous that every woman who adopted the new fashions of the shirtwaist and skirt ensemble could be identified as a Gibson Girl.[27] The popularity of the fashions thus enabled different interpretations and appropriations of the image. Even women who were not necessarily represented by the White, middle-class trope of the Gibson Girl could use her image to advance their own political agendas. By portraying themselves as other Gibson Girls, Black, working-class, and immigrant women expanded the meaning of the Gibson Girl to include other types of femininity and freedoms that expanded and diversified the meanings of the New Woman. Claiming access to the image by adopting the Gibson Girl fashions provided these women with a route to not only make claims on what the New Woman stood for but, most importantly, gave them the ability to shape their image as fashionable modern women.

For African American women in particular, adopting the Gibson Girl imagery offered a route to claim inclusion in American culture and to promote racial uplift. The strong association of the Gibson Girl with collegiate culture enabled African American women to appropriate the image to promote claims for racial equality as well as to assert personal liberation as both women and Black. They adapted the image as a manifestation of their worthiness as refined women, using fashion as a way to improve their position as Black women in their own communities while challenging structures of racism in White society. By appearing fashionable in an up-to-date style that matched the mainstream trends, these women expanded the boundaries of Black femininity, turning beauty culture into a political practice vis-à-vis both Blacks and Whites. Yet, Black women did face some challenges. Appropriating the term "Gibson Girl" posed a risk due to the dangers of associating themselves with her flirtatious and playful sexuality. Moreover, the Gibson Girl's athleticism proved to be problematic, as racist stereotypes portrayed the young Black girl as a muscular brute. However, adopting the image, if not the term itself, allowed a new model of Black femininity to challenge the prevalent racist images in the White media that ridiculed Black women's aspirations to enjoy the New Woman's freedoms and modernity.[28] Precisely because the Gibson Girl was never portrayed as a political activist but as an appealing and approachable middle-class young woman, her image, and more importantly her fashions, enabled African American women to lay claims to middle-class respectability and access to the privileges of White ladyhood.

The politics of fashion and appearance proved to be crucial to the emergence of the New Negro as a gendered experience, and they offered a space where Black women could not only claim their voice but also gain some control over their image and representation.[29] Fashion, and the mass-consumer market that made it accessible, enabled African American women to reinvent themselves as New Negro Women and to cultivate a look that was simultaneously respectable and modern, healthy and attractive, feminine and practical. Scholars have pointed to how the politics of respectability—a combination of morality, sexual purity, modesty, thrift, and hard work—were central to middle-class African American women's behavior and image in the early twentieth century. Many African Americans believed respectability was essential to racial progress and equality, viewing it mainly as a feminine duty.[30] Yet respectability connoted more than just a set of behaviors. It was also associated with a certain look and appearance. "On the streets, and as the street cars pass our homes, colored people should give the best pictures possible of themselves," reformer and activist Emma Azalia Hackley argued in a 1916 etiquette book for young Black women. "We are a poor people but we can be quiet, clean, becomingly and fittingly dressed," she claimed.[31] By using the visual power of fashion to convey a "respectable appearance," Hackley and other proponents of respectability constructed fashionability as crucial to the project of race progress. As Mary Church Terrell, the prominent reformer and the president of the National Association of Colored Women's Clubs asserted: "Every woman, no matter what her circumstances, owes it to herself, her family, and her friends to look as well as her means will permit, and a wise selection of colors to be worn plays an important part in securing the best results."[32]

African Americans seized on the fashionability and popularity of the Gibson Girl image to advocate broader demands for racial equality. The Black press and community leaders emphasized Black women's beauty and poise as a means of refuting derogatory White stereotypes that perceived Black women as uncivilized, masculine, and ugly or as a symbol of dangerous, promiscuous and available sexuality.[33] "We present the colored woman today as she impresses herself in the world as a growing factor for good and in her beauty, intelligence and character for better social recognition," wrote John H. Adams in a 1904 article in the journal *Voice of the New Negro*. According to Adams, the beautiful New Negro Woman, like the Gibson Girl, was the result of "careful home training and steady schooling," and her college training made her both dignified and modern.[34] By offering sketches to illustrate how the New Negro Woman was a version of the Gibson Girl, Adams supplied his readers with a visual evidence of his claims. These images not only suggested a link between modern fashion and upward mobility, but also served as a form of proof that Black women could indeed be fashionable, beautiful, and successful.

CHAPTER ONE

Black college girls, as the paragons of racial uplift, were held to the highest standards of middle-class respectability, and their appearance was understood as a reflection of these standards. Seeing students' fashion choices as more than just individual expression of taste, but as indicator for the entire progress of the race, colleges enacted strict dress codes that encouraged modest, simple, yet modern appearance devoid of showy and loud elements.[35] Students were encouraged to present an attractive fashionable appearance, to which the Gibson Girl fashions were particularly suited. Figure 1.3 offers an example: four African American women photographed on the steps of a building at Atlanta University.[36] Fashionably dressed in the Gibson Girl's ensemble of shirtwaist and skirt, these young women appropriated the Gibson Girl imagery to convey their own interpretation of the style. By portraying themselves as women of leisure who could contemplate the academic world, these women created a powerful image of African American womanhood that claimed the collegiate Gibson Girl as their own.

The emphasis on presenting a respectable appearance through popular fashion trends went beyond Black college women, however. There is ample photographic evidence that many middle-class Black women used the Gibson Girl fashions to reinvent themselves as modern and to distinguish themselves from working-class and rural Blacks.[37] Yet, fashion and appearance were not just about class concerns of elite women, but also carried immense political meanings for Black reformers and activists who styled themselves to gain equality and respect for their entire race. Civil rights activists Ida B. Wells-Barnett, Nannie Helen Burroughs, and Mary Church Terrell adopted the Gibson Girl styles to express their middle-class refinement. They created their own versions of the image, adopting her upswept hairstyle, but often paired it with more lavish clothes than the standard shirtwaist and plain skirt. They also tended to prefer more ornamented shirtwaists over simple white ones as a way to further distance themselves from the working class.[38]

Through their public appearances and the circulation of their images in the press, Terrell and Burroughs were among the women who became the new trendsetters of fashion and modernity. Terrell in particular provided a template for Black beauty. According to one woman who attended her 1916 "Modern Woman" lecture, Terrell, in her pink evening dress and long white gloves, and with her hair beautifully done, not only convincingly defined in her words the duties of the New Negro Woman to uplift the race but also embodied the Modern Woman and her values.[39] In presenting themselves as respectable middle-class modern women, Terrell, Burroughs, and other activ-

Fashioning the New Woman

FIGURE 1.3: Black women capitalized on the respectable association of the Gibson Girl in order to make claims for racial equality and access to privileges of ladyhood. (Thomas Askew, "Four African American Women Seated on Steps of Building at Atlanta University, Georgia," 1899, Library of Congress)

ists modeled racial uplift, situating themselves as fashionable New Women equal to Whites. In the process, they not only created the Gibson Girl as a more inclusive image, but also expanded her meanings, constructing respectability and fashionability as a political practice.

Working-Class Women and the Politicization of the Shirtwaist

African American women were not the only ones who took advantage of the popularity of the Gibson Girl fashions to enjoy the possibilities that the new mass consumer market offered. White working-class and immigrant women also tapped into the fashionability of the Gibson Girl to shape their own versions of the New Woman and to imbue the image with political meanings. These working-class women used the ready-made shirtwaist that revolutionized the women's fashion industry and became so identified with the Gibson Girl, and they turned it into the political symbol of their labor demands.[40]

CHAPTER ONE

By the mid-1890s, the shirtwaist became a national fashion and an essential item in women's wardrobes, coming in a variety of fabrics, colors, and styles. A fashion reporter for the widely circulated *Ladies' World*—a magazine that catered both to middle- and working-class women—announced in 1897 that "shirt waists made of every possible sort of material will be as much worn as ever. They do not diminish in popularity at all ... the wearing of shirt-waists is no longer a fad, but their usefulness and undeniable comfort have become so thoroughly well established."[41] By the 1900s, shirtwaists' styles became so diverse, ranging from mannish-tailored waists with basic lines to hand-embroidered elaborate silk versions with lacy inserts and frilly ornaments. Each woman could choose her own style according to her financial means, the event, and time of day (figure 1.4).[42] "Day by day the waist entrenches itself more deeply in the esteem of women," proclaimed the trade journal the *Cutter-Up* in 1899. "It is so easily managed and so much is possible with it that its permanency seems assured. It is worn by rich and poor alike, is ornate or simple, and lends itself to fashionable use, no matter what the occasion."[43]

While women wore shirtwaists under tailored suits since the 1860s, it was only in the 1890s that they were marketed as a separate item to be worn with just a skirt. The shirtwaist was structured as a female version of a man's dress shirt, and it retained the functionality and adaptability to mass production of the masculine garment even after its adaptation to the female body. The adoption of masculine elements into feminine attire was nothing new, but the popularity of the shirtwaist signaled the acceptance of the New Woman beauty ideal that was much more athletic and muscular than previously. Marketed as suitable for all occasions—work, shopping, and afternoon wear—the shirtwaist was particularly appealing to wage-earning women who could appear to have a diverse wardrobe without investing large funds.[44]

The shirtwaist's popularity and its ability to cross class and racial barriers was largely due to the simplicity of its design that made it both easy enough to be sewn at home by following a pattern, but also cheap enough to manufacture and to be sold as a ready-made. The increasing availability of affordable, easy-to-comprehend paper patterns made the shirtwaist an item that a skilled woman could sew without a lot of difficulties.[45] The paper-pattern industry, and particularly E. Butterick & Co. patterns, offered the household sewer, as well as the professional dressmaker, dependable ready-to-use patterns that presented the latest styles of Paris and New York.[46] At the same time, the rise of mail-order companies such as Montgomery Ward and Sears, Roebuck & Co., which looked to expand their markets to women's wear, offered affordable solutions to their customers. In addition, major immigration waves in

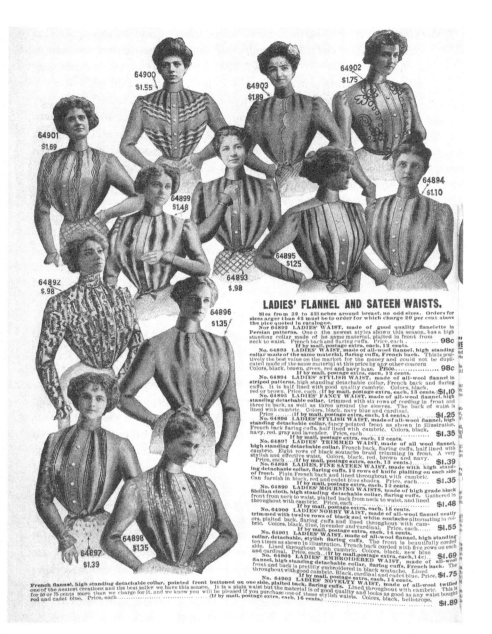

FIGURE 1.4: Becoming one of the most successful ready-made items at the turn of the twentieth century, shirtwaists became a marker of the "All-American Girl." (*Sears, Roebuck & Co. Catalogue*, no. 110, Spring 1900)

the 1880s that supplied cheap and unskilled labor turned the shirtwaist into a successful candidate for mass production. Although sewing a garment from a purchased paper pattern was often cheaper than buying a ready-made, fair-quality, reliable shirtwaists could be bought for less than a dollar.[47]

Unlike complicated, structured dresses, which needed to be fitted to the individual body, the shirtwaist did not require close fitting and hence was much easier to standardize, both in terms of styles and sizes. Changes in styles were very subtle, and were easy to update without investing much in production costs, but by adding gussets and pleats to the overall design.[48] Moreover, the implementation of Taylorist methods into the production process, together with the division of task labor that characterized the garment industry, contributed to the success of the shirtwaist as a mass-produced item.[49] The shirtwaist was largely responsible for the rapid expansion of the women's ready-made clothing industry, which grew in product value from $13 to $159 million between 1869 and 1899. It became one of the longest and most profitable trends in women's ready-made clothing as its popularity lasted for almost two decades, from about 1890 to the late 1910s.[50]

Differences in quality and durability were certainly obvious between a store-bought shirtwaist and a custom-made one, and among manufactured shirtwaists of different grades. Ella J. Cannady, the fashion reporter for *Ladies' World*, admitted that, "if one wants a supply of really good [shirtwaists], it is a good idea to make them at home."[51] However, the middle-class homemaker did not necessarily sew her own shirtwaists. Many middle-class women who could afford to hire a dressmaker regularly obtained their shirtwaists from her, in addition to more complicated dresses.[52] For those who preferred store-bought shirtwaists, the garment industry provided the latest fashions in a number of grades, so good-quality shirtwaists could be purchased, yet their prices could reach a few dollars each, which was beyond the reach of most working-class women.[53] In New York City, the more expensive shirtwaists could be bought in the fashionable Fifth Avenue department stores, while cheaper, lower-quality ones were available at less prestigious stores on First Avenue and from Hester Street's pushcarts, where most working-class women shopped.[54] Although most of the ready-made clothing within working women's budgets were so poorly made that they fell apart fairly quickly, the affordability of a ready-made shirtwaist—reaching as low as thirty-five cents (about ten dollars today)—enabled many working-class women to purchase several of them and thus to cope both with their rapid turnover rate, as well as with the demands of looking fashionable.[55]

Working-class women quickly adopted the shirtwaist, which enabled them to convey a respectable image without spending a week's pay. As one immigrant told the reporter of the *Sentinel*, a Chicago Jewish newspaper: "since [I am] learning to sew, [I] can have three waists for the price of one 'store waist' and the garments [I make] are prettier and wear longer too."[56] Yet, there was another factor that turned shirtwaists into what union leader and labor activist Rose Schneiderman dubbed as the "working girl's uniform."[57] For White working-class immigrants, the shirtwaist was instrumental in their assimilation into American society and culture. Sophie Abrams, an immigrant from Russia, recalled going shopping with her aunt on her first day in the United States: "She bought me a shirtwaist . . . and a skirt, a blue print with red buttons and a hat. . . . I took my old brown dress and shawl and threw them away! I know it sounds foolish . . . but I didn't care. . . . When I looked in the mirror . . . I said, boy, Sophie, look at you now . . . just like an American."[58] Adopting the shirtwaist ensemble marked women like Abrams as a modern New Woman, but first and foremost it enabled her to cast off her "greenness" and to appear as an American.

Indeed, the act of *buying* a shirtwaist, instead of *making* one, was a crucial marker for working-class immigrants' assimilation.[59] The ability to purchase a fashionable style that was equal in appearance, if not in quality, to middle- and upper-class fashions symbolized democracy to many immigrants. Yet, buying a shirtwaist not only marked these immigrants as Americans, but it also became a symbol of their economic independence. Although some immigrants working in the garment industry used their skills, and sometimes the factory's material and equipment, to sew their own designs, many others preferred to buy a ready-made shirtwaist, even if it meant compromising on quality or spending more money. In buying a ready-made, women could purchase other people's work and claim middle-class status instead of using their skills and time for so-called free to sew their own clothes. It was the act of consuming rather than manufacturing that symbolized freedom to these working-class garment workers.[60]

The identification of the shirtwaist with Americanism was not incidental. While shirtwaists were worn across Europe, the simplicity of the style and its mass-production were considered distinctly American. The shirtwaist never received strong approval from any Parisian style house, and, in fact, was one of the main U.S. export items during the 1900s. U.S. manufacturers exported shirtwaists to most countries of the world, including France, furthering the identification of the shirtwaist with America. In 1908, the total exports of shirtwaists to France amounted to nearly $1 million, making them one of the few designs to cross the Atlantic from West to East, rather than vice versa.[61] Identified as it was with the Gibson Girl image, herself an embodiment of the "American Girl," many young immigrant women saw the shirtwaist as a symbol of the wearer's successful Americanization.

However, the shirtwaist's popularity among working-class women could also present a problem in department-store settings, which relied on maintaining distinctions between working-class saleswomen and their middle-class clients. Most department stores enforced employee dress codes, using fashion as a way to maintain class hierarchies that reflected middle-class belief that working-class women's bodies and appearances needed to be controlled and regulated.[62] A 1902 rule book from the Chicago department store Marshall Field's claimed that "while we have never insisted, as have many stores, upon our saleswomen wearing black, we do desire that they shall appear in modest costume, and we deprecate the use of striking colors and patterns."[63] Although the manual claimed that Marshall Field's workers enjoyed greater freedom to fashion themselves, it also condescended their tastes, dissuading the workers from taking full liberty to express their personality as well as their financial independence.

By 1910, however, the popularity of the shirtwaist grew among both middle- and working-class women. As distinctions in styles and tastes became less obvious, Field's management, seeking to maintain class boundaries, changed its workers' dress code to make it more rigid than before. A rule book from around 1910 reversed Field's 1902 instructions and required that "all young women in the sales section will please dress in black, exception being made in the use of white or colored neck bands, if desired, which we will ask always to be held at the point of good taste." The manual specified, however, that "during the period when shirt waists are worn (from about the first of April until about the fifteenth of October) we shall not object to employees wearing neat shirt waists (white preferred)."[64] In 1912, the management was even more specific in its demands: "Waists must be white or black, white with black stripes or dots, black with white stripes or dots (stripes narrow and dots small) or natural color pongee or linen. Waists of very sheer, unbusinesslike material over colors, or white with great amount of insertion and black waists with pipings, pleatings, or bands of color must not be worn." Unable to fight the shirtwaist trend, Marshall Field's management attempted to at least control its employees' style choices. The notice also reminded workers that "good waists may be had on the sixth floor at $1.50, $1.75 and up, in the basement at $1.00 and up; all subject to employes' [sic] special prices."[65] On the one hand, this change in attitudes suggests that, by the 1910s, shirtwaists had become so prevalent that management had to enforce stricter codes in order to maintain class distinctions. But on the other hand, it also rendered such efforts futile, due to the variety of shirtwaists that were accessible to working-class women. These workers could, with their employee discounts, purchase good-quality shirtwaists that further blurred the same class distinctions the management struggled to uphold.

The shirtwaist thus become a useful means for working-class women to challenge class hierarchies and to claim their identities as modern American women. It became a site to both delineate and challenge definitions of gender and class propriety. Yet more than anything, the shirtwaist symbolized working-class women's growing politicized presence in the workforce.[66] As shirtwaists were the main item that female garment workers manufactured, their exploitive working conditions became intertwined with the clothing themselves. At the same time, since garment workers were both producers and consumers of shirtwaists, they used it to express and negotiate their status and rights as laborers. The shirtwaist thus became a political symbol of working women's plight as they embraced it as a badge of pride and protest.

Clara Lemlich—a shirtwaist maker and a union activist who was one of the leaders of the famous 1909–10 garment workers' strike known as the Uprising of the 20,000—utilized the shirtwaist imagery to mobilize support. As she told the middle-class *Good Housekeeping* readers in 1912, "The garments we work on are very beautiful, very costly—very delicate. Some of them sell for a hundred and fifty dollars. Such as you could never dream of buying for yourself."[67] By pointing to the discrepancy between shirtwaist makers and their ability to wear the waists they were making, Lemlich illuminated the real cost of shirtwaists while claiming workers' right to enjoy the fruits of their labor. In another article she proclaimed: "We're human, all of us girls, and we're young. We like new hats as well as any other young women. Why shouldn't we? And if one of us gets a new one, even if it hasn't cost more than 50 cents, that means that we have gone for weeks on two-cent lunches—dry cakes and nothing else."[68] As they claimed their right for both "bread and roses," and tapping into the multiple meanings the shirtwaist contained, working-class women were able to claim respectability while also protest their oppressive working conditions. Yet, by demanding their access to fashion, working-class women also framed fashionability as a political right. For these women, to be acknowledged as a fashionable person was intertwined with privileges of class and gender to which they argued they had the right to possess.

CHAPTER ONE

As Nan Enstad observes, the practice of ladyhood has shaped garment workers' understanding of their public identities, as well as their political claims. As they negotiated the tension between their aspiration to receive public legitimization as women, and their radical actions as strikers that challenge the very notion of respectable femininity, clothing became instrumental to their efforts.[69] In particular, the Gibson Girl image and its association with both middle-class respectability and consumer culture, enabled garment workers to shape their version of working-class ladyhood in ways that served their political goals. This is evident in a 1910 photograph of Lemlich, dressed in a white shirtwaist and plain dark skirt, her hair pulled back in a pompadour style, which offers a determined version of the Gibson Girl image (figure 1.5).[70] Lemlich in her appearance managed to capture both the romantic, athletic figure of the Gibson Girl, and to convey her demands to be taken seriously as a person, a worker, and a woman. By choosing to present herself as a shirtwaist maker while also wearing a shirtwaist, Lemlich literally wore her profession on her body, using fashion as a metonymy to her working-class politics. But in claiming the Gibson Girl image, Lemlich also expanded the meanings of the New Woman beyond collegiate culture and the middle class. Lemlich, as a working-class Gibson Girl, similar to the suffragists who used the image to popularize their agitation for women's rights, used this imagery to redefine the New Woman as both fashionable and political.

The ability of the shirtwaist to blur class distinctions might also have had a role in forming cross-class solidarity among women during the 1909–10 garment workers' strike. Cross-class cooperation was often fraught with tensions and class biases, despite the fact that middle-class reformers' participation in the strike offered a crucial financial support and public legitimacy for the working-class strikers and their demands. These tensions revolved around working-class women's fashions and appearance, which both sides saw as critical for the success of the strike. Working-class garment workers created a more exaggerated interpretation of the popular styles, using bold colors, large hats, and ornamented, fluffy accents in their dress. The appearance of the garment workers, which was an attempt to remind the public (and themselves) that despite their class status they were first and foremost ladies, proved to be a problem to middle-class reformers who sought to emphasize the poverty and helplessness of the strikers.[71]

However, it might also be that the strikers' ability to adopt the prevailing fashions, albeit in a radical interpretation, enabled them to imagine themselves as on par with their middle-class allies. Strikers' pleas for protection received public support and sympathy only after Mary Dreier, the Women's

FIGURE 1.5: Clara Lemlich (circa 1910) was among the White immigrant garment workers to use their positions as both producers and consumers of shirtwaists to appropriate the Gibson Girl image and demand their rights as workers and as women. (Kheel Center, Cornell University Library)

Trade Union League's (WTUL) socially prominent president, was arrested while walking the picket line.[72] Dreier and her WTUL colleagues certainly had their own grievances regarding the strikers' appearance and behaviors. However, the fact that she was arrested on the picket line might suggest that Drier's appearance was not so different from the poor garment workers', which caused the police to misidentify her. A *New York Times* article admitted: "The factory girl makes shirtwaists and the college girl wears them, and when they first walked Broadway arm in arm as pickets in the big shirtwaist strike that is now on, they both wore the garment of contention.... The public does not know and cannot distinguish the college girl who is walking up and down the sidewalk with almost every group of pickets."[73] Through fashion, both working-class and college girls could show their solidarity. But more importantly, the shirtwaist enabled both politicizing the New Woman and claiming the freedoms she represented. Thus, through this shared experience, created through the clothes they wore, working- and middle-class women politicized the shirtwaist, turning it into a symbol of their demands for rights and equality.

When they stood together, forming a united front with their fellow middle-class reformers both in their appearance and in their demands, strikers could imagine themselves as influential political subjects. By embracing the shirtwaist as a symbol of freedom, economic independence, and Americanization, and by surpassing and transforming its exploitive associations, working-class women turned their clothing into a political tool. Barred from using other means of influence, whether because they lacked economic resources or access to the vote, or simply because their class or race status excluded them from feminine respectability, working-class women used shirtwaists to gain a voice and to demand their rights not just as women and as workers but also as fashionable subjects entitled to be acknowledged as such.

Bicycle Fashions and the New Freedom for Women

If the shirtwaist's availability and its ability to cross class, race, and ethnic demarcations signaled working-class New Womanhood, the bicycle and the sartorial changes it brought to women's skirts defined the middle-class New Woman. Marking a new public presence and new possibilities of mobility, the bicycle and its fashions provided another visual image through which women could shape and reflect modern gender notions. "The typical girl of the present period is the bicycle girl," announced *Ladies' World* in 1896. "Like her Puritan predecessor, she too spins on a wheel, but her spinning is pleasure instead of toil, and its results are swift and healthful circulation of the blood instead of a homespun garment. The bicycle girl has become a collective, proper noun. She is no longer singular nor improper, even when she elects to ride a diamond frame wheel in a bifurcated apparel."[74] The "bicycle girl," with her relatively short skirt or bloomers became another visual type of New Woman—one that emphasized, above all, freedom of movement, health, and the luxury of leisure.

Although the "bicycle girl" was not necessarily a version of the middle-class Gibson Girl, the two images had much in common, and Gibson often portrayed his Girl as a cyclist. Moreover, the identification of the Gibson Girl with college and athleticism made the bicycle a particularly potent symbol of the New Woman. By the 1890s, sports became a socially acceptable activity for women, both as part of college curricula and as a leisure activity. Cycling in particular, as a new sport without long-standing traditions or gender affiliations (such as horseback riding or fencing), enabled women to adopt it more easily and to claim dominance in it.[75] Indeed, while both sexes shared enthusiasm for the bicycle, it was mostly women who contributed to cycling becoming a craze in the mid-1890s, furthering its association with the New Woman.

Bicycles were introduced in the mid-nineteenth century, but in the 1890s their popularity spread to the middle class, making them a national phenomenon. The bicycle's surging popularity in the early 1890s is often attributed to the introduction of the safety bicycle in 1886, which included two equally sized wheels with air-filled rubber tires. Perhaps more importantly, the safety bicycle also included a dropped-frame design that accommodated women's skirts while riding.[76] These technological advances made the bicycle lighter and easier to operate but also more affordable as a hobby and as a means of transportation to a larger number of people. As cycling enthusiast Mary Sargent Hopkins claimed in 1901, since "wheels are so reasonable in price now that they come within the reach of almost any purse, no matter how small," each woman could enjoy the benefits they brought.[77] However, despite being called "the people's carriage," bicycles were mainly a middle-class craze.[78] Most bicycles ranged from $85 to $100 (around $2,500 to $3,000 today), a considerable sum for many, although cheaper bicycles ranging from $10 to $40 (around $300 to $1,200 today) were available too.[79] This kind of investment was out of reach for most working-class people, but this did not mean that they never rode bicycles. Cheap bicycles could be bought on an installment plan or rented for an afternoon in the park. But it was largely middle-class women who became identified with the freedoms that the bicycle enabled.[80]

Contemporaries quickly saw the emancipatory potential of the bicycle. In 1896, Susan B. Anthony claimed that the bicycle has "done more to emancipate women than anything else in the world. . . . It gives woman a feeling of freedom and self-reliance." A woman riding a bicycle was, according to Anthony, the "picture of free, untrammeled womanhood."[81] Mary Sargent

Hopkins agreed, arguing in 1898 that "riding the wheel makes better as well as stronger women, makes them better wives and mothers. Riding the wheel strengthens the body and brightens the intellect."[82] For Anthony and Hopkins, the bicycle not only symbolized the New Woman but was the means through which she came into existence. Providing new possibilities to escape the physical confines of the domestic sphere, the bicycle offered the benefits of healthy exercise and mobility in ways that were not available before.[83]

Yet, it was not cycling alone that became the symbol of emancipated womanhood. "Talk about the emancipated woman!" exclaimed Hopkins. "The right to earn her own living on terms of equality with men, to vie with him in work, sport or politics, to vote, to hold office, to be president as well as queen and empress would never bring the blessed sense of freedom that an outdoor costumes, sans trailing skirts and entangling folds and plus a short skirt and bloomers, gives to the average woman."[84] According to Hopkins, it was the bicycle "costume," or outfit, that marked the New Woman's freedom. Another cycling enthusiast also credited the popularity of the bicycle outfit to women's liberation from their oppressive clothes: "Women have now the courage and fearlessness to emancipate themselves from the shackles of their present slavish dress," she argued.[85] Riding a bicycle gave a sense of freedom and mobility, but the bicycle outfit helped to popularize reformative ideas about fashion and its liberating potential.

Scholars have pointed to cycling, rather than sports such as tennis, golf, and skating, as being responsible for bringing the most *visible* changes and progress to women's fashions. Unlike sports such as swimming or gymnastics, which were activities that took place in specific and oftentimes private settings, cycling was a public activity and, as such, it was more influential on everyday fashion styles.[86] Most notably, the bicycle contributed to the loosening of corsets. Yet its more controversial contribution to women's fashions was the revival of bloomers, the infamous dress reform initiative of the 1850s that contained trousers and was associated with the agitation for women's rights.[87] In the 1890s, however, bloomers were marketed not as a feminist dress reform but as an appropriate garment to wear while engaging in cycling.

Woman's rights advocates welcomed the bloomer revival, feeling that their arguments regarding women's fashion and freedom might now find public acceptance. In 1896, Elizabeth Cady Stanton claimed that, since cycling had become so common, women who rode bicycles wearing conventional dresses appeared more "unnatural" to the "ordinary observer" than those who wore sporting bloomers. Not only were bloomers the most comfortable and safe choice for the cycling woman, Stanton argued, they were also the most "natural" and functional, since women were, just as men, "bifurcated animal[s]."[88] Frances Willard, the president of the Woman's Christian Temperance Union, shared Stanton's views. In *A Wheel within a Wheel*, her autobiographical account on how she learned to ride a bicycle at the age of fifty-three, Willard argued that the popularity of the bicycle and the "rational dress" that came with it finally "convinced the world that has [otherwise] brushed aside the theories, no matter how well constructed, and the arguments, no matter how logical, of dress reformers." She, like Stanton, believed that it was only a matter of time until bloomers became a prevalent fashion: "reason will gain upon precedent, and ere long the comfortable, sensible, and artistic wardrobe of the rider will make the conventional style of woman's dress absurd to the eye and unendurable to the understanding," Willard claimed.[89]

However, it would be wrong to assume that the bicycle popularized bloomers as a fashionable public attire. While women could purchase bloomers' patterns and some chose it as their favorite riding attire, it never became a widespread phenomenon.[90] The *Washington Evening Star* commented in 1895 that "Washington women... do not seem to be taking to the bloomers at all."[91] And in 1896, the *Ladies' World* fashion reporter admitted that, although the bloomer was the most sensible outfit for cycling and that in "France and Germany most women riders adopt the bloomers," American women were more reluctant to adopt it, and "will accept the bloomers only under cover of the skirt."[92] Although bloomers were a recommended and even essential part of the bicycling outfit, there was a common understanding that they should not be visible, especially not off the wheel. Constance Astor Choate, another fashion authority, wrote in *American Woman* magazine that "New York women who ride bicycles wear skirts. The bloomer style of dress skirts is practically unknown." According to her own observations when sitting on Riverside Drive one afternoon, "two hundred and sixty bicyclists pass a given point every ten minutes... and of the hundreds and hundreds of women riders only one appeared without a skirt, and she looked like a professional freak."[93]

Fashion magazines argued that bloomers were ugly, and advised women to refrain from wearing them. In the fashion section of the *Ladies' World* bicycle number of July 1896, the reporter claimed that "while some consider skirts dangerous and bloomers the only feasible garb... women certainly do not look well in them."[94] Adelia K. Brainerd, a columnist for *Harper's Bazaar*, also argued that the fact that bloomers were "most emphatically" *not* "pretty and becoming" became their "death-blow," since "women are too anxious about their personal appearance to be willing to wear what their own eyes tell them is ugly."[95] As cycling was an outdoor, public activity, often done in a mixed-sex environment, it was not only a leisure activity but also a courting activity. As such, it demanded certain dress codes and gendered etiquette that had to adhere to, not challenge, prevalent social norms.[96] When women rode their bicycles, they wanted to feel good, but they also wanted to look pretty and attractive, and at the turn of the twentieth century, this meant looking feminine. For most women, because cycling was not a political activity, they were more reluctant to adopt an attire so laden with political meaning.

Indeed, the bloomers' complicated history and meaning in the United States can explain their lack of popularity among American women. Despite the fact that nearly forty years had passed since the unsuccessful attempt of woman's rights advocates to position the bloomer as an alternative to fashion, the garment was still strongly connected to their political agenda of gender equality. Women, especially those who saw themselves as keeping up with the popular trends, could not overwrite the bloomer as the visual symbol of the masculine, unattractive, radical woman who threatened masculinity and wanted to abolish motherhood and family.[97] Moreover, for those who wanted to portray themselves as fashionable New Women, adopting the bloomer, even if only for cycling, posed a challenge. Thus, although the bloomers offered an opportunity to test the boundaries of conventional fashion by adopting more practical, and less feminine-looking outfits, for many women who wanted to maintain their social standing with the opposite sex, being associated with radicalism and masculinity was too high of a price to pay. As with the original bloomer of the 1850s, it was the disjuncture between reformative ideas of health and comfort, and ideas of beauty and femininity, that prevented bloomers from being accepted as legitimate public attire. While the bicycle managed to popularize some ideas regarding women's freedom and mobility in the public sphere, it failed, despite woman's rights advocates' hopes, to turn the bloomer into a fashionable style.

The Rainy Day Club and the Popularization of the Short Skirt

Even if the bloomers failed to become a mainstream fashion, women had a few more appealing alternatives. One was the divided skirt: a standard gored skirt front with a split pleat in the back, which enabled the wearer to straddle the rear wheel.[98] This option was a reasonable compromise for women who wanted to maintain the appearance of the skirt without relinquishing the convenience of bloomers. An advertisement in *Harper's Bazaar* appealed to this wish, describing the divided skirt as "stylish, graceful, absolutely safe . . . and . . . suppl[ying] important features of comfort and conveniences lacking in other skirts." The cycling outfit was "made with a gored skirt in front and divided in the back, but in such a manner that it has the appearance of an ordinary skirt." The ad emphasized that the garment's functionality was invisible, "the division not being perceptible either on the wheel or when used as an ordinary walking costume; at the same time has all the advantages of a full divided skirt." Although the bloomers attached to the skirt are visible in the illustration, the advertisement emphasized that they were not visible and thus should not be a cause of concern to the fashionable cyclist.[99]

The most popular outfit for riding however, was the "short" skirt with a length that varied according to the preference of each rider and the message she wanted to convey while cycling. More daring women, who saw the bicycle as a means of freedom and a way to advance women's status in society, chose to wear their skirts at knee length. Yet, the majority of women wore their short skirts between four to six inches above the ground. According to Choate, the *American Woman* fashion reporter, "New York women, the women who set the fashion for American women riders, wear skirts that are reasonably short; some reach to the ankle, some stop just below the knee, but the majority stop just below the tops of high laced cycling boots, which is just below the swell of the calf of the leg." *Harper's Bazaar* also commented in 1896 that the proper length for the skirt was considered to be about to the top of the boots, not shorter.[100]

Although the short skirt signaled a departure from previous fashions, it was less controversial since it still adhered to conventions of femininity. Dress reformers and women cyclists downplayed the connection between the short bicycle skirt and women's emancipation and instead stressed the importance of looking feminine and attractive. Mary Sargent Hopkins, for example, made sure to disconnect herself from the radicalism of the bloomer (as well as from its reputation and failure) and assured her readers that "right here I will say, for the benefit of those who do not know my sentiments and may think I am leading up to a plea for mannish clothing, that such a change I consider in very bad taste and not at all necessary. Bloomers, knickerbockers, or trousers of any kind are suitable only for undergarments and should be worn only as a substitute for a petticoat."[101] What Hopkins wanted to popularized was not trousers for women, but comfortable, yet feminine, attire. For her, the short skirt was the perfect solution as it both provided the required freedom and comfort to ride a bicycle and could still claim to be fashionable.

The popularity of the short skirt reached beyond bicycle riding. As women increasingly began to venture into public spaces, the workplace, and higher education, they sought to adjust their clothes to the new reality of movement and service. They took advantage of the fact that contemporaries became more accustomed to the presence of cycling women in public, and adopted these outfits in other contexts. Seeing the comfort that the short skirt afforded women in riding their bicycles, contemporary dress reformers, especially women who needed to walk and get around in city streets, viewed it as a potential solution to the problem of the ills of trailing skirts. The problem of long, voluminous clothes was especially acute during winter, they argued, when "it takes an exceptional 'handy' woman to successfully keep her skirt from dragging and touching the mud somewhere." The problem of long, wet, muddy skirts was according to reformers a health issue as well, since "the good sense of wearing long skirts on any day is questionable. The wearing of such disease and discomfort breeders on muddy days is no less than criminal."[102]

Encouraged by the increasingly commonplace, and unremarkable, sight of women riding their bicycles in short skirts, some New York society and professional career women formed a club to advocate the use of the short skirt not only for cycling but also for everyday use, especially on bad-weather days. In 1896, the Rainy Day Club was founded in order "to secure health and comfort by sanitary methods of dress and at the same time to encourage the use of costumes that are genuinely artistic, graceful, and modest." Members included doctors, literary women, reporters, and business women of high standing, among them Harriet Hubbard Ayer, a beauty entrepreneur; Mrs. Bertha Welby, a famous actress; and Mrs. A. M. Palmer, the wife of the famous theatrical manager and entrepreneur.[103] While there were some middle-aged women, the majority of members were under thirty, representing the generation of New Women who ventured into the workforce. These professional women who defined themselves as "business women," not as "women of leisure," searched for appropriate and comfortable outfits to wear in the streets, offices, and meetings. According to club members, suitable clothes were crucial in constructing a professional identity and pride around which women could form political solidarities.[104] In a sense, club members were an embodiment of the professional New Woman, who gained education and entered the workforce not as a poor garment worker, but as a career professional, often with enough income to afford a business wardrobe. In addition, as upper-middle-class women, they enjoyed sufficient clout and respectability to experiment with fashion without being censured too severely. These women formed a connection between fashion, beauty, and comfort, translating their ideas regarding women's freedom into sartorial reality.

From its beginning, the club drew a lot of media attention. Dubbed Rainy Daisies by the press, a nickname the club later embraced, the group used this publicity as a vehicle to promote their cause. The *New York Times* reported in 1897 that "the club is increasing rapidly in size and enthusiasm. It has now some 200 members, and at least 50 who are ready with a short gown for a rainy day, a few who wear their abbreviated skirts with dauntless courage every day, Sundays included." The club expanded to other places as well. In 1898, 150 women from Somerville, Massachusetts, "many of them leaders in society there," formed the first Rainy Day Association in Massachusetts. By the end of the year, there were branches in Philadelphia, Baltimore, Ann Arbor, St. Louis, and Syracuse, Buffalo, and Oneonta, New York.[105]

The main purpose of the club was "to establish ... a distinctive sensible dress for business women," alluding both to members' sense of fashion and their professional identity. In its inaugural meeting, club members resolved that since "the dress of to-day is an absurdity for business women," and "it is impossible for a woman to keep neat and clean even in dry weather," a change in women's attire was necessary. For club members, the ultimate goal was to try to induce women to abandon their trailing skirts and wear comfortable outfits at all times, regardless of weather. Their vision of a dress reform was for it to be "constructed so as to enable a woman to keep immaculately fresh on a dirty day, and neat on a wet day, [and which] will add to her self-respect as well as to her comfort, and thus contribute to her highest and noblest advancement." Taking their inspiration from "the wheelwoman in suiting her dress to her comfort when awheel," they constructed their own "rainy-day costume" that included a short skirt, jacket, and a high boot (figure 1.6).[106]

The utilitarian benefits of the outfit—ease of movement and better health—could not be contested according to club members. "I have worn my short skirt and high boots since the 5th of October, every day and Sunday," said Miss Welby, one of the club's founders, "and for the first winter in my life I have not had to spend a month nursing a cold." Yet the greatest joy that members had in wearing the rainy-day outfit was in the sense of dignity and confidence that wearing such an outfit gave them. As Miss Lillian Mack, a Newark newspaper journalist, argued, "it is very important that woman should be well dressed," justifying her choice in wearing a rainy-day skirt. "If I don't feel as well as I can, I find myself trying to get out of sight. Of course, a business woman should be well groomed, and she should look as pretty as

FIGURE 1.6: Seeking to differentiate themselves from previous unsuccessful attempts at dress reform, Rainy Daisies harnessed the popularity of the bicycle to promote their own liberating ideas regarding women's dress. One such "rainy-day costume" is depicted here. ("The Rainy Day Club," *New-York Tribune*, November 6, 1896, Library of Congress)

possible," Mack said. Mack's ability to dress in a way she perceived as both respectable and practical contributed to her own sense of accomplishment as a career woman. In wearing a short skirt while pursuing a career in journalism Mack was according to the *New York Times* reporter the epitome of the New Woman: rationally dressed and "very pretty."[107]

The question of skirt length was up to the member's discretion, as long as it was no less than four inches above the ground or more than eight inches above it. "The skirt . . . should be of a length that would accommodate the timid woman and yet allow the more independent ones to be comfortable also," one member commented. Members also emphasized that the club did not mandate a "uniform" and each member had the freedom to choose her own style according to her individual taste, although "a few rules regarding artistic effects, comfort, and hygiene" were kept. In general, the majority preferred a skirt rising six inches above the ground.[108] The emphasis on individual taste and the refraining from mandating a uniform attested to the importance club members gave to fashionable appearance, not only to health considerations. In order for an outfit to be suitable, it had to be appealing and be an expression of one's individual taste, not just to fulfill a function of comfort. Indeed, club members sought to start a new fashion trend, not a crusade against the fashion system.

Although club members advocated comfort and health as the most important aspects of women's clothes, they were no less convinced that "no great good could be accomplished unless the costume be one that the most particular husband, father, or brother could see nothing to object to, either in cut or make." They highlighted that their efforts in reforming women's attire should not be associated with previous attempts of "dress reform" that were identified with the bloomer failure. "Dress reform did not necessarily mean 'dress reform,'" member Mrs. Belle Gray Taylor urged other members not to associate the rainy-day skirt with radicalism or antifashion sentiment. Doing so, she argued, would be "one of the greatest obstacles in the way of any improvement in woman's dress."[109] For club members such as Taylor, the only way they could succeed was by popularizing the style and avoiding associations with masculinity and ugliness. "Nothing must be worn that could offend the most fastidious, or in any way make the wearer look other than a self-respecting, thoroughly womanly woman," another member argued.[110] Instead of seeing fashion as an oppressive element that needed to be resisted or ignored, club members understood that, in order to receive support and followers for their cause, they needed to present their ideas as part of the mainstream trends. For these women, the rainy-day skirt was an example of how the current fashion could combine "grace and utility more satisfactorily than anything worn in the previous period." The rainy-day skirt offered women sensible and beautiful solution to their needs. "Beautiful dress was suitable dress," Taylor asserted, "and . . . therefore short gowns in rainy weather were high art."[111] By insisting that their reformative skirt was both fashionable and comfortable, club members constructed a positive link between beauty and utility.

Along with the short skirt, club members also advocated other improvements to women's attire, such as the use of lighter fabrics, jackets, and boots. In 1897, Miss Marguerite Lindley, one of the club's members, designed a high boot that was endorsed by the club as an official part of the rainy-day ensemble.[112] The club also supported the introduction of pockets, which one club member defined as "women's greatest lack" and a major hindrance to women's progress. According to this member, the lack of pockets in women's clothing not only made carrying important items such as handkerchiefs, pocketbooks, and journals a nuisance, but it also proved a barrier for women's intellectual and professional development.[113] While pockets were no doubt indispensable, this member's grievances alluded to her privileged status. For her, the lack of pockets was a hindrance to her intellectual fulfillment, preventing her from taking part in leisure activities. Yet, in framing her grievances in such a way, she ignored the importance of pockets to working-class women who could use them to keep their belongings while working, for example, in factories.

Yet, although the majority of club members came from the upper-middle class, a fact that shaped their view and ways of action, they were not completely ignorant of their working-class sisters. In one of the club's meetings, Mrs. Y. B. Merrill suggested that members use their power to "induce saleswomen and factory women to join them and don the costume" by donating at least one rainy-day garment a year to those in need. This could have been a skirt or a jacket, but it had to be "made over neatly, so that when finished they will in no way resemble a charity contribution. These are to be given to women who could not afford to purchase them, and who perhaps have but one skirt in their wardrobe."[114] This particular effort might have been patronizing and was certainly suggestive of the class status of club members. However, it also implied that members saw themselves as part of a greater community of modern working women who were entitled to comfortable, healthy, yet feminine fashionable dress when they went out into the world. In fact, club members' insistence that their donations should be neatly made and not resemble "a charity contribution" suggests that they believed that working-class women laborers also deserved to be fashionable and should be respected as workers, not to be pitied as charity cases.

Club members took pride that they designed their own rainy-day dresses, again alluding to their class status, yet the pattern and ready-made industries also offered rainy-day skirts to the middle-class woman who did not want to make them herself. Rainy-day skirts could be purchased for as little as four dollars (around $120 today), a price that a middle-class woman could afford.[115] Rainy-day skirts and suits were also marketed as appropriate business attire in fashion magazines. For example, *Ladies' Home Journal* columnist Emily Wright recommended the rainy-day outfit for the "business girl" and saw it as one of the essential elements in her wardrobe.[116] However, despite their relative popularity and availability, rainy-day outfits—just as the bicycle and its fashions—remained mostly an upper-middle-class fad. The rainy-day skirt was associated more with the class status of the wearer and the fact she could wear the outfit without needing to worry for her reputation, and less with the needs of the modern working woman.

While the vision of Rainy Daisies storming the streets never fully materialized, nor gained the same currency and distribution as the Gibson Girl's shirtwaist, the club did have some influence in turning the "short" skirt into an acceptable mainstream fashion. The fact that magazines with relatively conservative agenda such as *Harper's Bazaar* and *Ladies' Home Journal* advertised rainy-day skirts attested to the acceptance of the short skirt as a fashionable trend, not as a notorious effort of an antifashionable dress reform. The rainy-day ensemble forged a positive connection between health, comfort, freedom, and femininity, proving, as club member Mrs. Whitehead claimed, that "if [a dress] was only carefully adapted to the purpose for which it was intended, beauty would be sure to follow."[117] As increasing numbers of women entered colleges and the workforce and engaged in exercise and sports, they demanded clothes that would be suitable to those activities. Yet unlike previous generations of dress reformers and woman's rights advocates who sought only to relieve the burden of what they viewed as oppressive fashions, the New Woman of the 1890s demanded her clothes also to be beautiful, feminine, and stylish.

Club members' insistence on combining both comfort and fashion in their skirt designs signaled the modern tendency toward simplicity of lines and the emphasis that form should follow function, not vice versa. In 1915, when asked to describe her vision of a universal dress for women, Rainy-Day Club member and past president, Mrs. A. M. Palmer, asserted that it "must be the strongest combination of beauty, simplicity, durability, and comfort.... It should be neither so scant nor so voluminous that it will be entirely out of harmony with the fashion of the moment, and ... it must be suitable for both light and heavy materials, comfortable for walking and attractive for drawing room wear."[118] As the twentieth century progressed, the club's approach and vision for women's apparel would gain popularity, not only among dress reformers and middle-class professional women, but also among feminists.

Seeking to express their radical ideas regarding women's sexuality and freedom through their appearance as well as their actions, these feminists would continue in the path that club members constructed for them, forming a positive connection between fashion and the advancement of women's freedom.

The Fashionable Legacy of the New Woman

The rainy-day skirt and the shirtwaist both contributed to the construction of a new notion of womanhood, embodied through the image of the Gibson Girl. Yet, as these fashions became more and more popular, they became more than just a visual attribute of the New Woman, but a fashionable look that defined her meanings. Although the mass production and mass distribution of the shirtwaist promoted some degree of conformity, it also gave women the possibility of infusing individual expression into fashion and playing an active role in shaping the image of the New Woman. White college students used the popularity of the shirtwaist to ameliorate public fears about women in higher education while also asserting their political views. African American women employed the respectable connotation of the Gibson Girl and her fashions to make claims for racial uplift and equality. For working-class immigrants, the shirtwaist provided ways to appropriate the Gibson Girl to claim their rights as workers and as American women, opening avenues for cross-class solidarity. The rainy-day outfit as well, albeit less popular than the shirtwaist, highlighted the strong connection between women's clothing and their experience of physical freedom, marking the path in which later feminists would follow. Indeed, the influence of the Gibson Girl's ensemble lasted long after the shirtwaist and the rainy-day skirt went out of fashion. A 1921 article, marking the twenty-fifth anniversary of the Rainy Day Club, pointed to the ongoing struggle of women to wear comfortable clothes consisting of short skirts.[119] Even as women increasingly progressed toward freedom and independence, both politically and sartorially, Rainy Daisies' crusade did not seem to be a relic of the past, but part of the contemporary modern effort to promote women's rights.

Although by the 1920s the Gibson Girl would symbolize more of a distant curiosity than an epitome of women's liberation, her ability to convey through her clothes an image of a freedom and feminine fashionability had an immense influence on the relationship between fashion and feminism. For the New Woman of the 1900s, the shirtwaist and the short skirt became both the epitome of and the terrain from which she could negotiate political, racial, gender, economic, and social equality. Yet, it was not the shorter hemline of the skirt or the looseness of the shirtwaist that made the Gibson Girl ensemble liberating. But it was the meanings that women gave the outfit, using it to express their own interpretation of fashion. Indeed, the New Woman and her fashions reflected her generation: women who were beginning to do away with ideas of gender hierarchy and to claim new statuses and freedoms but who were not completely ready to denounce the traditions with which they grew up. As the new century progressed, however, not only women's roles would be in flux. Women's fashions, as both a mirror and a catalyst to the increasing freedoms women would begin to enjoy in the twentieth century, also changed.

CHAPTER TWO

Styling Women's Rights
Fashion and Feminist Ideology

In 1911, a New York suffragist informed the *New-York Tribune* reporter of the new direction the campaign for women's suffrage has taken. "And now the latest move concerns the clothes question," she said. "It is a personal affair with most of us, but it is frequently hinted by the big leaders that the dress question is perhaps the most vital of all." As this suffragist explained, since the most pressing issue of the campaign was to gain public support by drawing a positive attention to the suffrage cause, it was decided that "the Suffragette . . . hereafter is to be the leading exponent of fashion . . . each and every one will dress as she never has before. It's all been planned and agreed to, signed and sealed."[1] This new attention to women's appearance and the emphasis on the need to look fashionable, feminine, and beautiful marked a change in the campaigning strategy.[2] After a decade of facing serious impediments to the broadening of the franchise, suffragists in the 1910s began utilizing theatrical and spectacular tactics—from outdoor gatherings, colorful parades, theatrical pageantry, and picketing—that pushed the issue of women's rights to the forefront of popular imagination and debates.[3] Fashion played a crucial role in popularizing these tactics and in shifting public opinion. As suffragists adopted the mainstream styles of the period, they not only fashioned a new image of the politically engaged woman that was palatable to the public, but they also turned fashion into a political tool.

Yet, the emphasis on fashionability was more than just a savvy campaign tactic. It pointed to a new understanding of the connection between fashion and women's rights that coincided with the rise of feminism in the early 1910s. While not all suffragists were feminists, there was considerable overlap between the two groups, as the suffrage movement provided a useful platform for many feminists to push for social change. Feminists, however, offered a more radical vision for society than just the access to the vote. Indeed, the novelty in the term "feminism"—a neologism that entered the American vernacular around 1911–12 as a signifier of what was then called the woman's movement—was that it described a comprehensive ideology that went beyond struggles for voting and political participation.[4] Marie Jenny Howe, a self-identified feminist, argued in a 1914 *New Review* article: "Feminism is not limited to any one cause or reform. It strives for equal rights, equal laws, equal opportunity, equal wages, equal standards, and a whole new world of human equality." According to Howe, feminism was an encompassing ideology that included a gendered social critique intertwined with a call to change the entire social system, not only the lives of women. In order for women to achieve equality, Howe argued, a complete social, psychological, and political change in the position of women was needed.[5]

Howe's understanding of feminism centered on ideas of self-fulfillment and self-expression that were intertwined with modernist aesthetics and mass culture.[6] Like their suffragist friends who harnessed fashion to promote their campaign, Howe and her peers, many in the radical and bohemian circles of New York's Greenwich Village, viewed fashion and appearance as integral in their struggle for equality and freedom. "Dress seems, at first glance, to be the least important of the questions which modern women are taking up; but the ... examination into its practical aspects reveals ... that it affects all their other interests," Nina Wilcox Putnam, a self-proclaimed Greenwich Village feminist, argued in 1914.[7] For these young, usually White, educated, upper-middle-class, politically radical feminists, clothing was a critical social issue as well as a matter of personal choice, identity, and self-esteem.[8] Seeing themselves as New Women and active feminist reformers, these women used fashion to express their ideas regarding sexual freedom, independence, and women's social roles. For them, their clothing and appearance constituted their identity as feminists. Yet their call for more comfortable clothes and freedom of choice was entwined with an aesthetic awareness and emphasis on beauty, thus marking a new relationship feminism forged with fashion.

This chapter examines how fashion functioned both as a political strategy to popularize the suffrage cause and as the sartorial expression of feminist ideas, pointing to the shifting role of fashion in early twentieth-century feminism. While nineteenth-century woman's rights advocates sought to distance themselves from the associations of fashion with frivolity, irrationality, artificiality, and volatility—all negative gendered qualities equated with femininity—suffragists and bohemian feminists in the 1910s did not reject fashion per se, nor did they believe that it hindered women's progress.[9] On the contrary. For them, fashion was associated with modernity, rationality, and innovativeness—values that symbolized their identities as New Women and feminists. Thus, instead of being relegated to the margins, or seen as frivolous issues, fashion and appearance became an important component in a range of feminist efforts and an important site where feminist ideology was shaped in this period.

Changes in fashion styles throughout the 1910s, as well as the sartorial and social changes that World War I brought by the end of the decade, opened up a room of experimentation and expansion of appropriate feminine appearance. As mainstream fashion became more compatible with reformative ideas regarding women's bodies and freedom of movement, clothing became useful means to negotiate gender and sexual politics. Both suffragists and bohemian feminists adopted and adapted the popular fashions and presented themselves as stylish modern women. However, while there were overlaps between suffragists and bohemians, these two groups differed in how they utilized fashion and in their understanding of its social and political roles. Greenwich Village feminists adapted the mainstream fashions, most notably Oriental-style dresses, to create an alternative, even avant-garde form of dress that communicated both their identities as modern women and their feminist ideas regarding women's gender roles. For them, clothing was a way to express their uniqueness and creativity as independent individuals. They fashioned their appearance according to their own personal taste and political values, free from external commercial decrees, viewing the making of clothes as a feminist practice.[10]

Suffragists, on the other hand, generally saw fashion not as a form of gender critique but as a tactical means of gaining public support for their cause.[11] By emphasizing the aesthetic values and feminine elements of their clothes, they sought to separate themselves from the popular derogatory images of women activists that portrayed them as masculine and unattractive. Suffragists thus harnessed fashion and fashionability to present their respectability as women and their worthiness as voters.[12] Although suffragists differed in both their political tactics and their fashionable tastes, most tended to adopt mainstream fashions without changing them, thus embracing the gendered conventions these clothes conveyed. Black suffragists in particular, adopted more conservative styles of dress that emphasized their feminine qualities and did not challenge gender norms. They harnessed fashion to advance their cause, combining efforts for gender equality with racial uplift.

Nevertheless, whether they adhered to the mainstream fashions or adapted them to create more alternative forms of dress, both suffragists and Greenwich Village feminists forged a more positive relationship with fashion. Both in their writings and sartorial practices, these feminists sought to combine emancipatory ideas with fashionable appearance. Arguing that women's attire could be comfortable, functional, *and* beautiful, they pushed the issue of fashionability, not only of clothes, to the center of feminist concerns. For these suffragists and bohemian feminists, fashionability became crucial for promoting women's independence and visibility in the public sphere, and they used their clothes to advance this political message. In the process, they did more than transform the image of "the feminist" in the public eye. They expanded feminism's scope beyond struggles for equality into the material everyday lives of women. But more importantly, through their use of clothing to express their politics, they claimed fashion as a feminist means of resistance.

Changing Attitudes toward Fashion

By the second decade of the twentieth century, the feminist agenda placed more emphasis on visual appearance and its cultivation through clothes. Calls for more comfortable clothing became increasingly intertwined with a fashionable awareness to appear attractive and in style. In a paper presented at the biennial meeting of the General Federation of Women's Clubs in 1912, the suffragist Maud C. Hessler argued that "the question of dress cannot be separated from artistic standards," and that women's dress should not only express "physical comfort, but also . . . gracious harmony and beauty which gives pleasure to the beholder and expresses in visible form an inner beauty of orderliness of spirit."[13] This emphasis on aesthetics reflected the growing importance of appearance and personality in popular culture. The rise of the mass consumer market and the increasing dissemination of visual images through periodicals, opulent department-store displays, and advertising created a more visually oriented society than in earlier decades.[14] Realizing the social and political importance of images to shape public opinion and attitudes, suffragists pushed this issue forward in their campaigns through a revived interest in clothing. Instead of hampering their goals, suffragists found that fashion, if utilized properly, could be used to popularize and advance their cause.

Thinking that their political message would be more palatable if delivered by attractive messengers, suffragists emphasized the importance of cultivating a feminine, appealing, and less threatening public appearance through fashion. According to Dr. Anna Howard Shaw, one of the National American Woman's Suffrage Association (NAWSA) leaders, this meant avoiding any attribute that would associate one with the "freaks"—the short-haired woman, the long-haired man, and the woman who smoked and played bridge—or any other behavior that did not conform to the mainstream gender notions of how one should look and behave. Only in this way, Shaw believed, could suffragists avoid being identified as masculine, dowdy, and unattractive, an accusation women faced as they began to demand equality with men, and which proved to be a serious obstacle for gaining suffrage.[15] As one activist confessed, the mannish-looking suffragist "has done more to hurt the cause than anything I know of. . . . Our salvation will be the effeminate woman, the average woman."[16] In emphasizing their femininity by appearing dignified, attractive, and fashionable, suffragists implied that they were likable and virtuous women, thus undermining the association of political participation with a threat to gender hierarchies.[17]

Inez Milholland, one of the leaders of the National Woman's Party (NWP) whose beauty made her a celebrity within suffrage ranks and beyond, styled herself as a fashionable "beauty" with brains and independence. Understanding that her status as a charmer proved beneficial to the suffrage campaign, she admitted to press reporters in 1910 that "it might be considered good politics for those in the suffrage ranks to put their most attractive members forward when it was sought to influence legislators."[18] Milholland used her fashionable reputation to redefine the image of the suffragist as a modern, fashion-savvy woman. Yet she also harnessed her fashionable reputation to expand the acceptable gendered boundaries of appearance for women in public and to promote a more subversive, albeit subtle, image. In 1912, Milholland launched with her friend the actress Fola La Follette a Throw-Away-Your-Corset campaign, calling on women to emancipate themselves "in matters of dress as well as in politics." Despite the radical message, Milholland's reputation as "one of the most beautiful young women in the suffrage cause" led the press to embrace the initiative rather than framing it as a threat.[19] The fact that both she and La Follette, who was the daughter of a famous politician, could receive such positive reaction from the public when promoting radical initiatives attested to the cultural influence these women had.

Milholland believed that voting was a tool to enhance women's beauty, arguing that "the opportunity for thinking and for occupation which will be given to women by the granting of the ballot will do much to make them beautiful."[20] Other suffragists also pushed forward the idea that voting was a beautifying force and refuted arguments that suffrage agitation masculinized women. The suffragist Maud Wood Park announced that "if a woman wishes to be beautiful let her take a real interest in the things of the great world outside her home. I might almost say that to retain her beauty she should become a suffragist, for that movement offered the greatest field for living, purposed interest." Supporting suffrage demonstrated the intelligence and progress of a woman, Park claimed, but most importantly, it also helped her stay young and beautiful.[21] The feminist intellectual Charlotte Perkins Gilman also argued that political independence and freedom would enhance women's beauty. Once women would gain equality with men, Gilman argued, their clothes would reflect their humanity instead of their sex appeal, which she believed was society's way of keeping women dependent on men.[22]

The claim that suffrage had the power to enhance—rather than diminish—one's feminine beauty became a central strategy in promoting the suffrage cause, in gaining public support, and in refuting anti-suffragists' accusations of gender transgression.[23] Suffragists used two main arguments in their campaign, which were in constant, unresolved tension with each other. On the one hand, suffragists demanded equality on the basis of their humanity (or their likeness to men) and sought to eliminate sex-specific limitations, such as access to the vote. On the other hand, suffragists, especially in the last stages of the campaign, also stressed the benevolent qualities women could bring into society (differently from men). They underlined the qualities that defined "female" or "womanhood," arguing that the vote would allow them to bring these qualities into the political system and to "clean up" (and feminize) politics.[24] Suffragists' emphasis on feminine appearance thus can be understood as a strategic decision to favor "the difference argument" in order to achieve public support for their goals. In appearing fashionable and appealing to the eye, suffragists believed they could celebrate their femininity without giving up their call for equality. As suffragist Lydia Commander declared, women were "determined to take an active part in the community and look pretty too."[25]

However, by favoring these kinds of arguments, suffragists also undermined some of the radicalism that feminist ideology contained and weakened the possibility that access to the vote might change gender structures.[26] Emphasizing the feminine aspects of their dress and appearance revealed these suffragists' gender conservatism and their shortcoming in offering a more radical feminist critique. Viewed through the lens of their fashion choices, suffragists saw the vote not as a tool for social change but as a means to expand their influence in the public sphere while still maintaining the current gender system.

One strategy where fashion played an important role in aiding suffragists to counter accusations of being manly was to increase their visibility in the press, mainly through photography.[27] In a 1912 *Good Housekeeping* article, for example, Mary Holland Kinkaid used photographs of prominent suffragists to refute the "popular misconception" that suffragists were "strident creature[s], mannish in attire and of unattractive personality." In addition to describing the superb domestic skills—including cooking, sewing, and decorating—of famous suffragists such as Elizabeth Cady Stanton, Carrie Chapman Catt, Anna Howard Shaw, and Inez Milholland, Kinkaid presented photos of suffragists as fashionably dressed, charming, and motherly. These photographs offered a tangible proof that suffragists were as accomplished in keeping their homes as they were in politics and that they truly adhered to the romantic, feminine, and appealing image they claimed to present.[28] Although many of the militant suffragists were young, single women who represented an updated version of the athletic Gibson Girl, Kinkaid chose in her article to emphasize the "woman militant's" more domestic and motherly qualities. The photograph of Milholland, for example, was taken from a suffrage pageant in which she was depicted as Cornelia, the classical Roman figure surrounded by children. While Milholland herself did not have children, it was important for Kinkaid to present her not just as an "unusual beauty" but also as the prototype of the devoted mother.[29] Kinkaid also identified married suffragists using the protocol of the day: tacking "Mrs." onto the names of their notable husbands and omitting the women's first (and maiden) names. This was the case of the society woman turned suffragist Katherine Duer MacKay, who, despite being the organizer of the Equal Franchise League, was identified in the article as Mrs. Clarence MacKay. MacKay's interest in politics was also framed as a domestic endeavor. "Like many of the other suffragists," Kinkaid explained, MacKay's suffrage activism "may be traced to the instinct of improving home conditions and whatever . . . fails to contribute to the highest welfare of the family."[30]

Kinkaid's choice to highlight these gender attributes reflected the relatively conservative view of some suffragists, as well as the magazine's readers, that women must maintain a feminine appearance despite their political activism. But it also suggests the power of anti-suffragist propaganda claiming that giving women the vote would cause them to abandon their husbands and children, and that overall suffragists were hysterical, unsexed, or bad mothers.[31] Fearing that a celebration of more defiant appearance would avert support from the suffrage cause, suffragists chose to highlight their feminine attributes through adhering to popular fashions, rather than promoting alternative styles. Even Milholland, who was known to present a more radical appearance, was celebrated as a romantic figure and not as an extremist.

Black activists, like their White counterparts, also had to harness their appearance to gain public support to their ideas, and they too emphasized their feminine and domestic traits. Yet, in general, the African American community was in favor of women's suffrage, seeing it as part of a broader struggle for universal suffrage and racial equality. Thus, the emphasis on feminine and respectable appearance was geared more toward uplifting messages and White audiences than an attempt to convince Black men that women were entitled to vote. Black suffragists were more concerned in convincing Whites of African Americans' worthiness as humans, rather than trying to ameliorate fears that they were "desexualizing the race" or that the vote would masculinize women.[32] As racist stereotypes already identified African American women as masculine brutes, Black suffragists needed to claim their humanity by presenting genteel femininity as they made their case for granting suffrage. "The mannishly attired, short skirted, short haired woman, who, for so many years was the butt of the satirist and the cartoonist, has been shoved off the board," argued the suffragist and activist Mary Church Terrell. Praising her substitute, "the cultured, womanly woman ... [who] in her dress ... keeps pace with fashion," Terrell also emphasized that she was a mother who "boasts of it and the home which she ennobles."[33] By cultivating not only feminine, but also fashionable appearance, Black suffragists demonstrated that they too could bridge the gap between political activism and beauty. Arguing that gaining the vote was a crucial step for overcoming both gender and racial stereotypes regarding Black femininity, African American suffragists framed fashionability as a tool of racial progress.

Fashion thus became part of both White and Black suffragists' engagement with class and racial politics of respectability. As the majority of White suffragists came from the upper and middle classes, maintaining a fashionable appearance was an indication of their respectability as women, even when they engaged in activities that challenged the gendered divisions of the private and public spheres. In a response to an anti-suffragist who complained about the indecency of suffragists' clothes during a parade, the suffragist Elizabeth Newport Hepburn claimed that she saw "only self-respecting women dressed in the fashion of the day. The clothes of these marching women were ... essentially up to date." Alluding to the fashionable tastes of the marchers, Hepburn maintained that their appearances alone roundly discredited the anti-suffrage argument that "nobody who stood for woman's rights could by any chance represent the charms and beauty of women." Suffragists' fashionable tastes attested to their respectability, not to their indecency, Hepburn argued.[34] Even though questioning women's sexual respectability was a common tactic to discredit working-class women's struggles, middle-class White suffragists were protected by their class privilege when they went out onto the streets. Suffragists needed to face more accusations of transgressing gender hierarchies and being "freaks" than of being prostitutes or sexual deviants.[35]

Whiteness was another category that enabled these suffragists to claim their respectability while stretching the boundaries of what was considered to be appropriate feminine behavior. Although White suffragists had to counter accusations of being masculine, their Whiteness enabled them to challenge more fiercely notions of gender propriety without having their femininity, and their access to its privileges, questioned. An example for that can be found in Milholland's appearance leading the March 3, 1913, Washington, D.C., Woman Suffrage Procession, the first national parade that put the suffrage cause on the front pages of newspapers and in the forefront of public attention.[36] The image of Milholland dressed as Joan of Arc with a long cape, a crown on her head, and demonstrating her horse-riding skills (figure 2.1) became associated not only with the parade and with Milholland herself, but also with the NWP and suffrage in general. Even while appropriating the symbolism of the masculine white knight on a horse, Milholland was able to capitalize on her reputation as a beauty to convert the image of a pants-wearing woman into an attractive one instead of a radical threat.[37] In presenting herself as a noble woman, wearing a crown and flowing hair, adopting a medieval myth of female heroism and adding modern meanings to it, Milholland constructed a new image of womanhood. She was strong yet elegant, romantic yet modern, determined yet likeable—an embodiment of the New Woman that the NWP and the press used to popularize the suffrage cause.[38]

Black suffragists, however, could not enjoy Milholland's entitlement.[39] For them, maintaining a fashionable feminine appearance was crucial not only to their ability to advance the suffrage cause but to take part in the struggle to begin with. Because African American suffragists could not escape racist stereotypes that deemed Black women as hypersexual and promiscuous, they

FIGURE 2.1: Suffragists deployed fashion and other spectacular tactics to promote their cause by presenting themselves as honorable, beautiful women, such as the example of Inez Milholland, who led the 1913 Woman Suffrage Procession in Washington, D.C. (Bain News Service photograph collection, Library of Congress)

had to fashion a distinct form of female propriety as they engaged in political advocacy.[40] Indeed, fashion fulfilled a dual political function for Black suffragists. Their emphasis on feminine and fashionable appearance was not just about claiming racial equality and access to the privileges of White womanhood. It was also directed inward, toward the Black community, as Terrell and other Black activists used their appearance to push for greater visibility of women in politics.

Clothing and appearance thus played an important role in the suffrage struggle, shaping tactics and attitudes among suffragists. Yet, the ways in which both Black and White suffragists styled themselves also influenced the reception of their ideas in public. By cultivating a feminine and fashionable appearance, suffragists transformed their image and gained support for their cause. But looking fashionable also created a mutual terrain from which they could form cooperation in advancing their goals, as fashion offered at least a potential to create a feminist solidarity that was based on ladyhood. However, suffragists' need to counter the sexist and racist images as part of the opposition's propaganda, as well as the racism of many of the White suffrage leaders, limited the degree to which they could form such coalitions. Moreover, the anti-suffrage propaganda also influenced how much suffragists were willing to push against it to promote more radical visions for women's roles in society. Instead of seeking alternative looks that might have challenged or upset the public, suffragists chose to adhere to more conventional gender norms and to adopt the mainstream fashions.

Suffrage Styles and the Politicization of Fashion

Luckily for suffragists, developments in clothing styles and manufacturing facilitated their ability to appear fashionable without compromising on comfort or mobility. By 1908, the year in which suffrage parades began, new fashions, which reduced the numbers and weight of undergarments, and marked an end to the famous Edwardian petticoats with their frills and flounces, entered the mainstream. Moving toward simplification, the new styles created a narrower and straighter silhouette than the famous S-shape of the 1900s by reducing skirt circumference and train length.[41] *Vogue*'s fashion reporter commented on the new silhouette: "the fashionable figure is growing straighter and straighter, less bust, less hips, more waist, and a wonderfully long, slender suppleness about the limbs.... How slim, how graceful, how elegant women look!"[42] Although the shirtwaist-and-skirt ensemble would remain popular, its prominence declined in favor of one-piece dresses and tailored suits, which became the latest word in fashion. These styles created a new fashion ideal that, according to fashion historian Elizabeth Ewing, symbolized "the start of modern fashion."[43]

These developments did not happen in a vacuum. Designers were not immune to the changes resulting in the modern reality of women in work and leisure that demanded new and appropriate clothing. Responding to these trends, they incorporated loose, simple, and more flowing elements—similar to those advocated by nineteenth-century dress reformers—into their designs.[44] Haute-couture designers, most notably Paul Poiret, Jeanne Paquin, Lucile (Lady Duff Gordon), and the Liberty & Co. store in London stood at the vanguard of these changes. They brought back the concept of the natural figure by introducing and popularizing the Empire-style dresses: those with high waistlines falling just below the bust and often made from drapey, transparent silk or silklike fabrics that produced loose and linear silhouettes. A 1911 article in *Harper's Bazaar* commented: "more *en vogue* than ever before are the smart and serviceable one-piece dresses of navy-blue silk serge, surah silk, or French serge.... The sense of security at the waist-line and the peace of mind assured by the possession of a simple all-in-one gown which can be slipped on at a moment's notice are hard to estimate in dollars and cents."[45] By the mid-1910s, these couture one-piece dresses became so popular as their dissemination reached beyond the upper class. Department stores, mail-order companies, and fashion magazines quickly adapted haute-couture designs and created cheap versions and patterns that offered working-class women opportunities to keep up with the latest Parisian modes.[46]

The fascination of designers as well as consumers with Oriental styles during the 1910s also contributed to the simplicity and looseness of clothes. Drawing from various cultures and periods ranging from Russia, Turkey, China, to Japan, the Oriental style was eclectic and diverse in character, sometimes combining different cultural motifs in the same outfit.[47] By 1914, inspired by Leon Bakst's designs for Serge Diaghilev's Ballets Russes, the shirtwaist would turn into a tunic worn outside the skirt, providing a less restrictive waistline than in the previous decade. East Asian influence on fashion, mainly those inspired by the Japanese kimono, also contributed to the popularization of the loose-fitting styles and facilitated less constricting corsets and undergarments.[48]

The Oriental style also espoused a more sensual ideal of female beauty, as the narrow silhouette emphasized women's curves and legs. Christening in 1910 the "hobble skirt"—a long skirt with a narrow hem inspired by the traditional Japanese costume—Poiret declared, "Yes, I freed the bust, but I shackled the legs."[49] Despite restricting women's freedom of movement to some extent, the narrow skirt created a sensual image that emphasized women's sexuality. Unlike the wide skirt of the previous century, which removed a woman's lower body from sight and desexualized women, the hobble skirt highlighted women's bodies and accentuated both the functional and sexual elements of the legs. Moreover, despite its confining name and look, the skirt's original design was soon modified with slits and slashes, so that, although the skirt remained extremely narrow, it became less restrictive in terms of movement, which contributed even more to its sexual appeal.[50] Even Irene Castle, the Grande Dame of the dance halls and a fashion trendsetter, admitted that "the Tango may be danced in the narrowest of skirts" and recommended that dancers wear hobble skirts with slits in order to remain fashionable while dancing.[51]

Whereas the Empire and the Oriental styles celebrated a sense of eclectic romanticism and feminine gentility, the new tailored suit—with its loose-waisted jacket, and the straight, mid-calf or above-ankle length skirt—represented a practical modernity with which many women identified (figure 2.2).[52] According to the *New York Times*, the functionality of the suit appealed specifically to women who were "interested in other things besides society—even though [they] be in and of society," with philanthropy, suffrage, and art constituting those "other things." These women turned the tailored suit into an appropriate all-day outfit to wear, both for walking and running errands during the day, and for afternoon formal receptions, making it one of the most popular fashions of the period.[53] The outbreak of war in Europe in 1914 and its mobilization efforts also contributed to the popularity of the tailored suit. Much due to its functionality and utility as military uniforms, designers popularized the suit by lowering the waistline and shortening the skirt hemline, providing a practical outfit for the war effort.[54]

As the ensemble of the 1890s had been, the tailored suit of the 1910s was deemed strictly American. The suit accommodated developments in the ready-made fashion industry, which pushed for simpler patterns and loose-fitting styles that were more easily adjusted to standardized measurements. A *New York Times* article praised U.S. ready-made manufacturers, noting that "the ready-to-wear tailored suit is sold in all classes of shops . . . even those that do not serve the highest class of trades are showing excellent tailored suits of moderate price." Calling the ready-made tailored suit the "American woman's National dress," the article claimed that "year by year it has improved in style and workmanship, until it has made possible our oft-repeated boast that more well-dressed women are seen on American streets than anywhere else in the world."[55]

These new styles appealed to suffragists, who readily embraced them into their everyday and campaign wear, finding them useful in their promotion of the suffrage cause. Many embraced the functionality and easiness of the tailored suit, which despite being more masculine in look than Oriental-style clothing, conveyed professionalism and respectability. Recognizing the appeal of the design to the busy suffragist, the American Ladies Tailors' Association presented in 1910 its own version of a tailored costume, calling it the "suffragette suit."[56] The suit contained a plain shirtwaist under a short jacket and a divided skirt, and resembled the earlier rainy-day outfit. Although the

FIGURE 2.2: The tailored suit became a popular fashion during the 1910s due to its functionality for walking, while still maintaining a professional look. After 1914, silhouettes became looser and wider and were influenced by military uniforms as well as by women's political activities toward suffrage, as in this example from circa 1917. (76.97.1, Chisholm Halle Costume Wing, Western Reserve Historical Society, Cleveland, Ohio)

bifurcation of the skirt alluded to more radical ideas regarding women's bodies, by the 1910s it was no longer viewed as a threat to the gender system. The popularization of cycling turned bifurcated clothing into fashionable items in women's wardrobes. Seeing it as a utilitarian solution to their needs, suffragists welcomed the divided skirt of the "suffragette suit," embracing both its fashionability and the reformative feminist ideas behind it.

However, what distinguished the suit as a feminist attire according to reporters was less of the fact that the skirt was bifurcated, but that the suit contained pockets, and plenty of them. "This garment has two pockets in front and two behind," the *New York Times* article informed the readers. "The whole costume has seven or eight pockets, all in sight and all easy to find," the reporter concluded.[57] Whereas pockets were considered a utilitarian, and even essential, clothing element to the walking suit, they became in the 1910s a metaphor to women's rights and suffrage. The suffragist Alice Duer Miller, in her series column "Are Women People?," published in 1914 a short piece titled "Why We Oppose Pockets for Women." In it, Miller mockingly detailed anti-suffragist arguments, substituting the word "vote" in "pockets" in order to show the absurdity of preventing women of their rights.[58] Yet, despite her sarcastic tone, Miller purposely substituted "votes" for "pockets," acknowledging that both had the potential to enable an independent and mobile lifestyle. Suffragists, like dress reformers before them, were well aware of the feminist meanings of pockets, allowing women independence and mobility, and they framed their demand for sartorial freedom as part of their political demands.[59] The association of pockets with suffragists' agitation for the vote became so prevalent that every outfit that contained multiple and visible pockets was deemed as a "suffragette costume," not only the tailored suit. In 1913, the trade journal *Women's Wear Daily* (known at the time as *Women's Wear*)reported on two one-piece dresses consisting of "mannish pockets on each side," up to the total number of four pockets, identifying them as "suffragette gowns."[60]

Suffragists adopted the "suffragette" version of the tailored suit both because it was more suitable to women's active lifestyles, and because they could easily use it in their assertion of their political presence in the public sphere. In addition to the benefits of greater comfort and health that the tailored or "suffragette" suit provided, the circumference of the skirt—which was not too wide and not too narrow—together with the ankle-length hemline, made marching in city streets more convenient and more feasible, thus turning parades and other suffrage spectacles into a popular publicity tactic. "Marching costumes" as the one in figure 2.3, consisting of tight trousers underneath a mid-calf-length skirt with a deep slit, enabled suffragists to march comfort-

FIGURE 2.3: Changes to clothing styles not only enabled suffragists to present themselves as beautiful respectable women but also made tactics such as marching and parading much more feasible. ("Woman Modelling Marching Costume for Chicago's Suffrage Parade, June 6, 1916," George Grantham Bain Collection, Library of Congress)

ably, even for a few miles, without being worried that their attire would get dirty or wet or become a health hazard. Although the suffragist's pose in figure 2.3 revealed her legs, while marching she would have looked very feminine with the trousers concealed under the long skirt, thus not exposing her to negative public reaction—at least not on that account.[61]

Indeed, although suffragists did not oppose reformative ideas regarding women's dress, they were reluctant to adopt styles that challenged gender norms of femininity in more overt ways. While divided skirts, or marching outfits such as the one in figure 2.3 would have been acceptable, the trouser or pantaloon skirt—an Oriental-influenced garment based on the Turkish harem pants—was firmly opposed. Trying to avoid the association with the radical bloomerites of the nineteenth century, suffrage leaders denounced the trouser skirt as ugly as well as uncomfortable, and refused to approve the outfit or to associate it with the suffrage cause.[62]

The suffrage press also advertised specific suffrage designs, such as the "suffrage blouse" advertised in the NAWSA publication the *Woman Citizen* in 1917. The blouse had no distinct feature beyond being "ready-to-wear-to-anything-and-not-at-all expensive," a characteristic the magazine identified as distinctively suited for suffragists' needs.[63] Like the "suffragette suit" or the "suffragette gown," comfort and utility were the elements that defined a fashion item as a suffrage design, not a particular style or brand. Indeed, even though suffragists showed a preference for certain styles such as the suffragette suit, it would be difficult to identify a unified appearance that suffragists promoted. Some preferred the suit, some opted for a one-piece dress, while others alternated between different styles.[64] As mainstream fashion in the 1910s became more suitable to their activist lifestyle, suffragists felt they could adopt the popular modes to convey their political message without having to create a special style of their own. In fact, Mary Ware Dennett, the secretary of NAWSA, insisted that "there is nothing uniform about suffragists, except the desire for the power to vote."[65] Citing individual taste and sense of fashion as the main motivations for choosing an outfit, Dennett and her fellow suffragists used their fashion choices as an argument for gaining suffrage.

By adhering to the popular trends, suffragists expressed their superior fashion sense, thus countering the myth that they were masculine and unattractive. But by cultivating their own individual tastes, these suffragists also proved their independence of mind. Although following the latest fashions implied conformity and feminine frivolity, suffragists framed their adherence to fashion as the expression of women's independence as well as their feminine virtue, rather than an organizational decree they must follow. In a message to marchers in 1912, Harriot Stanton Blatch announced that "a white or light dress and a small hat are desirable. They are not obligatory." Arguing that large numbers of marchers are more important than uniformity of dress, Blatch went further by claiming that "any regret some may feel for lack of uniformity

... should be outweighed by the thought that distaste for conforming may be but the promise of independence in a future voter."[66]

The only garment that ever came close to becoming a suffrage uniform was a replica of prison garb that NWP activists wore during their time at the Occoquan Workhouse in Virginia after being arrested for picketing in front of the White House in 1917. While in Occoquan, suffragists resisted the dress, viewing it as a sign of the denial of their rights as political prisoners and a deprivation of their middle-class, privileged status. "It takes a dominant personality to survive these clothes," Doris Stevens recalled.[67] However, once released, suffragists turned the same garb into a badge of honor of their political determination. In 1919, two years after their jailing first began, the NWP organized a cross-country "Prison Special" speaking tour in which suffragists recounted their experiences in jail as a way to promote their cause. Speakers on the tour wore "calico wrappers designed exactly after the pattern of those which they were forced to wear in the work-house, thereby making the accounts of their experiences in the jail more vivid."[68] These suffragists used the prison dresses as a visual rhetorical tool, turning their own bodies into a political site for advocating suffrage and gaining public legitimacy for their claims. By creating their own fashionable versions of the original prison garment, suffragists stripped away the connotation of criminality and powerlessness inherent in the prison dress and turned it into a symbol of struggle and power as well as into a political performance.[69]

Moreover, by dressing up in their prison garbs replicas, NWP suffragists, who were mostly upper- and middle-class women, were able to project a classless image that posited a solidarity, even if only imagined, with working-class prisoners. However, as with other historical and theatrical outfits that suffragists employed in their pageants and parades, the prison replicas remained a publicity tool and a gimmick, not an attempt to create a new fashion or to harness the mainstream modes to shape their image.

Clothing silhouettes and designs were not the only fashion elements that helped suffragists popularize their cause. Color, and particularly the suffrage colors—white, purple, and golden yellow—proved to be a central technique through which suffragists managed to convey their ideas visually.[70] Glenna Tinnin, one of the organizers of the 1913 Washington, D.C., suffrage parade, explained that "an idea that is driven home to the mind through the eye produces a more striking and lasting impression than any that goes through the ear."[71] The 1913 parade plan specified the order of the marchers, divided by professions, countries and states, and the color of their dresses, hats, and banners. Social workers were supposed to wear dark blue, writers wore white and purple, and artists wore pale rose.[72] The overall picture created a compelling and organized sight of color and harmony that advanced the point that suffragists had excellent fashionable taste. It also highlighted the argument that, with the vote, suffragists could wield their competence and skills in fashion and beauty in the service of the common good.

Through color and arrangement, suffragists thus turned their clothes and their bodies into a tangible manifestation of their arguments.[73] In addition, the use of colors and banners enabled suffragists to transform the urban landscape into a site of visual politics. In marching in their costumes and holding their handmade sashes and slogans, which exhibited their womanly talents of embroidery and fashion, suffragists asserted their political presence in what was considered to be a male territory. A photograph of a 1915 parade in New York City exemplifies this idea, showing suffragists marching in formation, their bright clothing contrasting sharply with the sidewalk crowds of men in dark-colored suits (figure 2.4). This visual contrast—between women and men, bright and dark, order and disorder—provided a perceptible manifestation to suffragists' arguments and conveyed to viewers the possible contribution women might make to politics after receiving the vote.

While suffrage parades often created a colorful image, white in particular became popular among the many suffrage organizations.[74] In 1911, the New York Woman's Political Union parade committee appealed to manufacturers to process an order of white dresses for their spring march, deciding it was a useful color to express their appeal. The National Woman Suffrage Parade Committee also instructed marchers to wear white blouses and skirts for their 1915 parade while carrying yellow banners.[75] By adopting white as a signature color, suffragists conveyed a message of unity, emphasizing their shared gender identity and plea, despite differences in class and backgrounds among them.[76] However, despite this unified image, color could not overwrite racial distinctions among suffragists. Although Black women participated in parades and other theatrical spectacles, they were often relegated to the back of the processions and photographs of them almost never appeared in the mainstream press, thus giving the illusion that only White women marched in parades.

Nevertheless, Black suffragists adopted the fashionable imagery of the suffrage colors and silhouettes, using it as a political means to advance racial equality, and to reclaim their bodies, their humanity, and their respectability as women. White suffragist Mary Beard, who headed the education division in the 1913 Washington, D.C., parade, where Mary Church Terrell marched

Styling Women's Rights

FIGURE 2.4: The use of suffrage colors, and particularly white, was instrumental in constructing a unified suffrage imagery, creating not only a sense of solidarity among activists but also making a powerful political statement. ("Pre-election parade for suffrage in NYC, Oct. 23, 1915, in which 20,000 women marched," George Grantham Bain Collection, Library of Congress)

with a group of students from Howard University in a segregated section, commented on the dignity of the marchers and the positive responses they received from the crowd.[77] Ida B. Wells also famously integrated the 1913 parade, when—despite resistance from the organizers to march with her fellow state suffragists—she joined the Illinois delegation from the crowd, wearing their matching hats and banners.[78] By dressing like her White counterparts, Wells not only asserted her right to equal citizenship as a woman, but she also promoted racial equality as an African American, laying claims to middle-class respectability.[79] Thus, as they adopted suffrage styles, suffragists such as Mary Church Terrell and Ida B. Wells could show support for suffrage and at the same time challenge the prevalent racism and class bias of many of the suffrage leaders.

In particular, Black suffragists capitalized on the association of the color white with sexual and moral purity—qualities long deprived from African American women in public discourse—to show they were honorable women.

Yet, they utilized the suffrage imagery and colors beyond the struggle for the vote. Black suffragists found the visual language of suffrage to be useful in advancing a broader activist agenda that sought to better the lives of all African Americans, including universal suffrage, economic equality, and fighting against Jim Crow and lynching. In 1917, in response to race riots in Waco, Memphis, and East St. Louis, the National Association for the Advancement of Colored People (NAACP) organized a silent parade to protest the discrimination and oppression of Black people in the United States.[80] Using similar tactics to those in suffrage demonstrations, eight thousand protesters marched in silence down Fifth Avenue in New York City, carrying signs against segregation and lynching. Women wore white dresses, just as in the suffrage parades, emphasizing their feminine respectability as they marched, causing the *New York Times* to declare that "the parade was in all respects one of the most quiet and orderly demonstrations ever witnessed in Fifth Avenue."[81] By utilizing suffrage parades' imagery to make claims for racial equality, Black activists employed fashion to expand the suffragist agenda to include not only them but also broader issues than the vote. The NAACP's ability to exploit these tactics to their favor also suggests how by 1917 images of women marching in white became part of the mainstream visual urban political landscape that Black women could utilize without risking their respectable status as middle-class women.

The streets were not the only place where suffragists showcased their fashionable sense of adornment. Using their position as consumers as a legitimization for their presence in the downtown districts, suffragists formed a strong connection between fashion and politics through their "voiceless speeches" tactic. This was a staged protest in store windows where a young, fashionable suffragist would hold changing signs. Shop display windows, and particularly those of women's clothing stores, were associated with the accepted feminine activity of shopping. As such, suffragists could use them to promote their political agenda without transgressing gender conventions regarding women's roles in the public sphere.[82] Yet by turning themselves into live mannequins, showcasing not only suffrage slogans but also their clothes and beauty, suffragists framed suffrage as a fashionable trend or as a product to be consumed. These suffragists employed fashion simultaneously as an advertising stunt to allure people to the notion of women voting, and as a commercial tactic to advertise the latest in fashion, thus solidifying the connection between women's rights and fashionable appearance.

Department stores were not just a site of protest, however, but also a place where suffragists could purchase their outfits. Specialty suffrage stores sold suffrage regalia that included sashes, hats, dresses, and blouses, and offered a variety of styles for the fashionable suffragist who wanted to create her own image. In 1912, R. H. Macy's department store was designated the official headquarters for suffrage supplies by the Women's Political Union and NAWSA, a deal that benefited all sides.[83] Other retailers also exploited the growing popularity of suffragists and tried to make a profit by incorporating suffrage symbols, colors, and commodities into their store window decorations.[84]

Macy's and other stores offered official suffrage costumes, and suffrage organizations encouraged women to buy specific outfits as a form of financial contribution and support. Yet, the fact that a woman could be identified with the suffrage cause by wearing mainstream fashion in specific colors expanded participation in suffrage parades and activities to women who did not necessarily come from the middle and upper classes. One could have a suffrage ensemble by buying or making an ordinary white dress or blouse and then adding a decorative accessory in purple or yellow. As the suffragist Elizabeth Newport Hepburn explained, "many of us buy our frocks at department stores, and special suffrage regalia is not, alas, a specialty of these stores."[85] Indeed, for suffragists who were excluded from the mainstream movement due to their class or race, adopting suffrage styles and colors was the easiest way to assert their role as partners in the cause. Through clothes, they could claim access to the privileges of ladyhood and of fashionability that many of the White, upper- and middle-class suffragists enjoyed.

Fashion was thus instrumental to suffragists' success in transforming their public image. The creative use of fashion and the increasing visibility of suffragists in the streets, as well as the circulation of suffragists' photographs in national magazines, provided contemporaries with tangible evidence that suffragists were not "devilish amazons" but ordinary women wearing fashionable styles.[86] "Wherever suffrage parades have been held it has been conceded that they have proved potent object lessons," claimed suffragist Gertrude Halladay Leonard in an internal memo of the Massachusetts Woman Suffrage Association in 1913. "Advertising our cause, arousing interest and favorable sentiment, breaking down prejudice, stirring the imagination. Everywhere they have impressed upon the crowds of spectators that many women care for suffrage, that they are the right women,—normal, sensible and high-minded,—and that they are willing to offer this public proof of their devotion," she explained.[87]

And indeed, suffragists' efforts to turn their image into a positive, fashionable, and likeable one in the public eye seemed to bear fruit. In 1911, the *Independent* commented that "suffrage speakers no longer appear upon the platform in short hair and bloomers. The present-day advocates of the exten-

CHAPTER TWO

FIGURE 2.5: Suffragists used fashion to counter the image of the feminist as a dowdy, masculine-looking woman and to present a new relationship between fashion and women's rights. ("The Type of Suffragette Has Changed," *New-York Tribune*, February 1911, Library of Congress)

sion of woman's sphere are . . . wiser than their grandmothers. . . . They wear all the hair they are entitled to or more, and their gowns are in the height of fashion."[88] The *New-York Tribune* also acknowledged that the "type" of suffragist has changed (figure 2.5). Instead of the masculine, dowdy, suffragist, with oversize clothes, untidy short hair, and a masculine hat, the new type of suffragist, as the illustration showed, was an attractive young woman dressed in a fashionable one-piece dress, wide hat with feathers, and a sash draped over one shoulder.[89] By 1915, it seemed that at least on the fashion front, suffragists could claim a success. An editorial in *Century Magazine* announced: "In the campaign for woman suffrage now being waged in New York, it has been observed ... that the suffrage speakers have a conspicuous advantage over their opponents in point of personal charm; that, in fact, the 'anti' more often looks like the strong-minded suffragist of caricature than the suffragist does."[90] In their ability to become less outrageous in the public sphere yet still remain noticeable for their sense of style and organization, suffragists pushed women's suffrage into the cultural mainstream and, eventually, into a constitutional amendment.[91] As they employed the popular modes in the creation of their image, suffragists refashioned the ways in which urban politics were played out, contributing to the creation of a modern political landscape based on appearance. Yet in the process, they also formed a positive connection between fashionable appearance and feminist ideas, which marked a new relationship between feminism and fashion. No longer seen as opposing feminist goals, but as a useful way of achieving them, fashionable attire in the 1910s became a part of the suffrage agenda and the fight for women's rights.

The Style Politics of Greenwich Village Feminism

If most suffragists viewed fashion mainly as a tool to popularize their cause, self-proclaimed feminists—many of them belonged to the radical and bohemian circles of Greenwich Village—saw fashion and clothing as part of a broader gendered critique regarding women's role in society. Clothing's ability to serve both as a symbolic language and as material experience fitted feminists' understanding of feminism as both ideology and practice. For them, women's political equality, economic rights, and wearing comfortable, healthy, and becoming clothes were intertwined. In 1914, in a feminist mass meeting titled "Breaking into the Human Race," fashion was discussed along with marriage, motherhood, equal opportunity in the workforce, unionization, and housework as key issues of modern feminism.[92] According to Nina Wilcox Putnam, one of "the country's leading feminist[s]" and a speaker at the meeting, the freedom to wear clothing that expressed the wearer's individuality, sense of style, and independence was a fundamental feminist right. "The true feminist recognizes that one woman may like to swathe herself in draperies, and the next may prefer the plainest, freest form of garment; and that one should be made to feel uncomfortable or ill-at-ease because big financial interests have approved one rather than the other, is outrage upon the right to mental and physical liberty!" argued Putnam.[93] Titling her talk the "Right to Ignore Fashion," Putnam did not negate the pleasure or the power of clothes but sought to free them from external interests and decrees of the fashion industry.

Although the topic of dress reform was certainly not new on the feminist agenda, twentieth-century feminists believed that women's clothes could be both aesthetic and practical and that one should not come at the expanse of the other. For them, fashion was not just a means to an end but a material expression of their feminist identity. In a series of essays on "The Dress of Women" in her journal the *Forerunner* in 1915, Charlotte Perkins Gilman offered an intellectual discussion that attempted to bridge the gap between beauty and health without compromising on aesthetic principles. But clothes and appearance were not only theoretical matters for Gilman.[94] For her, and other bohemian feminists, fashion was an everyday practice of resistance and a tangible way to experience new bodily and mental freedoms. "This matter of the dress of women is mainly important as it affects the minds of women, and so the mind of the whole world," Gilman argued.[95] Female beauty and fashion could be powerful, and these feminists used this power to expand their freedom by designing, adapting, and consuming styles that constituted their identities as modern women.

However, Gilman and others did not frame their efforts as a call for a new movement for dress reform. According to Gilman, "the coming change in the Dress of Women [was] not so much a change of costume as a change of mind." For her, as for Putnam, the ability to cultivate an individual taste, free from economic or sexual interests, reflected women's progress. Only when women could choose the most suitable clothing to their lifestyles and bodies would they become beautiful, Gilman argued. "The hope of the world in this matter of clothing is not in some revelation of A Perfect Dress; it is in the development of a personal taste, an educated taste; and with it, a strong effective will," she wrote. Believing that an "extremely comfortable and pretty kind of dress" was available even in 1915, Gilman advocated for a comfortable attire that remained within the boundaries of acceptable feminine appearance, urging women to find a style that would fully reflect their sense of power and personal dignity.[96]

Bohemian feminists were in agreement that women's clothing should be both comfortable and becoming. "Not for an instant is it suggested that people should cease to make themselves attractive in appearance, or that uniformity of dress ought to be adopted," argued Nina Wilcox Putnam. "On the contrary, a greater individuality is to be desired, but, above all, comfort and convenience," she maintained. What counted as becoming or attractive did not follow a specific, unifying standard, Putnam argued, but was to be adjusted according to the wearer's personal figure and taste. "One should be able to wear what one pleases without coercion of any kind or the impertinence of criticism from someone whose tastes happen to differ," Putnam claimed. As clothing should express the wearer's unique and free personality, Putnam argued, there was not one feminist fashion that women needed to adhere to in order to express their politics.[97]

The emphasis on individual choice and independence of mind, not only in choosing one's clothes but also in other realms of life, reflected the individualistic nature of early twentieth-century feminism and its focus on the importance of personality. Influenced both by liberal traditions that saw the individual as the most important political unit, and by the popularization of psychological theories that revolved around the happiness of the self, feminists turned their attention to self-fulfillment and self-expression in their construction of their identities.[98] This stress on individuality, however, did not hinder collective efforts to improve women's status. Indeed, feminism, as historian Nancy Cott argues, was an ideology that sought "individual freedom by mobilizing sex solidarity."[99] Only as free individuals, these feminists argued, could they demand equality as a group and fight discrimination on account of sex. And as one of the most tangible expression of one's personality, clothing provided a ready and valuable tool for expressing just that. Since clothes can simultaneously express conformity and individuality, feminists used them to convey both their unity as a class and their uniqueness and creativity as independent individuals. "Clothes must differ as people differ," argued Gilman, "else they fail of one great function, that of personal expression."[100] Looking to fashion themselves as modern women advocating progressive ideas, bohemian feminists turned their clothing choices not only into the expression of their own personal tastes, but more importantly into a feminist practice.

By the 1910s, Greenwich Village had become a hub for radical and bohemian lifestyles that included socialism, feminism, and new ideas regarding sexuality and marriage. It also became a laboratory for women and men to experiment with different forms of sexual relationships, household settings, and dress. Bohemian feminists saw fashion as part of their modernist effort to create a new society, a new relationship between men and women, and, most importantly, a New Woman.[101] When the feminist Henrietta Rodman founded the Feminist Alliance in 1914, the organization had a special committee on dress reform that sought to promote an alternative style that would align with the alliance's goals.[102] Such a style, feminists argued, should be practical and compatible to modern life, express the wearer's personality and individuality, protect the wearer's health and be comfortable, *and* also be aesthetically appealing. "The modern active woman wants to be artistic, and she wants to be practical," argued Milholland, one of Rodman's peers in one of her speeches. To achieve this, Milholland claimed, a woman needed a dress that was "simple in outline, artistic in color and cut, and comfortable for all practical and healthful purposes."[103]

Feminists argued that every woman should fashion herself according to her own individual taste and inclination. Curiously enough, however, it was Oriental-style clothing, particularly that influenced by East Asia, that many Greenwich Village feminists found suitable to express their identities as modern American women. "No costume for women has been evolved which is more convenient, decent, comfortable, and in its own way, beautiful, than the Chinese," agued Gilman.[104] Other feminists found Japanese-style clothing more inspiring. These feminists' fascination with Japan was not coincidental. Japan has occupied a special place in the Orientalist imagination as both an exotic culture, and, especially after 1905, as a military and imperial power. Japan's isolation from Western influence until the mid-nineteenth century and its rapid modernization under the Meiji turned Japanese culture into both a symbol of a picturesque, romantic past and an emblem of modernity.[105] The Japanese aesthetics of clean and simple lines, two-dimensional conception, and blurred gender differentiations had a great influence on many artists and bohemians, many feminists among them. Additionally, the Western tendency to equate the East with the feminine and the West with the masculine enabled feminists to capitalize on the popularity of the Oriental styles to challenge gender roles, while leaving racial and class hierarchies intact.[106] Since Japanese-style clothing did not include clear masculine markers such as pants, feminists could employ them to express their politics and still maintain a feminine and fashionable appearance.

By the early 1910s, Japanese influence gained an increasingly central position in women's apparel through the adoption of kimonos, the straight Japanese silhouette, Japanese fabrics, and ornamental motifs.[107] While actual kimono robes were marketed as gowns to be worn at home or as sexualized lingerie, Japanese-inspired afternoon and evening dresses incorporated motifs such as the kimono cut, sleeve, collar, and the obi into their designs, creating kimono-style dresses that symbolized the newest trends of the era.[108] Nina

Wilcox Putnam, Henrietta Rodman, Edna Kenton, and other Greenwich Village feminists found the flowing, loose style of the kimono most suitable to the liberated image they wanted to convey, and they created their own versions of the Japanese dress that suited their lifestyles as active feminist reformers. They took the design of the kimono and appropriated it to their own needs, thus endowing it with a new set of meanings that expressed their feminist values.[109]

Putnam claimed to have created a one-piece kimono-style dress in 1913, because "the question of feminine dress, its discomfort, its disproportionate expense, has been troubling me ... and the result of my contemplation ... has been the somewhat tentative wearing of a garment which seems to meet with most, if not all, of my requirements."[110] Putnam thought a reformative dress should express the wearer's personality and individuality by adhering to ideals of beauty as well as to principles of comfort and health. In her autobiography she described her design: "I could not see why discomfort was necessary in women's dress. Nor did I perceive any added beauty in the figure as formed by a corset ... so after a deep thought I designed what I christened the one-piece dress." Putnam's design was influenced by the kimono. "It had the V neck now so almost universal, and slipped on, over the head, without fastening of any sort, while the sleeves were slightly defined ... or else simply fell from the shoulder for evening wear." According to Putnam, her dress was both fashionable and sensible, and thus expressed her identity as a modern woman (figure 2.6).[111]

Putnam's design was not just the sartorial expression of her feminist views, however, but also a form of feminist activism. By designing and sewing their own clothes, adapting the Oriental style and giving it their own interpretation, Putnam and other feminists asserted their individual tastes and gained control over their images. Indeed, in a period when home sewing was as common as buying ready-made clothing, designing and making one's clothes contained a message of empowerment and an expression of independence, as women could modify and accommodate the pattern design to their own taste and purpose.[112] By claiming sewing as a feminist activity, Putnam used fashion as a tool of self-definition. However, given that for many working-class women sewing was not leisure or political activity, but an unrewarding job for wages, the call to make one's clothes contained class bias with regard to its empowering messages.[113] Feminists such as Putnam could experiment in designing clothes and alternative styles precisely because they enjoyed the time and privileges that their upper-middle-class status provided them. Their class privilege also shielded them to some extent from criticisms about their

FIGURE 2.6: Nina Wilcox Putnam was among the Greenwich Village bohemian feminists who found Asia, particularly Japan, as a source of inspiration, adapting Oriental style to express their identities as feminist reformers. (Nina Wilcox Putnam in her own design, *American Magazine*, May 1913)

appearance, and thus they could negotiate more easily the popular reactions to their alternative styles of clothing.

Putman was not alone in adapting popular Oriental styles as an expression of her identity as a feminist. Other Greenwich Village feminists also utilized the Oriental style in their outfits. The feminist educator Henrietta Rodman's "working uniform," as she called it, was "a straight skirt of two lengths, front and back, and a sort of jerkin, which is also of two lengths, hollowed out a bit under the arms to form the kimono sleeves."[114] Greenwich Village–based feminist author Edna Kenton also saw the advantages of the kimono style that suited stout women like her and did not take a lot of time to make: "the larger woman doesn't need a corset any more than the thin woman does... the bliss of having every limb free and untrammeled is one I wouldn't barter for anything."[115] The loose and flowing dress style changed women's silhouettes, as well as their posture and way of movement. This in turn created an image of a free, independent woman that suited the bohemian feminist's values.

Kimono-style dresses freed feminists from tight corsets, gave them a greater freedom of movement, and protected their modesty, while also enabling them to challenge gender norms and to promote their agenda of sexual liberty and free speech.[116] Rather than embrace a masculine attire to make their gendered critique, feminists stuck to dresses, however loose or exotic, when they conveyed their message. Unlike the bloomer of the 1850s, the reformative ideas regarding women's dress that feminists promoted in the 1910s were in accordance, not in opposition to the contemporary fashion trends. "I was comfortable, clean, not unbeautiful," claimed Putnam, "for these new clothes were full of color, and above all I was safeguarding my health, and I knew it."[117] Kimono-style dresses succeeded in combining both aesthetic qualities and reformers' values, and thus proved to be useful in countering long-lasting negative stereotypes about the antifashionable feminist. According to Putnam, kimono-style dresses enabled feminists to "[abandon] all the nonsensical claptrap of dress with which women unconsciously symbolized their bondage."[118] Yet in adopting kimonos, feminists did not abandon their desire to appear fashionable. On the contrary, they could adhere to the popular fashions while also expressing their identity as radical feminist reformers.

Greenwich Village feminists altered the function of the kimono, which was mass-marketed as a sexualized garb with "Oriental allure" suitable for the home, and turned it into everyday street-wear.[119] Putnam claimed that her design—which had "the kimono effect," as it was "a one-piece dress, made of the straight breadths, with a girdle at the waist and a little coat of the same design"—was the perfect "street suit."[120] In shifting the meaning of the kimono from private attire to be worn at home to an everyday outfit suitable to wear in public, feminists challenged through their garb the gendered division between the private and the public spheres. When feminists took kimonos out of the boudoir and into the streets, they expressed yet another political message: an image that celebrated women's sexual freedom in public. Fashion thus became a tool through which these feminists asserted their sexual drives as women, offering legitimization to their radical ideas.

The image of the Greenwich Village feminist draped in kimonos became one of the main images of the bohemian feminist and her radical lifestyle.[121] Rodman became famous for her "sandals and a loose-flowing gown exactly like a meal sack," an attire that the press and contemporaries identified as the marker of "radical women."[122] Rebecca Hourwich Reyher recalled in an interview about her experiences with Rodman in the Feminist Alliance: "Nowadays when women wear very handsome caftans from the East, they wouldn't be surprised to see a woman draped in a piece of material just flowing with the head cut out in the center and her figure showing, striding easily. But in those days... for a woman to wear that kind of robe, particularly of some kind of rough material so that she looked as if she were dressed in a gunny sack, was most unusual."[123] However, although Rodman's clothes were identified as politically radical, the fact that her outfits were inspired by the Oriental style also made them fashionable. Instead of attracting public ridicule or even hostility, contemporaries found feminists' kimonos attractive and appealing.

The notion of greater personal freedom and expression, especially as it manifested in feminists' promotion of "free love," appealed to many young people who found these "sex-radicals" exciting and intriguing.[124] For these young women who were enthralled by the bohemian promise of a liberated life, radical feminists' attire offered a way to imagine themselves as liberated and modern, even without committing themselves to bohemian lifestyle. The "Village smock," the dress item most associated with Greenwich Village feminists, became a popular fashion worn both by artists and young women who wanted to be associated with bohemian culture.[125] Although Rodman herself opposed the use of ornamental and rich fabrics, arguing that simple brown or gray linen was a more feminist form of dress, decorated fabrics soon became part of "the uniform of the New Freedom." Rodman's Village smock was adopted by other Greenwich Village bohemians and, later by the mainstream market. Greenwich Village shops sold smocks and hand-printed tunics and dresses as part of the tourist attractions of the neighborhood.[126]

Indeed, feminists' kimono style became a mainstream fashion. However, although bohemian-style dresses gained some popularity among big retailers and the general public, it was mainly Greenwich Village feminists who used them as a means of expressing political views. In their fashionable choices, feminists in the early twentieth century demonstrated that the meanings they gave their clothing were not superficial or unimportant, but served as the basis for constructing modern identities, negotiating freedoms, and engaging in politics. By adapting the popular fashions and in attributing to them political and cultural meanings, Greenwich Village feminists, like suffragists, participated as producers as well as consumers of "the feminist" image. And, as had suffragists, they managed to make this image and its politics attractive. As their styles became more commercialized, however, the ideas that they carried also entered the mainstream. No longer seen as a threat, radical feminists now became fashionable trendsetters.

The Mainstreaming of Feminist Styles

Feminists and suffragists' agitation for women's rights, equality, and social change did not cease once the United States entered World War I in April 1917. Nor did fashion or appearance take a back seat in public debates. On June 1917, only two months into U.S. involvement, the *New York Times* acknowledged the war's impact on women's styles, arguing that "all wars have left their traces in the clothes worn by women, and it is not to be supposed that this most supreme war of all will merge itself into peace without being reflected in the fashions following those of 1914."[127] To a certain extent, the *Times*'s prediction was accurate. Women's appearance at the end of the war was very different from the beginning of the decade. However, while the industry reacted swiftly to the new situation and began marketing styles influenced by the military and patriotism, changes in women's fashions were less caused by the war than enhanced by it. Already before U.S. entry into the war, suffragists and feminists promoted looser and more comfortable fashions that reflected their political values and helped them in shaping their public image.

Yet, not only women's appearance was transformed over the course of the 1910s. Women also continued their forays into the workforce, education, and politics, changing public perception of women's appropriate place and role in society. As suffragists and feminists sought to expand their rights, they also forged a positive link between feminism and fashion, making the latter an important element in their efforts. Rather than denouncing fashion as frivolous, they turned fashion into a feminist issue and feminists into fashionable women. By offering tangible ways for women to express their individuality through clothing, they positioned women as artistic creators, producers of meaning, and interpreters of their own image.[128] Thus, by taking fashion seriously, feminists complicated and broadened the meanings of feminist politics in the early twentieth century. Fashion was no longer just an object women purchased, or a designers' decree they had to comply with in order to be fashionable—now it was a political means through which they created themselves as modern, liberated, New Women.

Although by the end of the decade kimono-style dresses and the "suffragette suits" began to lose their popularity, the simple and straight silhouette of the Japanese style and the functionality of the tailored suit continued to dominate women's fashions in the 1920s. Putnam forecasted back in 1914 that feminist reformative ideas regarding women's clothing would gain success, since instead of appealing only to the personal taste of "a few scattered individuals," they would address the "collective consciousness" of a "large body of people." The meanings of freedom, independence, and modernity that feminists gave to and expressed through their clothing appealed to many women who identified with these values. "When such a body begins to murmur a reform," claimed Putnam, "that reform is almost certain of accomplishment."[129]

By the 1920s, the alternative styles feminists advocated, as well as their ideas regarding women's personal freedom and sexuality, had entered the cultural mainstream, embodied in the youthful image of the flapper. "Whenever a style comes in that is comfortable, clean, not unbecoming, and that is a step in the direction of freedom, it comes to stay," the feminist Crystal Eastman explained women's endorsement of her alternative styles.[130] As more women in the 1920s broke new ground in politics, employment, and sexual behavior, they embraced the fashionable ideas feminists promoted in the 1910s and adopted, like them, a style that expressed their freedom, independence, and modernity. No longer needing to persuade men to accede them political rights, women in the 1920s used their clothing and appearance to expand their political freedom to other realms. In the process, they did not depoliticize fashion but made it an inherent part of what feminist politics came to stand for in the interwar period.

CHAPTER THREE

Dressing the Modern Girl

*Flapper Styles and the
Politics of Women's Freedom*

In 1921, feminist and suffragist Mary Alden Hopkins reminded contemporaries that, although the campaign for women's suffrage was over, the feminist struggle was about more than achieving political equality. "Votes and jobs and citizenship have not lessened for women one jot of the importance of clothes," she said, pointing to the important role she thought fashion played in women's emancipation. "Because women found [clothing] important, because they are the expression of her sex, because her clothes are her second self," Hopkins explained, fashion and appearance became a central route through which women expressed and experienced their freedom in the post-suffrage years.[1] By insisting on wearing comfortable clothing that allowed physical mobility, and by demanding being able to celebrate their sexuality without being reprimanded for it, young women in the 1920s turned their clothes into the visible symbol of their changing political and social status, of the freedoms they were beginning to claim, and the new moral values they promoted.

Although young women bobbed their hair, donned makeup, and wore uncorseted dresses before the end of World War I, only in the 1920s did these fashions become mainstream and identified with the figure of the flapper, or the "modern girl." Sophisticated, sexually liberated, and independent, the flapper represented the culmination of processes that the war escalated and highlighted, especially with regards to the mobilization of women into the workforce and the political changes that suffrage brought.[2] Her image challenged prewar gender, class, and racial hierarchies and symbolized the rise of a new youth culture that emphasized individuality, pleasure, and sexual expression. This new culture was part of what historians deem as the sexual revolution of the 1920s, which shattered Victorian stereotypes of the passionless White middle-class woman and brought greater public visibility and positivity regarding female eroticism and sexual expression.[3] Also associated with urbanism, skyscrapers, the growing numbers of automobiles, and modern aesthetics in art, the flapper became more than the quintessential image of the New Woman in the postwar decade. She became the visual representation of a modern cultural consciousness that defined the 1920s.[4]

Like images of youth before her—notably the Gibson Girl—the flapper was intertwined with a gendered understanding of modernity defined by mass consumer culture, popular magazines, and the ready-made industry. This culture encouraged both the consumption of new products and new patterns of consumption.[5] Clothing, cosmetics, and hair products provided women with a means of shaping their identities and demanding new freedoms, turning modernity into a distinctly feminine experience.[6] Indeed, flapper fashions served, as historian Mary Louise Roberts argues, "a maker as well as a marker" of the modern woman and the values she represented, not only reflecting but also constructing gendered ideas and understandings.[7] And as the flapper gained cultural importance throughout the decade, her fashions and appearance became a contested site where contemporaries debated and redefined the meanings of modern femininity.

Whereas in popular imagination the flapper was U.S.-born, White, middle-class high-school-aged or college-going woman, the availability of relatively cheap, durable, and fashionable apparel enabled the image to cross races, classes, and regions. Depictions of the flapper in the mainstream media concentrated on her sexuality and quest for fun, varying in terms of class and race association. Some depictions, such as those in F. Scott Fitzgerald's stories, portrayed the flapper as a young society woman or college student, who did not need to work for a living but spent her time in leisure activities. Others depicted her as an independent secretary or salesgirl, or as a young aspirant with rural origins who came to the big city to find success in theater or the movies.[8] The Black press presented the flapper's fashionability as an epitome of the New Negro Woman—a modern racial identity and political consciousness that was quintessentially urban and emphasized consumption rather than labor. These depictions tended to celebrate flappers' middle-class and respectable origins rather than their overt sexuality. Yet, Black newspapers also celebrated more brazen appearances of Black sexuality, thus legitimizing the image for young Black girls.[9] Despite these class and race differences, however, flappers looked very similar, both visually and sartorially, contributing to the dissemination of the image nationally and even globally.[10]

However, the flapper was never a fixed image, but one that reflected both women's progress toward greater freedom and equality, and the shortcomings of this progress.[11] She was simultaneously young and ageless, middle-class and working-class, boyish and feminine, conformist and individualistic, liberated and oppressed, harmless and threatening. The flapper's fashions also conveyed conflicting messages. Although her clothing afforded women with new physical, sexual, and spatial liberties, the flapper's close ties with consumer culture also set the boundaries of these freedoms and limited them. Moreover, one's class and race often determined the extent to which women could participate in consumer culture and the level of control they had in shaping and styling their own image.

This chapter revisits the flapper and her fashions in order to highlight the social and political meanings attached to her styles, as well as the economic, cultural, and political processes that generated them. As they fashioned their understanding of modernity through the clothes they wore, flappers used their appearance to demand new freedoms. For White women, these freedoms included the right of self-expression, the celebration of sexual desires, and the possibility of economic independence. But for Black women, freedom also meant refuting degrading racist stereotypes of Blacks among Whites, while promoting claims for inclusion in White society. Furthermore, the demographic and economic changes brought by the end of the war and the first Great Migration opened new possibilities to redefine racial, gender, and class identities. Black women used fashion also to challenge intra-racial notions regarding female propriety and sexuality, asserting new images of Black modernity.[12] These multiple meanings that women gave their clothing pushed fashion into the center of struggles to carve new positions of power and agency in the postwar period and imbued them with political significance.

Some scholars interpret women's growing focus on fashion and consumerism in the 1920s as evidence of the abandoning of a commitment to feminism in favor of an illusionary and superficial sense of freedom.[13] The rising influence of mass consumer culture and media co-opted the feminist struggle into commercial interests and helped to diffuse the movement's achievements and influence, which eventually led to feminism's decline as a compelling ideology in the post-suffrage era.[14] However, by overlooking the ways in which feminist ideas function and permeate beyond organized structures of politics, these studies neglect an important cultural component of feminism in this period. Clothing and appearance, as Mary Hopkins argued in 1921, were not disconnected but intertwined with feminist ideas of independence, liberation, choice, and sexual agency.[15] Indeed, feminism—as ideology and praxis—became inherent to Americans' understanding of modernity in the 1920s, primarily due to its connection with consumer culture.[16] A closer look at 1920s fashions and the meanings women gave them reveals that rather than symbolizing the depoliticization of women by consumer culture, fashion enabled feminism to penetrate into the cultural mainstream. In their insistence to maintain the popularity of short skirts, bobbed hair, and loose-rectangular silhouettes, flappers expanded and redefined the meanings of women's freedom, turning the radical feminist ideas of the 1910s into a fashionable cultural style. These women, by using their power as consumers in political ways, turned fashion into an important site where feminism was shaped and popularized in the post-suffrage period.

The Ready-Made Industry and the Popularization of Flapper Fashions

The popularity of the flapper was very much connected to her styles and their dissemination among diverse populations across class and race lines. In general, 1920s fashions were a continuation and simplification of the styles that had emerged both before and during World War I, evident in the emphasis on simple vertical lines, loose silhouettes, and the blurring of female curves.[17] The rectangular silhouette—created by a loose-fitting cut of the dress, and the dropped waistline that made the bust and waist almost invisible—was the most evident and constant marker of the flapper style throughout the 1920s. The period between late 1925 and 1929 became the most identified with "flapperism," contributing to a misconception that styles remained constant throughout the decade. However, despite the late 1920s being a rare period of stability of styles—due mostly to women's insistence on keeping to the fashions they found most suitable—fashions did change from the beginning of the decade to its end. Skirt hemlines in particular tended to fluctuate in height, rising in 1921–22 to mid-calf, and dropping again in 1923 to ankle length. Then, around 1925 hemlines began their constant rise, until they closed in on knee height around 1926 (figure 3.1).[18]

Moreover, variations existed between daywear, marked by simplicity and functionality, and more sexually expressive eveningwear, which used transparent fabrics and low cleavage lines.[19] Women who shied away from the

FIGURE 3.1: The rectangular silhouette and the dropped waist remain fairly constant throughout the 1920s, becoming the most recognizable markers of the flapper style. Skirt hemlines, on the other hand, tended to fluctuate. (Drawing by Einav Rabinovitch-Fox)

sexuality of the narrow rectangular look turned to the robe de style alternative in eveningwear. This type of dress, which was most associated with the French designer Jeanne Lanvin, maintained the youthful dropped waistline yet featured a full skirt reminiscent of the hoop skirts of the nineteenth century. Varying the skirt length created a more modern look for this bouffant style. And since it was restricted mainly to formal and festive wear, not everyday clothes, its lack of functionality and the hindrance to mobility due to its voluminousness was less of a concern.[20]

Parisian couture designers—particularly Coco Chanel, Madeleine Vionnet, and Jean Patou—began to look at the so-called average woman and her lifestyle as inspiration for their designs. "Fashions, nowadays, develop slowly, and more logically than they used to do. This is because, nowadays, they bear closer relation to the lives of their wearers," argued *Harper's Bazaar*'s fashion reporter Marjorie Howard in 1927.[21] Chanel, a self-made woman who took pride in her work and was unashamed of her sexuality, epitomized the flapper image both in her designs and in her persona. Her dresses and suits were characterized by an extreme simplicity and casualness that suited women's lives of work and leisure. Together with her tendency to mix high and low elements (such as silk with plastic jewelry, or jersey cotton for an evening dress), she provided women with practical sartorial solutions to their active lifestyle.[22] "I make fashions women can live in, breathe in, feel comfortable in and look younger in," Chanel attested about her designs.[23]

Whereas Paris remained the main source of styles, developments in clothing manufacturing and distribution caused the American ready-made garment industry to rise to power in the postwar decade. As a result, fashion became more accessible to various demographics. Unlike Parisian haute couture, the domestic industry was not inhibited by strict traditions of handcraft manufacturing, the influence of trade guilds, or by professional working standards. The U.S. structure, in contrast, was based on piecemeal sewing and sweatshop factories that proved especially suitable to mass production. This structure enabled the industry to introduce technological improvements to production—such as electric-powered cutting machines—more easily than its European competitors.[24] The industry also benefited from mass immigration waves in the late nineteenth and early twentieth centuries, which delivered the cheap labor crucial for sustaining its growth. Although the early 1910s saw important victories for workers in the garment industry—through the founding of unions, the implementation of safety regulations, and labor protective legislation—at the end of the war the industry could still rely on a massive labor force that was often poorly paid and poorly skilled, and thus easily exploited.[25] This in turn enabled manufacturers to keep costs low and profit margins high, even when investing in technological improvements that raised the quality of standardized clothes but could also incur significant expenses.

Technological developments in fabric production, and especially the increasing use of manmade fibers, also contributed to the growing influence of the American ready-made industry. Coined in 1924 as "rayon," manufacturers promoted this semisynthetic fiber made of regenerated cellulose as a cheaper or artificial alternative to silk. Rayon enabled the creation of pretty, inexpensive dresses with the look of the glamour of silk, which facilitated the industry's efforts in producing cheap versions of couture designs for a mass market. Rayon also had an important role in reducing the weight of undergarments, as well as in boosting the hosiery industry, which saw a period of increasing popularity due to the shortening of hemlines. As a result, both the quality and the durability of ready-made clothing increased, which caused them to become a viable option for consumers.[26]

From the consumer side, the conditions after the war created a vast market for ready-made fashions. The relative affluence in the United States in comparison to war-devastated Europe, developments in transportation, as well as the growing numbers of women in the labor force all served as catalysts for growth. The increasing numbers of women in white-collar jobs during the 1920s (25.6 percent of employed women)—a trend that was accelerated by the war but not caused by it—triggered a demand for both office and business attire and the wages to afford such a wardrobe. Manufacturers adjusted the industry to meet increasing consumer demand by adding seasons of sale cycles, altering the buyers' system, and encouraging a local industry based on style piracy.[27] The result was that, by the 1920s, Parisian styles crossed the Atlantic much faster and more easily than before, as department store buyers and U.S. local manufacturers offered women inexpensive U.S.-ready-made versions of haute couture models adjusted to American tastes.[28] These shifts in turn contributed to the growing prominence of the American ready-made industry and the spread of standardized clothing, evident in a threefold increase in profits from $473,888,000 in 1914 to $1,406,684,000 in 1923.[29]

The simplicity of styles accommodated them for mass production, but the loose-fitting silhouettes also made them adjustable to a wide range of sizes and figures. The fact that dresses did not require careful fitting to one's body curves marked another form of democratization of fashion. "Manufacturers turn out gowns in sizes by the gross, and almost any figure can wear them with little or no alteration," one reader wrote to the editors of the *Literary Digest*, noting that even in her forties she could find a becoming outfit that suited the prevailing modes.[30] According to the dressmaker Lane Bryant, who built a business empire by catering to stout women, the loose style of the flapper's dresses suited not only the slim silhouette but also fuller types of women. Bryant used her catalogs to reassure her potential customers that they need not compromise on their appearance because of their weight, and that they, too, had the right to dress fashionably. "Stout women like to dress smartly. Why shouldn't they?" the 1926 spring and summer catalog read. "There's no reason why you cannot wear exactly the same youthful styles that are worn by women who are slim of silhouette," Bryant asserted.[31] A page in her 1928 catalog offered four models "Designed Especially for Short Stout Women," which were not "old" or outdated but instead used "slendering" methods such as the use of narrow strips or thin belts.[32] Bryant offered stout women fashionable dresses by adjusting the prevalent modes to suit a larger range of sizes. But in turn, she also provided women with the possibility of imagining themselves as modern liberated flappers, even if they did not necessarily fit the media's popular depictions of the image.

Flapper styles and the ready-made industry offered variety not just for different body shapes. Fairly priced mass-produced clothing could be bought in stores and through mail-order catalogs, enabling women from different ethnic, regional, and socioeconomic groups to dress like the fashionable women in Paris or New York.[33] Especially for African Americans, mail-order catalogs provided ready access to the latest fashions, avoiding the limitations of discrimination and racial segregation. In a period when many department stores did not welcome Black consumers, or refused to allow them to try on the clothes in the store, mail-order catalogs proved to be the easiest way to forgo such obstacles. By buying from a mail-order catalog, African Americans asserted their right to participate as equals in the market, turning the act of shopping via the mail into a political act of resistance to a racist system.

Moreover, although this form of consumption necessitated cash on hand—a fact that often circumscribed the purchases one could make—mail-order catalogs also functioned as fantasy literature. By displaying images of the latest in fashion, these catalogs offered a route for anyone to participate, if only by imagination, in the mainstream consumer culture.[34] Mail-order companies and clothing stores routinely advertised in the Black press, suggesting that they recognized the potential of the African American market and courted it deliberately.[35] While these advertisements were often for White-owned companies that depicted White models, they nevertheless offered a democratic vision manifested in standardized clothing that could be potentially shared by Blacks and Whites alike.

Indeed, the popularity of ready-made clothes that were similar in style if not in quality to custom-made apparel, reflected the continuous democratization of fashion and the erosion of cultural and class distinctions. But they were also the ones that enabled the flapper image to spread quickly and become part of the fashionable mainstream. By bringing "within the reach of moderate and modest incomes wearing apparel which previously only the wealthy could afford to buy," the ready-made industry enabled women from different socioeconomic classes to actively engage as equals in the creation of national, and even international, fashion trends. Thus, ready-made clothing became not only an agent of modernity, but also of democracy.[36] Clothing styles gradually ceased to be a definitive marker of class. As one businessman remarked, "I used to be able to tell something about the background of a girl applying for a job . . . by her clothes, but today I often have to wait till she speaks."[37] Differences still existed, with the quality of fabrics and sewing varying from custom-made to mass-made clothing. However, style—and the ability to appear fashionable—became within the reach of more people than in previous decades.

The prevalence of ready-made fashions, moreover, contributed to a change in the influence of traditional cultural trendsetters. Mary Alden Hopkins acknowledged in 1922 the increasing economic power of working women: "Fashions in this country are no longer ruled by a few leaders of society. They are determined by the purchases of several million working women. . . . The girl with the pay envelope sets the styles for the women who dressmake at home." Hopkins pointed to a shift in cultural influence from top-down to bottom-up and identified the wage-earning flapper as the one who set the styles for American women in general. "So long as the wage-earning flapper insists on practical and comfortable frocks, the rest of us are safe," she wrote. According to Hopkins, not only was the working flapper the arbiter of styles, but she also signified a transformation in the relationship between women and the fashion industry. Women no longer followed blindly the industry's dictates, but were actively shaping fashion trends through their consumer choices.[38] "Women realized their status in life. They demanded independence, and they got it... when they went shopping they asked for what they wanted, instead of what they saw," explained fashion consultant Margery Wells in *Women's Wear Daily*, corroborating Hopkins's observations.[39]

Furthermore, it was the young American woman, rather than the French chic matron, who was heralded as the harbinger of taste. "It doesn't matter what queens or beauties do. The young woman of to-day insists on dressing to suit her own life as well as she can with the available materials," argued the *Literary Digest*.[40] Attributing the changes in fashions to the independent mind of ordinary consumers, contemporaries recognized that Paris designers no longer had a monopoly on styles, and that it was American women, asserting their power and freedom as consumers, who set the fashions.[41] The writer Muriel Draper noticed that the American woman of fashion, whose clothes "combine suitability with elegance, freedom of line with perfection of detail, and a vitality and boldness of design and color," has caused the French dressmaker to respond with as "much speed and invention as could be summoned" to fulfill her needs.[42] The designer Patou in particular was known to cater to the American consumer and her taste by using American models to display his designs, or by favoring U.S. buyers and clients in his fashion shows, often creating two separate collections, one for the American consumer, and one for the French.[43]

Magazines also courted the working flapper, contributing further to her status as a fashion trendsetter. Fashion and sewing advice columns offered women practical solutions for all their activities as modern women: leisure, evening, and most importantly, work. The *Ladies' Home Journal*, for example, began in 1923 to dedicate a section in its fashion pages to the "business woman," seeing her as a separate consumer segment. In such a column from 1924, the journal offered "attractive frocks" one could wear to the office, emphasizing the utility of these dresses to function as appropriate attire both during and after office hours.[44] By acknowledging, as a column from 1929 did, that "the business woman finds her appearance may be a determining factor in her business career," the *Ladies' Home Journal* used fashion to legitimize women's place in the workforce. It constructed the fashion-savvy flapper as an office worker who "is particularly interested in the smart and the new."[45] Thus, through the celebration of the working flapper as the new fashionable role model, magazines not only helped in popularizing her fashions, but also normalized women's work for wages by framing it as a desirable fashionable pursuit.

For those who did not buy their clothes in stores or through trade catalogs, the simplicity of styles and the availability of easy-to-follow patterns made it easy to follow trends, further contributing to the dissemination and democratization of fashion styles. "Do you know how a woman is very likely to make herself a frock today?," asked Hopkins of *New Republic* readers. "She lays on the floor a length of cloth, doubled over. Shears in hand, she shapes it like a paperdoll's dress, gouging skillfully in under the arms, and cutting a circular opening in the neck." With styles so plain and dresses so easy to construct, Hopkins suggested, every woman could be a designer.[46] An example to Hopkins's observations can be found in a dark orange silk crepe dress from the mid-1920s (figure 3.2). On the wearer, the dress looks very plain, falling on the body like a sack and blurring the wearer's body features. Yet, laying it on the ground, the simplicity of the cut becomes even more obvious. The gown's rectangular shape attests to the uncomplicated pattern and the minimal skill required to sew it.[47]

Pattern companies such as Vogue, McCall's, and Butterick stressed that following a pattern was an attainable task for the young business woman or the modern flapper, not just her mother. They offered designs that copied Parisian styles models and gave women the opportunity to create their own variations—as well as their own versions of the flapper.[48] "Dame Paris . . . caters now to the modern woman's varied occupations and demands," announced a 1926 article in *Woman's World* magazine. Haute-couture designers' "most charmingly practical, neat and wearable models . . . may be so easily copied," the article explained and provided its readers with detailed instructions on how to make four "Paris gowns that are easily made at home."[49] Mary Brooks Picken—the founder of the Women's Institute of Domestic Arts and Sciences and an influential authority on fashion and dressmaking—put the principles of easy dressmaking and time saving into practice when she invented in 1923 the "one-hour dress." The design was according to Picken, "a proof that with proper instructions you really can make pretty, becoming dresses at wonderful savings, right at home, no matter how little spare time you have."[50] As an enthusiastic supporter of home sewing, Picken argued that self-made clothes

FIGURE 3.2: The simplicity of the silhouette made the flapper-style dress extremely adaptable to both mass production and home sewing, leading to the further democratization of styles in the 1920s. ("Dark orange silk crepe dress, American ca. 1925–1929," photo courtesy of the Kent State University Museum)

were not only cheaper but also more beautiful than ready-made, as they better suited the wearer's figure and personality.[51]

Whereas it was White-owned pattern companies that controlled the market, the Black press also offered practical solutions to the home sewer and the fashion consumer. Fashion columns were published regularly in Black newspapers and magazines, keeping readers informed on the popular trends and major debates in the fashion world.[52] Even the politically radical Universal Negro Improvement Association publication *Negro World* featured a survey of the latest fashions in a column titled "Dame Fashion" by activist and journalist Amy Jacques Garvey.[53] In addition to its informational columns, the *Baltimore Afro-American* offered its readers useful sewing patterns. And the *Half-Century*—a magazine for Black women—offered both its own shopping service and a pattern service, enabling women to purchase every design from the magazine's covers and its fashion pages.[54] *Half-Century*'s pattern service enabled new migrants to appear fashionable, but it also provided fashionable solutions to its rural subscribers, thus contributing to the dissemination of fashionable trends all across the country. One such reader confessed: "I want to express my thanks for the pattern service. . . . Even if we are country women we like to look well when we go to the city to shop. . . . Your fashion page is fine too, and helps us to make over our own clothes and to comb our hair nicely. By wearing becoming clothes we feel more like 'somebody' and by making them over from time to time we save money to buy more property with."[55] Black women could find in fashion a sense of pride and self-improvement, but they could also use clothing as a financial investment to compete with Whites in the market and achieve economic mobility.

Thus, whether women sewed their clothes or bought them ready-made, the growing accessibility of fashion was a route for them to reshape notions of gender, race, and class while taking an active role in articulating the meanings of the flapper. The dissemination of fashion styles via the ready-made industry turned the flapper, as well as the liberating meanings she entailed, into a popularly shared image. As styles spread across regional and even national boundaries, they contributed to a more democratic understanding of the flapper. But more importantly, the availability of ready-made clothes enabled many women across class and racial lines to make claims to fashionability and to their right to participate in a fashionable discourse, letting their voices be heard and their bodies be seen.

Flapper Styles and the Meanings of Freedom

As the flapper began her cultural ascendency in the early 1920s, clothing and appearance became central to her definition. "She is a very pretty girl," Bruce Bliven described the flapper to the *New Republic* readers.

> She is frankly, heavily made up, not to imitate nature, but for an altogether artificial effect. . . .
> Her dress . . . is cut low where it might be high, and vice versa. The skirt comes just an inch below her knees, overlapping by a faint fraction her rolled and twisted stockings. . . .
> Jane's haircut is also abbreviated. She wears of course the very newest thing in bobs. . . .
> The corset is as dead as the dodo's grandfather. . . . The petticoat is even more defunct.[56]

Although Bliven's tone is sarcastic, reducing her to a mere caricature, the flapper was not just the sum of her clothes—or lack thereof. Despite his condescending descriptions, even Bliven recognized that the flapper's clothing was the visual expression of a generational shift in moral values and political views. Indeed, flapper's fashions served as a realm where women could negotiate new roles and identities, including the assertion that women "have highly resolved that they are just as good as men, and intend to be treated so." For flappers, clothes went together with "independence, earning your own living and voting," and they were not ready to give up any of these symbols of freedom.[57]

Flapper styles and their meanings were thus bound up in the social, cultural, and political processes that brought changes to women's lives during and after World War I. In particular, the flat, tubular silhouette, together with short hairstyles, created a new and more youthful beauty ideal than previous generations.[58] The flapper was identified mainly as a young girl in her teens or twenties who lived a libertine and mobile life, and thus her youthfulness was intertwined with modernity. Her image both constituted and represented a distinctive youth culture that emerged in the 1920s that exalted sexuality and mobility. However, youth became less a marker of age and more a state of mind that valued novelty and innovation.[59] As *Vanity Fair* asserted in 1921, "Flapper is a limitless, a widely embracive term, to such a point that serious men have observed . . . that all women between the ages of fourteen and fifty—make it sixty, if you wish—may be called 'girls.'"[60] "Flapper" and "youth" were no longer references to a stage in life but markers of sophistication and fashionability. Through the use of clothing and makeup, every woman could become a flapper—regardless of her age—and could assert her identity as a modern woman who holds progressive views on women's sexuality and gender roles.

In addition to conveying youth, the rectangular silhouette created a slenderer and flat body ideal that constructed a boyish, even androgynous, look. Some critics understood this look as a threat to the gendered social order, arguing it was a result of women's masculinization due to the war.[61] Yet, while the flapper adopted some traits considered to be masculine, such as short hair and smoking, to most contemporaries she did not symbolize the masculinization of women or a rejection of womanhood as much as a newly mobilized and sexualized femininity.[62] In fact, that many observers called the look "boyish" rather than "masculine" indicates that they responded more strongly to the look's youthful connotations than to its possible challenges to gender norms. The boyish flapper was portrayed not as a danger to be avoided but as a celebration of youth and modernity.[63] Particularly, the raised hemlines that revealed women's legs and knees expressed a new understanding of female sexuality. By drawing the attention to women's legs, rather than to their bosoms or their waists, the short skirt created a conceptual shift from equating women's sexuality with maternity (as bosoms were associated with breastfeeding) to a new feminine identity in which sexuality was severed from motherhood and was based on pleasure.[64] Thus, more than a rejection of womanhood, as some critics argued, the flapper ideal symbolized a rejection of the gendered expectations that came along with motherhood.

However, although the flapper represented a new definition of female sexuality, it was still very much a heterosexual one. The boyish look of the flapper, despite its name, did not suggest an option for gender transgression or crossover. On the contrary, rather than point to openness regarding homosexual expressions, the 1920s were a period when heterosexuality, and particularly female heterosexuality, became a much more rigid standard. Women's sexuality was supposed to be expressed only within marriage, which was framed as a "compassionate relationship" based on friendship and sexual fulfillment. Female homosocial relationships and homosexual desires did not draw much attention or criticism in the nineteenth century. Yet by the 1920s, with the rising popularity of Freudian theories, female companionships lost their cultural legitimacy and began to be deemed as both a medical problem and a social peril, identified as "lesbianism."[65] Although no doubt many queer women adopted the flapper look in the 1920s, the image itself did not carry subversive connotations at the time. Boyish or even masculine garb for women—the extreme short bob, masculine hats, neckties, or monocles—did not necessarily register an identification of a lesbian identity; rather, it conveyed adherence to the period's trends of blurring gender roles and the assertion of female sexual desires.[66] In fact, in popular imagination, the image of the lesbian was usually of a trouser-wearing woman, quite different from the short-skirted flapper. Trousers for women as public attire were still considered a taboo in the 1920s, yet contemporaries did not interpret the adoption of other masculine attributes as an attempt to "pass" either as a man or as a lesbian. As long as the flapper wore a skirt, critics were more concerned about her overt (hetero)sexuality and lack of morality than the threat of sexual transgression.

The rising youth culture in the 1920s played an instrumental role in shaping this new understanding of female sexuality. The increasing popularity of mixed-sex, age-based socialization, as well as the growing availability of automobiles, created a space to experiment with new courting customs and sexual practices away from parental control. This new understanding marked a clear break with the prewar generation of middle-class White Americans. However, many of the features that characterized the "new sexual order" of the 1920s—premarital sexual activity, greater sexual expression, and the commercialization of sexuality—had already existed among working-class, immigrant, and African American urban communities before World War I.[67] When White middle-class flappers adopted these manners and appearance, they popularized these ideas for mainstream society, but they did not invent new styles as much as incorporate them to their middle-class culture. White flappers' great contribution was thus in turning a youth subculture into a mainstream one, giving it the mark of fashionability and legitimacy.

Yet, the growing public acceptance for more overt expressions of female sexuality and the liberating meanings that were attributed to the flapper and her styles still differed along class and racial lines. Both White and non-White flappers needed to negotiate the tension between their desire to display a freer expression of one's sexuality and the need to maintain respectability. However, this was a far greater challenge for African American women, due to the deeply embedded racist stereotypes that casted Black women as sexually deviant. Thus, although by the 1920s respectable middle-class Black women began to wear light makeup and jewelry, when it came to clothing, they presented a more conservative taste.[68] "Conservative styles are best unless you are strikingly pretty—and comparatively few of us are," argued a writer in a 1922 *Half-Century* article, suggesting that readers would adhere to more con-

CHAPTER THREE

servative cuts and silhouettes that eschewed deep cleavages and very short skirts. The writer, perhaps as part of a continuous attempt to counter White accusations of Black women being morally loose, discouraged readers from adopting "a dress loaded with beads, embroidery, ribbons"—a conspicuous appearance that could have drawn unwanted attention.[69]

Nevertheless, as the 1920s progressed, young Black women began to push against these conservative views, adopting a more brazen appearance that challenged intra-racial notions of middle-class Black respectability. Like their White counterparts, young Black women adapted their appearance to suit the popular flapper styles of the period. Wearing short skirts, makeup, and bobbed hair, these Black flappers embraced a modern image of womanhood that was much more sexually expressive yet conveyed both sophistication and propriety.[70] The Black press was instrumental in legitimizing this kind of appearance and making it part of the aesthetics of respectability. Images such as the one that appeared in the *Chicago Defender* in 1928, presenting members of the Unique Fashion Club showcasing the latest styles, helped to normalize the flapper's sexuality within the boundaries of racial uplift and respectability politics (figure 3.3).[71] Indeed, the image of the Black flapper did not reject notions of respectability but expanded the concept's boundaries by accommodating a consumerist, modern, and fashion-savvy perspective of Black women.

Beyond youth and sexuality, 1920s fashions were also associated with physical mobility and freedom of movement. The short skirt in particular symbolized this understanding. Not only did it endow women with two visible legs, but the short hemlines also afforded unprecedented ability to use them.[72] "Skirts can't be too short for me," claimed Mrs. H. Fletcher Brown, who defined herself as "'one of the girls' in [her] forties, who has struggled through all the difficulties of the past styles." The freedom of movement the short skirt enabled was a physical, palpable progress for women like Brown who were old enough to remember the days of long, cumbersome skirts. For Brown and other women of her generation, the ability to use one's legs without being hindered by uncomfortable clothes represented the essence of women's advancement.[73] Offering both an actual sensation and a visual symbol for women's mobility, the short skirt, according to the *Nation*'s editors, became "more than *a* fad. It typifi[ed] this generation."[74]

While the short hemlines bestowed new mobility to the legs, sleeveless dresses with wide armholes enabled unprecedented freedom of the upper limbs. Deep cleavages also freed the neck, especially in comparison to previ-

FIGURE 3.3: By the mid-1920s, African Americans could enjoy greater access to consumer culture and leisure practices that turned the image of the flapper, and her fashions, into a respectable one, despite its overt sexuality. (Unique Fashion Club members "Display Many Styles at Fashion Show," *Chicago Defender*, 1928. Image published with permission of ProQuest LLC. Further reproduction is prohibited without permission.)

ous high-collar styles. The popularity of lightweight fabrics such as chiffon and silk, together with the continuing trend of undergarments being lighter and fewer caused the overall weight of clothes to cease from being a concern for women. According to one study, women's clothes in 1929 averaged 2 pounds, 10 ounces, while men's averaged 8 pounds, 6 ounces, causing some to suggest a dress reform for men.[75] Lighter clothing and fewer underwear not only allowed women to engage in physical activities more easily, but they also simplified traveling, further contributing to women's increasing mobility. Instead of traveling with several trunks of clothing, women could now "pack twenty dainty costumes in a bag," which offered more spontaneous travel and enabled women to break the confines of domesticity that put them in the home or under the supervising eye of men.[76] Women's clothes thus no longer impeded their mobility and freedom; it now facilitated these, and in the process it normalized women's movement and presence in the public sphere.

The modification and at times even elimination of tight corsets—as well as the rising popularity of the brassiere—also contributed to the liberating image that 1920s fashions presented. In 1922, Eleanor Chalmers, the fashion editor of the *Delineator*, reported that "'Let Go' is the law of the new corset and corsetless figure." Chalmers noticed that more and more young women chose to discard their corsets altogether or replace them in favor of very light supportive girdles or a bra.[77] Examples of brassieres from the 1920s shows that they gave only minimal support, and in fact functioned more as an extra layer underneath the clothes than as a means to mold a woman's torso. While these brassieres had a flattening effect, their boneless structure was still less confining than the corset (figure 3.4).[78] Even women who chose to keep their corsets could enjoy the new styles that were "molded into new and more plastic shape . . . so soft and supple that it seems almost boneless, very slender but round, and neither flat, thin, or angular."[79] Indeed, the majority of women opted for a boneless, unrestrictive brassiere rather than a corset, thus conveying an image of bodily freedom. As they wore their flapper dresses, which both accommodated corsets' disposal and provided visual evidence for such an act, they expressed their freedom in material ways.[80]

Flapper styles enabled more than just asserting physical mobility, however. For Black flappers in particular, adopting the short styles became a means through which they could claim their rights to participate in the growing youth culture and the promises it entailed. The availability of ready-made fashions and the growing access to urban leisure enabled young Black women to assert through their appearance their equality with Whites. Indeed, the

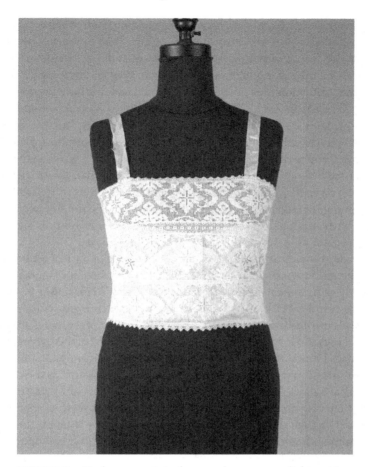

FIGURE 3.4: Undergarments in the 1920s became very light and less restrictive compared to those in previous decades, allowing women more freedom of movement. (Brassiere ca. 1920s, photo courtesy of the Kent State University Museum)

issue of fashion and appearance was very much intertwined with civil rights battles to gain equal access and status in mainstream culture.[81]

Yet, by arguing that the flapper's styles improved women's health, contributed to their beauty, and expressed their freedom, Black flappers also challenged intra-racial gendered and class notions of propriety.[82] Dorothy Ilone Embry, the leader of the Harlem Sub-Debs association claimed in 1927:

"Hurrah for shorter skirts—they give more freedom of movement.... Hurrah for less clothes—they give more health.... You don't find many twentieth century girls fading away or swooning as it seemed the style to do in the 80's and 90's. No, they play golf, tennis, basketball, they go out for track teams, swimming and numerous other beneficial exercises that have improved the health of the female sex." Embry also connected the physical mobility of the flapper's fashions with broader claims for gender equality. "It's the same old freedom men have had since the world began. But it has just been passed on to women, and men, in their supercilious ego, think it is profane for mere 'woman' to have the same rights and privileges that man-made laws gave men," she asserted.[83] In demanding their right to wear short skirts, while also maintaining their standing as respectable girls, Embry and her peers challenged both structures of racism and African Americans' notions regarding women's place in society and their expression of sexuality.

Female students at Fisk University also made the connection between their demands to participate as equals in the White consumer market and a gendered criticism aimed toward their community. In 1925, they protested their treatment by Fisk's White president Fayette McKenzie, focusing their grievances on the institution's strict dress code. Instead of the mandatory cotton stockings and long-sleeved dresses—which for many of them represented an outdated moral system—these female students demanded the freedom to show "long necks and [wear] dresses made of silk or satin," as their White counterparts did at other colleges. These female students were not only protesting their discrimination as Blacks by gaining control over their appearance and asserting their rights to be recognized as fashionable women. They were also claiming their right to be treated equally as their male colleagues who were not subjected to a similar strict code of appearance and behavior.[84]

These college students' class and education certainly facilitated their participation in the fashion world. However, working-class Black women also adopted the flapper's fashions to challenge gender and racial structures. They used the flapper styles to perform a "public self" that contrasted their reality of work and poverty while expanding and redefining notions of respectability. Although many southern migrants who worked as domestics or factory workers did not have the time or the opportunity to dress according to their personal preference during weekdays, they used the custom of "strolling" during weekends to display their fashionable tastes. As a June 1928 *Inter-State Tattler* photograph showed, these "nifty bunch of damsels, nattily dressed for their Sunday afternoon stroll," used their public display of fashion to reinvent themselves as modern women (figure 3.5). By taking off their work uniforms

FIGURE 3.5: By adopting flapper styles, African American women claimed their right to participate in the mainstream youth culture as their white peers did, turning their appearance into political expression. ("A Nifty Bunch of Damsels...," *Interstate Tattler*, June 1928. Image published with permission of Readex, NewBank.)

and putting on their best clothes, these women constructed an identity that was starkly different from not only their rural origins but also from their weekday work routine.[85] As they wore the latest trends of short bobbed hair and knee-length hemlines, these women could both put aside their everyday troubles and assert control over their bodies and appearance, far from the supervising eye of their White employers or the confining realms of middle-class propriety.[86] Even if they could only do so during weekends, Black flappers' insistence on wearing short skirts, donning makeup, smoking, dancing, and hanging out in dance halls and clubs enabled them to participate in the same kinds of liberated social lives their White peers enjoyed.

Similarly, for second-generation Mexican, Japanese, and Chinese women, adopting the flapper style was a means of claiming American identity and demanding their right for inclusion in White society. As with African Americans, their ability to adopt the flapper fashions was compromised, as their fashionable choices became a source of intergenerational tensions between parents and their daughters. These flappers thus needed to negotiate between their aspirations to participate in the White youth culture, and their commitment to their ethnic communities and identities.[87] Although adopting the flapper image did not necessarily mean assimilation, the ability of fashion to transcend class and racial differences also made it a common symbol for female freedom and modernity. Both White and non-White women could share a common culture and look. This joint experience, even if only potentially, enabled young women of color to claim their equal right both to participate in redefining ideas of femininity and sexuality and also to expand women's place within their communities.

Indeed, for the women who adopted them, 1920s fashions conveyed multiple emancipatory meanings: redefinition of gender identities, sexual agency, independence from parental control, and a new sense of physical mobility and pleasure. However, it would be wrong to assume that fashion was entirely an empowering or liberating force.[88] Whereas the standardization of ready-made clothing across diverse and multiple groups of women enabled the dissemination of the flapper's image, popular culture and advertising pushed for a more unified, conformist, and ultimately limited ideal.[89] Moreover, despite the effortless look, maintaining the flapper ideal required much time and effort. Keeping a bob entailed frequent visits to the head dresser, and, with the popularization of makeup, beauty routines also became more time-consuming. In addition, the rectangular silhouette that favored a slim figure required the molding of the body and controlling it to achieve that look. If slender women could easily replace their corsets with a loose brassiere, curvaceous women opted to shape their bodies with more structured corsetry that minimized their proportions.[90] Dieting in particular, which became popular in this period, can be interpreted as a step that further limited the freedoms the flapper was associated with. Whereas flattening brassieres were an external form of policing the female body, similar to the ways corsets and crinolines once did, dieting became an internal means to check women's freedom and independence—and thus more effective.[91] Additionally, those who opted for the voluminous robe de style had to compromise on their mobility in order to achieve a more feminine look. Keeping up with the appearance that the flapper image dictated thus proved to be challenging for women who could not conform to the flapper ideal, particularly non-White, older, and stouter women. For them, adopting "flapperism" also required adopting a strict regimen of dieting, grooming, chest binding, and makeup wearing.

Additionally, although the stability of the rectangular and short silhouette enabled many women to remain fashionable without investing large sums of money every year, not everyone had the means to keep up with the life of leisure that flapperism promoted. In 1927 the fan magazine *Motion Pictures Classic* estimated that the cost to look like a "well-dressed flapper" was about $346.50 a year, the equivalent of "equip[ping] completely a reasonably well-furnished three-room flat."[92] Thus, for working-class single women whose own salaries did not permit such outlays, being a flapper usually meant participating in some form of "treating," whereby men paid for women's leisure and lifestyle in return for sexual favors. Such women then had to negotiate a space between their respectability and their desire to participate in leisure activities, which often also required them to relinquish their independence and control.[93]

Women had to contend with these contradictory messages, bridging the tension between the emancipatory meanings they gave their clothes and the pleasure they derived from fashion, and being expected to uphold a beauty ideal that demanded the constant policing of their bodies. They had to reconcile feeling empowered by the vote and the economic opportunities that have opened up to them in the 1920s, with the message they received from magazines and advertisements that the most important thing for a woman was to be attractive in order to secure and settle down with a husband. They had to navigate between their desire to celebrate their sexuality and femininity, and maintaining their respectability and social standing within their own communities. And they had to mitigate the tension between their will to express their individuality with a profound social pressure to conform. Although a century later it is difficult to trace how individual women managed these negotiations, recognizing the possibilities and limits expressed in popular images of the flapper allow a better understanding of women's experience of modernity in this period. Indeed, the liberating aspects of the flapper style were not intrinsic to the clothes themselves. Rather, it was the meanings that women gave their clothes that made them instrumental to the redefinition of modern femininity in the 1920s. By wearing short skirts, short hair, and by discarding corsets, flappers not only created a new image of femininity, but they also invested fashion with political meanings.

Debates over the Flapper and the Meanings of Her Fashions

As the ability to appear fashionable no longer belonged to the elite few but became a nationwide and even global phenomenon, clothing and appearance gained cultural and social importance as indicators of national trends and attitudes. Debates over the length of skirts and hair, the numbers of underwear, as well as the amount of makeup and exposed skin, exceeded the realm of fashion magazines and served as a means through which contemporaries—men and women alike—could delineate and redefine the meanings of modern femininity.[94] As the author Richard Le Gallienne observed in 1927, "usually changes in fashion go deeper than a matter of clothes or ways of wearing the hair. They are barometric of changes in the social, the spiritual and intellectual atmospheres."[95] For contemporaries, women's fashions in the 1920s symbolized, for better or worse, a modern youth culture that sought a radical break with the past, and they used fashion as a conduit in their attempts to regulate this culture and shape its meanings.

The thing that concerned the flapper's critics the most was the moral implications of her fashion choices. The less clothes women wore, opponents claimed, the fewer moral values they retained.[96] "The modern girl is extremist. She dresses in the lightest and most flimsy of fabrics. Her dancing is often of the most passionate nature, and I believe the modern dance has done much to break down standards of morals," claimed the managing editor of the *Pennsylvania Punch Bowl*, a University of Pennsylvania magazine.[97] For Barton W. Currie, the editor of the *Ladies' Home Journal*, "flapperism" included all "modern manifestations" that had been associated with the "'dreadful' side of youth": jazz, short skirts, bobbed hair, the "immodest" abandonment of corsets, cigarette smoking, petting parties, car riding, psychoanalysis, Greenwich Village follies, Ziegfeld chorus girls, one-piece bathing suits, modernism in art, birth control, eugenics, and Bolshevism.[98] Others blamed the flapper's short skirts for causing male office clerks to lose their morals and adopt improper behavior.[99]

Black leaders were equally concerned about the flapper's immorality.[100] "One of the great problems we are facing today is immorality in our whole social structure. Modesty and kindred virtues have been thrown to the winds and not a few of our younger generation are allowing their baser natures to dominate," a *Chicago Defender* editorial described some of the worries that leaders had regarding youth's moral values.[101] The boyish ideal of the flapper, which created a redefinition of female beauty and sexuality, proved to be challenging to those who emphasized Black women's more traditional feminine traits. According to the Reverend J. Milton Waldron, pastor of Shiloh Baptist Institutional Church, bobbing one's hair "cause[d] women to lose their feminine identity and destroy[ed] the personality and beauty of a woman."[102] Instead of viewing the flapper's figure as an opportunity for social inclusion, as her appearance and lifestyle were similar to the general youth culture of the

1920s, Black middle-class reformers feared she would be a cause for further stigmatization by Whites.

In their attempts to prevent the further degradation of morals, some municipalities proposed legislation to regulate women's clothing in public. In 1921, the *Literary Digest* reported a proposed ordinance in Utah that set a fine and imprisonment to any women who wore on the streets skirts higher than three inches above the ankle. Another bill in Virginia proposed banning skirts higher than four inches above the ground and prohibited dress cleavages that displayed more than three inches of a woman's throat.[103] Whereas these bills never became law, efforts in regulating women's beach attire proved to be more successful. Chicago, Cleveland, and even Atlantic City were among the cities that issued ordinances and regulations regarding appropriate swimwear for women. Although these regulations varied greatly from one place to another, almost all of them banned the one-piece bathing suit that revealed women's arms as well as hips.[104] Municipalities' insistence that women's appearance was a matter of public interest pointed to the anxiety the flapper stirred about women's new political power. Under the cover of moral policing, critics of the flapper sought to curtail women's political gains by controlling their appearance and limiting their sartorial freedom in the public sphere.

Likewise, the flapper's defenders also imbued her clothes with political meanings. Young flappers defended their sartorial choices by claiming that their clothes conveyed freedom and health, not the lack of morals. "The flapper isn't the terrible, wicked thing she's supposed to be," contended Myrtle Heileman, a self-proclaimed flapper from the Chicago suburbs. "Analyze her dress. It's the most sensible thing since Eve. She wears rolled sox and why shouldn't she? They are extremely cool and comfortable. . . . Her bobbed hair is cool, sensible and sanitary, and it has nothing to do with her brain," Heileman protested.[105] Although not necessarily using their fashions as a direct political or feminist statement, for Heileman and her peers, flapper styles were an expression of their confidence, power, intelligence, and competence. "The flapper—meaning the modern girl—is not immodest, but she wants all that life has to offer her, and what's more, she gets it too. She has not lost the attributes of sentiment and tenderness, but she is protecting and enhancing them with a cloak of sophistication," an editorial in the *Flapper*, a magazine that served as an arena for young girls to share their thoughts, corroborated Heileman's claims.[106] For these flappers, fashion conveyed modernity, sophistication, and progress, and not, as their opponents argued, social decay or moral regression. Black flappers also used arguments similar to Heileman's.

"In spite of all that the censors say and think about the present-day styles, the styles today are unquestionably the prettiest, sanest, and most healthful ever decreed," argued Gemma James in the *Half-Century*, asserting that beauty was mainly in the eyes of the beholder.[107]

Debates over fashion were not limited to questions of morality and the perils of youth, however. Contemporaries were also quick to make the connection between flapper styles and women's newly won political status. "Woman's independence has manifested itself nowhere else as sensibly and as sharply as in her relation to her wearing apparel," argued essayist Ann Devon. "In fact, it seems to be one of her new accomplishments of late years to which she can point with unrestrained pride."[108] Associating the flapper styles with the political, social, and sexual freedoms of women in this period, contemporaries understood her image as implicated in, rather than disconnected from, feminism. The writer Alexander Black correlated women's political enfranchisement with the emancipation of their bodies, arguing that "what a girl could and could not do had been settled in a huge percentage of instances by the length of her skirts." Now, after gaining suffrage, Black claimed, the "unhampered mind of women has chosen to acquire an unhampered and describable body."[109] Self-identified feminists such as Emily Newell Blair also defended the flapper, acknowledging the liberating image her clothes conveyed. Since different qualities demanded different looks, postures, and gestures, she argued, it only made sense that "women, even feminists, who wish to succeed in any of these departments of work, business, politics, or domesticity will naturally follow the fashion that seems to have the best chance of getting her what she wants." For Blair, that fashion was the short hemline dress styles, as it proved more appropriate to women's modern lives of "driving a car in traffic . . . pushing one's way through a subway mob, keeping alert for bargains, making engagements, filling positions on committees, even playing good bridge."[110]

This embrace of the flapper's fashions represented the different route feminism took in the 1920s, which was based more on personal appearance and individual fulfillment than on participation in politics.[111] The feminist suffragist Mildred Adams pointed to this change in attitude, claiming that suffrage has become a "sort of feminine Holy Grail" for the old generation of feminists. Yet the young generation of the 1920s, who did not fight for suffrage, preferred to concentrate on "short skirts, cigarettes, free speech—all these modern manifestations." However, while it was more individualistic in its character, this type of feminism was no less political than the previous struggle for suffrage, Adams claimed.[112] Indeed, the popularity of short hemlines and loose silhouettes made feminism fashionable and feminists appealing. The typical feminist, "1929 model," according to the suffragist Ida Clyde Clarke, "revealed in all of her pristine prettiness, level of head, clear of vision, strong of will, and yet, none the less feminine for a' that."[113] Dorothy Dunbar Bromley, another feminist, argued that the "Feminist—New Style" knew both how to work her feminine charms without compromising on health or comfort, and to fight for her place in politics.[114]

No longer associated with lack of fashionable taste or with the inability to look beautiful, feminists and their ideas of freedom were now popularly fashionable. "The modern girl has learned to wear both high heels and blue stockings. She has taken the curse off the blue stockings; she wears them in their place, attractive, and if occasion demands it, sheer," argued Elise Jerard in the *Pictorial Review*.[115] The growing popularity of the flapper styles enabled the entrance of feminism into the cultural mainstream. Whereas most women in the 1920s did not belong to feminist organizations, by expressing their individuality and freedom through fashion they validated these ideas culturally. In their defense of the flapper and her styles, these women participated in the creation of their identities as modern, liberated, and sexual women. But they also redefined feminism as a cultural style and popularized its ideas.

The Battle of the Skirts

Debates over the flapper's character and fashion were thus more than just debates over fashion styles. Contemporaries attached multiple meanings and values to the flapper, seeing her fashions as intertwined with the social, cultural, and political processes that changed women's status after the war. As flapper styles became associated with ideas of youth, physical mobility, and sexual freedom, they functioned—as historian Mary Louise Roberts has noted—as a "visual language of liberation" that was imbued with political meanings.[116] As such, when the fashion industry sought to lengthen skirt hemlines in the late 1920s, women's reaction was also invested with politics. Rather than just accept the industry's decree, a heated battle erupted between those who favored the change in styles and women who saw it an as an attack on their political and sartorial freedoms. Using their power as consumers and their new position as fashionable trendsetters, these women pushed against calls to alter their style, turning fashion into a site of political activism.

Economic interests played a major role in the hemlines debate in the late 1920s. Despite a few supporters among big manufacturers and retailers— mainly from the hosiery industry—many in the fashion business who depended on the volatile nature of fashion for making profits were much concerned about women's adherence to the short skirt. Warning that the stability in styles would lead to the ruin of businesses, loss of jobs, and poverty, many manufacturers pushed for a drastic change in styles that would, they argued, ensure the vitality of the national fashion industry.[117] As the editors of the *Nation* observed, "though a healthful desire for variety may have something to do with [attempts to change styles], the only real reason, so far as we can make out, is to force women to buy a complete new wardrobe."[118]

However, economic interests were not the only ones that stood behind the industry's push to lengthen skirts. *Harper's Bazaar*'s fashion reporter Marjorie Howard observed in 1928 that "some of the couturiers, and more especially those of the male sex . . . have made a determined effort, this spring, to get us back into clothes that they call 'more feminine,' which seems to mean more difficult to get into, and more difficult to wear."[119] By 1929, Howard used the magazine pages to warn her "fellow countrywomen" of "a conspiracy against [their] sartorial liberty." She cautioned her readers that "a return to uncomfortable clothing is in the air" and called women to resist the male plot to "get you into tight bodices and long skirts." According to Howard, it was appropriate to treat the proposed changes as a male-planned conspiracy, "because the houses directed by women are not nearly so stringent in their proposed reforms. Many of those directed by men, however, are determined to force us into what they call femininity at all costs."[120]

Not everyone shared Howard's concerns. The essayist Ann Devon, for example, believed that just as in previous years, women would prove their independence of mind and would not succumb to the industry's whims. "If this were the first or even the second attempt to persuade or coerce us, the optimism of the conservative might not be warranted," she claimed. "But the trick has been tried each season for the past three or four years. And having stoutly resisted thus far it seems more than probable that women will continue to do so." Moreover, Devon argued, the new mode had little chance of success as the current style made women look young and thin, and a "woman is not going to relinquish her youthful appearance simply to solve the economic problem of merchants."[121]

However, despite this confidence, Howard was not alone in fearing a male conspiracy against women's freedom. Many women, and feminists in particular, worried that designers and manufacturers were plotting to "imprison modern women in the sartorial shackles of [the past]" and put women back into the confinements of corsets and trained gowns, and by extension also back into their "submissive" social standing.[122] They understood this move as an intentional backlash against women's achievements. "One great good the

World War accomplished was to free women from the curse of stupidity in the matter of clothes, and now comes this effort to set women back a century," protested the New York–based fashion designer Ethel Traphagen.[123]

The feminist Mildred Adams complained that "under the combined attack of couturiers and corset makers, manufacturers of silks and velvets, advertising artists, stylists, window decorators and fashion magazines, women are to be made feminine, no matter what the cost to comfort or bank accounts." She protested that the new styles and the people who advocated them defined femininity "in its narrowest and more thoroughly traditional sense. Not what the American women are in 1929, but what French women are supposed to have been before they were contaminated with modern ideas."[124] For Adams and other feminists, the debate over skirt length was not about comfort or style but about what and who defined modern femininity. "The battle, as we see it," the editors of the *Woman's Journal*—the official organ of the League of Women Voters argued—"is between the weight of modern propaganda enforcing the standardization of a new fashion, and the new freedom of women."[125] For them, skirt length was intertwined with their political rights. As one flapper suggested, "Would we passively give up the vote, or any other rights finally obtained after long struggles? Then why give up the comfort, economy, and freedom of movement which the short skirt has meant to us?"[126] By correlating women's rights with sartorial freedom, these feminists politicized fashion and turned it into a site of contest.

Feminists' sense of urgency was not completely overrated. Attempts to regulate women's clothing, and more specifically to lengthen hemlines, were of course not new.[127] However, by the late 1920s, the flapper and her lifestyle came increasingly under scrutiny, as the social atmosphere that heralded women's progress changed. Contemporaries began questioning the actual achievements of suffrage, given the fact that women failed to form a voters' bloc and to become influential political power. Some veteran suffragists also acknowledged the inability of suffrage to significantly change women's status and situation, admitting that equality lay not in getting the vote but in equal opportunities in jobs, education, and marriage. These suffragists recognized that, although women did penetrate traditionally male-dominated realms such as the job market, they did not enter as equal partners.[128] Others have used the "new style" feminist, with her indifference and even boredom toward politics, as evidence that women's struggle for equality had disappeared. The young generation, critics claimed, appreciated the vote and the great sacrifices that suffragists went through in order to get it. But they had no interest in continuing the previous generation's battle, preferring instead to concentrate on personal happiness and individual fulfillment.[129] As popular support for the flapper and the freedoms she represented eroded, feminists feared that not only their hemlines were in danger. Indeed, the backlash against the flapper's fashion choices was mainly directed toward the freedoms associated with them, and feminists sought to protect both.

Reacting to the effort to lengthen skirts, a call for a women's rebellion against the new styles took form. "'Down with the corset and up with the hemline!' should be the slogan of every woman who doesn't want to be bullied into doing something as undesirable as it is unwelcome," appealed the feminist journalist Fannie Hurst. "Organization against the oligarchy of industries is all that can save her from the predicament that is about to send her backsliding," she argued. Hurst warned that "at the moment, the ridiculous spectacle is seen of millions of women about to climb back into corsets, trains, long gloves and coiffures.... Here is one of the most important emancipations of woman in the past twelve years, about to go for naught." If women would not rebel, Hurst cautioned, then "fashion, emboldened by signs of success, suddenly trumpets her triumph. Long Skirts. Trains. Corsets. Larger hats. Eleven yards to the gown instead of four or five. Long Gloves. Long Hair." All of what women gained since suffrage, Hurst warned, would be lost if women accepted Paris's decrees.[130] The suffragist and founder of the League of Women Voters, Carrie Chapman Catt, also supported women's action against the longer styles. "Women are just awaking to the inaptness of the [long] styles ... and if you will listen you will hear the far-off rumble of coming rebellion. ... It is bound to be supported by the masses of women who think."[131]

Feminists' call to organize against the long skirt reached beyond their circles. The Jersey City YWCA members asserted that "the new long skirt is neither efficient nor healthful" and called other branches to join them in a boycott campaign on the long styles.[132] College students also joined the boycott movement. At Hunter College for example, 70 percent of the female students declared themselves fashion rebels, announcing that "[the long skirt] is impracticable, uncomfortable and uneconomical ... it banishes the sense of freedom and comfort ... [and is] 'a long step backward in the progress of women's emancipation.'"[133] *Women's Wear Daily* reported that rebellion against the long skirt was not limited to big cities such as New York and Chicago but spread across the nation, stretching as far west as Longview, Washington.[134] The rebellion even reached as far as the courts, when a woman in Los Angeles sued for a divorce on account of cruelty, after her husband made her wear long skirts when she wanted to wear them short.[135]

There was also a class component to women's rebellion against the long skirt. Although many college and professional women were at the forefront of the campaign, working-class women who held jobs that required them to move freely or to travel on public transportation—saleswomen, secretaries, and garment workers—were "the group most benefited by the short skirt" and the physical mobility it enabled. They also had great interest in sticking to the prevailing mode. "Modern life demands simple and convenient clothing," one reader explained to the *New York Times* editor. "Paris forgets that millions of young American women are in business and are not going to be pestered by tangling skirts that catch in subway doors nor sleeves that drag in and out of typewriter keys."[136] Working-class women also had the most to lose if styles were to change, as they had the fewest funds to completely change their wardrobes and also could not afford to look unfashionable for fear of losing their jobs.[137]

The campaign also crossed racial lines. "Don't give up a sensible skirt for one that is not sensible—style or no style," declared a *Baltimore Afro-American* article. "If enough women will laugh at the stylists, their fads will die overnight," promised the writer.[138] The *Pittsburgh Courier*, paraphrasing Shakespeare's *Hamlet*, announced that whether or not to adopt the long skirt was the question that most occupied Pittsburgh's female population. Opinions were divided, but it seemed that, overall, African Americans, like many of their White counterparts—especially young women living in major cities—stuck to the short skirts.[139] In a survey on the question whether to adopt the long style, most of the interviewees told the *Baltimore Afro-American* that they preferred their skirts short. "I don't like the long skirts for anything. I think they are horrid," answered one respondent. Another women went even further, suggesting hanging "the person who first thought of bringing the 19th century styles back for women."[140] In a period when lynching was a pressing issue among African Americans, the fact that this woman resorted to this metaphor suggests the great importance women placed on their short skirt. For them it was not just a fashionable question but a crucial route through which they claimed racial equality and personal freedom.

The skirt debate, which initially appeared to be confined to the pages of women's magazines, received by late 1929 a growing attention from the public and popular press. Ann Devon observed that "the new mode has displaced prohibition as the popular dinner topic.... Discussion of the new fashion is divided pro and anti, a sure signal of battle. Normally, nothing bores the average man so much as a pow-wow on women's wear. Yet at the moment he not only listens to but joins in the argument, and even offers sporting odds on the outcome."[141] An editorial in the *New Republic* concurred with Devon. "Although styles are rarely important in themselves," the paper editors explained, they decided to cover the "skirt debate" with great interest since the question of "will the new styles—the tight waists, the long skirts—symbolize [women's] return to bondage?" was an important social question. Editors, retailers, and readers all shared their concerns and predictions of whether women would agree to depart from their short skirts and by extension, their freedoms.[142]

Despite some uncertainty, it first seemed as if the campaign to keep skirts short was a success. Retailers complained that the "new" long skirts did not sell and that they had to comply with market demands for shorter skirts.[143] J. J. Goldman, founder of Associated Dress Industries, argued that women, dissatisfied with the long skirt style, were refraining from making purchases.[144] "The difficulty in selling comes on the question of length," an executive buyer commented. "The average woman is now willing to wear a dress that covers the knees or is just a little bit below, but the extra two or three inches is often the cause of considerable delay in concluding a sale."[145] Some retailers complained that the new fashions proved to be even less profitable, as "retail stores found their alteration expenses going up because women bought the longer dresses, wore them once and then had them shortened at the store's expense."[146] Other retailers, who chose to put the alteration expenses on the consumer, found that the increased price of the dress pushed customers away. One buyer pointed out that the long styles also made waists and curves visible and demanded fitting, which in turn posed a problem for large-size women who found them less flattering than the previous mode and refrained from buying them.[147] "Women don't like the styles and I don't blame them," said a buyer for one of Chicago's largest department stores. "They make their wearers look older, and who wants to take in 10 years overnight these days? No woman exists—except the very young—who isn't in quest of youth. Why should she put on draperies and long skirts?"[148] The fact that the new styles made the wearer look older also did not help in making the long skirt more popular, but it was not only maintaining youth that was in the minds of women who resisted it.

However, not all women showed a united front. Some women were quite happy with the return of the long skirt. After some months of resistance, retailers in Columbus, St. Louis, and Philadelphia announced that sales were picking up and that women seemed quite happy to accept the new mode, not just for eveningwear but also for daytime.[149] In addition, although students at Radcliffe, Smith, and other colleges rejected the long skirt for daywear, the

New York Times reported that Wellesley students adopted wholeheartedly the dictum of Paris in both day and evening gowns.[150] This kind of support alluded to the power of the fashion industry to determine styles and influence women's choices. Although many women resisted, many others accepted fashion decrees. Yet, despite supporters of the long skirt mode, most retailers admitted that women just did not seem to wear for daytime a skirt longer than four inches below the knee. "The acceptance of a longer skirt length is not to be confounded with a long skirt," *Women's Wear Daily* advised its readers.[151]

Reaching its culmination in the winter season of 1929–30, the skirt debate seemed to conclude by the early 1930s, as women had the upper hand. "The American woman can say triumphantly and loudly that she has won her fight against the Paris couturiers; no longer will she be bound in what she shall wear by the captious and arbitrary notions that emanate from Paris," claimed the *Nation*'s editors.[152] Feminists announced that American women had proven their independence and power against the strong pressures of the fashion industry. "The first round in the Battle of the Skirt seems to have been won by women," announced the *Woman's Journal*'s editors. "Women have the upper hand as buyers. They are wide awake today. They like their freedom."[153] In January 1930, *Outlook* magazine declared that "it was a great war," and it had ended "with emancipated women, fashionable women, and flappers getting approximately what they wanted."[154] Women's victory was meaningful and important, enabling feminists to show that, despite the lack of interest in politics, women were still determined to keep their sartorial freedoms. That it was women who in their determination shaped fashions, and by extension, also their image and identities.

However, the outcome of "the battle of styles" was more complex than feminists wanted to admit. In fact, the result of the "battle" was more of a compromise, as skirts for evening became long, with trailing hemlines. This compromise was welcomed by retailers and manufacturers, who were able to portray women's acceptance of the longer mode for eveningwear as a victory. A complete change in fashion was not needed for the fashion industry to recover financially. All that was needed was to increase women's choice and to offer them more variety. If once a short skirt would have been appropriate attire for both work and evening leisure, now women were compelled to change their outfits if they wanted to remain fashionable.[155]

The economic Depression also played a role in maintaining skirts short. Since people buy less clothes during economic downturns, feminists' so-called victory of maintaining shorter lengths was not just a result of their campaign efforts, but because many women decided to postpone updating their wardrobes and spend their money on other things. As the Depression wore on, an emphasis on the versatility of a dress, or what buyer Amelia Rosenau described as its "wearability," became the main focus of consumers. "Reduced incomes and the necessity of doing little thinking before each purchase has made the American woman practical-minded about her apparel," she maintained.[156] Although styles demanded more variety, women preferred to stick to their older clothes, or they sought out solutions like the Lord & Taylor's "versatility dress" that contained two skirt lengths in one dress and could be used, according to the ad, as a suit, afternoon frock, dinner dress, and evening dress.[157]

Although the variety of skirts lengths alluded to the difficulty feminists had in influencing fashion trends, the skirt debate nonetheless proved that the fashion industry did not have complete control over women's tastes, looks, or consumer decisions. "We have freed ourselves from the tyranny of one iron-bound fashion at a time. Fashion is no longer tied down to just one skirt, one sleeve, one neckline, as it was before the War. In spite of all the talk about returning to the restrictions of our mothers, of being tied again to their corset strings, the new latitude in skirt length is really an additional defiance to tradition, not a return to it," argued Marjorie Howard in 1930.[158] Skirts in the 1930s remain fairly short, as the accepted length for daywear appeared to be at most four inches below the knee. Waists reappeared, but the bias cut that characterized 1930s styles still afforded the comfort that the flapper styles provided.[159]

More importantly, the skirt debate normalized fashion as a legitimate arena for political activism. While there was nothing directly political, or even feminist, in the decision to wear the short skirt, the social and political context of the debate rendered it as such. If the industry believed that "freedom" would be a fading trend that could be changed according to manufacturers and designers' whims, women proved that they were willing to fight for their political gains, whether it was their political representation or the length of their skirts. By conflating short skirts with their political rights, women demonstrated that freedom and equality lay not only in political participation or in access to education and jobs. It was also in wearing comfortable clothing that allowed physical mobility, in the ability to celebrate women's sexuality, and in their power as consumers. Although they shifted their attention from the ballot box to the realm of fashion, the women who fought to keep their skirt short did not abandon their commitment to feminist ideas. For them, fashion was not a matter of frivolity but a central tool to express one's identity as a modern woman and the freedoms that went along with that identity.

The Fashionable Mainstreaming of the Flapper

As contemporaries debated the flapper's clothing, behavior, and lifestyle, they imbued her image with great political significance. Discussions over the proper length of skirts, the feminine charms of bobbed hair, and the effects of the corset on women's health became an arena for both women and men to delineate their perceptions of what it meant to be a modern woman. Moreover, the flapper's image had an important role in popularizing feminist ideas and in making them part of the mainstream discourse. That women could wear sheer dresses and expose their legs in public legitimized their sexuality. And as women fought to keep their skirts short, they translated ideas of mobility and freedom into sartorial expression, expanding their actions beyond protecting a fashion choice. Indeed, when the flapper turned mainstream, so too did the meanings she represented. Instead of dissolving feminist ideology by concentrating on clothes, fashion played a role in turning feminist ideas and attitudes into a popular cultural style. The mainstreaming of the flapper sheared away some of her radical character and the threat she posed to gender norms, but it also made these same ideas popular and acceptable.

Additionally, the distribution of clothing styles turned fashion and the flapper into a shared experience that crossed class and racial barriers. Ready-made clothing might have promoted conformity, but it also enabled women to exert their power as consumers and to act as a political group. By adopting and adapting the flapper's fashions and lifestyle, women could stretch the boundaries of respectability and propriety and could construct new images of femininity that represented their new experiences and realities. These images expanded definitions of beauty and appropriate body display, enabling women to carve new spaces and to assume new positions from which they could actively participate in the public sphere. Especially for women of color, using fashion in the construction of their image gave them some control over how others perceived them and judged them, as well as new means of claiming equality and taking part in racial uplift projects.

While not every girl who wore a short skirt identified as a sexually liberated flapper or as a feminist, we should not dismiss the power of clothes to convey liberating, empowering messages or to articulate a sense of group identity. Although fashion could not offer women the power that a constitutional amendment gave them, it created a space to negotiate freer, more independent, sexual identities, adding a cultural and material component to the politics of women's freedom in the 1920s. By the end of the decade, as the country stepped into grave economic depression, much of what the flapper represented became, like all fashions, outdated. Still, the liberating meanings of her fashions did not lose their power nor their popularity. The flapper might have changed her appearance, but she did not change her values. And whereas her clothes underwent transformation, what they meant to her did not. Despite the hardships of depression and war, women continued to demand clothing that provided them with comfort and mobility. And they continued to use attire to express their independence and political rights and thus also to redefine feminist visual culture in a time of great change.

CHAPTER FOUR

Designing Power

The Fashion Industry and the Politics of Style

In 1951, Dorothy Shaver—the president of New York City's department store Lord & Taylor—paid tribute to female American designers, who, she argued, captured through their creations both the American spirit and the modern American woman: independent, active, and feminine. The female designer was instrumental in shaping the essence of modern femininity, she asserted. "Because of the American designer's ability to interpret social change in feminine terms, the American woman's clothes are an expression of herself as an individual yet also as a representative of a cultural pattern." According to Shaver, the new roles that American women were taking in business, civic life, and the home also demanded new clothing needs. "It isn't only when she goes to a ball that she wants to look well. It's when she is shopping, or cooking, or bicycling, or voting," Shaver pointed to American designers' success in creating functional, comfortable, durable clothes for the masses that also look feminine and attractive.[1] For Shaver and her audience, American design was the sartorial expression of feminist ideas of freedom, modernity, and democracy, and it was the American female designer who put these ideas into a material form.

Shaver gave this speech in front of the Fashion Group, an all-female organization that she helped found that sought to promote the American fashion industry and women's role in it. And indeed, in 1951 she had a lot to celebrate. In the two decades prior, the domestic fashion industry rose as an influential creative force and as an important fashion center. American designers, and especially women such as Elizabeth Hawes, Vera Maxwell, Bonnie Cashin, and Claire McCardell, transformed the fashion world by popularizing casual styles for everyday wear, which received the name "sportswear." Partly inspired by constraints imposed by the Depression and World War II, and partly because of designers' desire to create beautiful and practical clothes for the masses, sportswear brought a new design language and feminist aesthetics grounded in comfort, versatility, and accessibility.[2] It created a new ideal of fashionable femininity as a source of power that became increasingly associated with Americanism. This ideal lionized the working, on-the-move woman who became the epitome of American modernity, rather than the elite matron principally interested in decorative luxury. This design language continued trends for clothes to express ideas of mobility, independence, and freedom, representing the culmination of these efforts from the early twentieth century. No longer seen as alternative or radical styles, the feminist aesthetics that sportswear espoused became part of the fashionable mainstream and a mainstay in women's lives and culture.

Shaver credited the American designer in creating the "American Look" that "reflects our striving for functionalism yet... also captures our yearning for beauty."[3] However, she and the Fashion Group were no less instrumental in popularizing fashion as a marker of both national and feminist pride. These female designers, journalists, and retail executives managed to gain prominent roles and influence in the fashion industry. Aided by the growing influence of Hollywood's film divas such as Katherine Hepburn, Greta Garbo, and Marlene Dietrich, they turned fashion into an important vehicle to redefine modern femininity and gender roles in a period of economic depression and war. Viewing themselves as leaders of taste, these women sought to express "publicly our views, or shaping, or helping to shape the views of many women in America." They saw it as their mission not only to promote women in the industry but also to advance the life of women around them.[4] In the process, they turned fashion into an important site where feminist ideas continued to percolate and even thrive, especially during a period in which other political arenas of feminist activism seemed to be in decline.

Scholars have successfully challenged perceptions that feminist organizing and activism disappeared after the passing of the Nineteenth Amendment. Even so, they have rarely given attention to women in creative industries, and especially in fashion.[5] Yet, these were not insignificant realms. Although neither the women of the Fashion Group nor designers like Hawes and Mc-

Cardell identified with the women's movement at the time, their role as cultural producers was instrumental to shaping ideas regarding women's freedom and independence. By creating professional networks, advancing the status of American design, and offering women affordable clothing cut for comfort and a busy lifestyle, these women helped feminism remain a popular idea in mainstream culture.

This chapter shifts the attention to this group of designers and fashion professionals to reveal how they created fashion as a realm of women's empowerment, both as workers and as consumers.[6] The vision these women created through sportswear offered a conceptual as well as tangible framework to popularize and legitimize feminist ideas of freedom, economic independence, and mobility. As designer Claire McCardell declared, "sports clothes have changed our lives—perhaps, more than anything else, made us independent women."[7] While she was mainly referring to White middle-class women like herself, McCardell and her peers helped consolidate a consumerist feminist ideology that became prominent in the interwar years and part of a national identity. For the women of the Fashion Group and the designers who promoted American sportswear, women's right to enjoy the same professional, educational, and political opportunities as men did not come at the expense of their appearance. On the contrary, it was through fashion that these women could redefine and re-create what feminism meant to them.

Carving Professional Fashion Networks

The Fashion Group was founded in 1930, but its idea was born during a luncheon in 1928, at which seventeen prominent women decided to create a forum that would advocate for American fashion. Representing all realms of the industry—manufacturing, retail, design, advertising, education, and the press—these women signaled the extent to which White middle-class women managed to reach high-level positions in the business.[8] The original founding group included fashion editors Edna Woolman Chase of *Vogue*, Frances Hughes of *Mademoiselle*, Julia Coburn of *Ladies' Home Journal*, and Carmel Snow of *Harper's Bazaar*, as well as Virginia Pope, the influential *New York Times* fashion reporter. Other prominent founders were designers Claire McCardell, Clare Potter, Edith Head, Nan Duskin, and Adele Simpson, as well as beauty culturists Elizabeth Arden and Helena Rubinstein. Interior designer Eleanor LeMaire, Tobé Coller Davis—the founder of the Tobé-Coburn fashion school—and Dorothy Shaver from Lord & Taylor were also among the founding group.[9] Estelle Hamburger, a retail executive who owned a fashion advertising consulting business, was not part of the original seventeen founders but joined as a board member shortly after.[10]

The most significant outlier in this cohort was Eleanor Roosevelt, the only original founder who did not come from the industry. Yet, her presence in the meeting was not surprising because, as a fashion-savvy woman, she had formed close and personal connections with many female executives in the fashion business. Roosevelt was instrumental to the Fashion Group's efforts in advocating for American ready-made designers. She used her prominence as First Lady to publicize the Fashion Group's exhibition at the 1939 World's Fair in New York City. And in 1940, she joined the advisory committee of the organization's annual event Fashion Futures, a promotional fashion show that featured American design.[11] Roosevelt was also a big proponent of working women, which can explain her interest in forming a group that would advocate for women in fashion. The April 1930 issue of *Vogue* carried an article by Roosevelt calling for young women to seek creative careers, not just temporary jobs "with a pay envelop at the end of the week." Targeting her message to the *Vogue* readership of young, professional, middle-class women, Roosevelt claimed that finding a fulfilling career would not hinder one from getting married, as it did in previous generations. In fact, she argued, women's use of their creative talents would only lead to better homes, in which both boys and girls would "grow up with two personalities as parents, each of them contributing something of interest to the lives of the young." According to Roosevelt, a career in fashion was not only a route for self-fulfillment but a manifestation of a feminist vision of equality and economic independence, and she saw the Fashion Group as a useful forum to advance these goals.[12]

While most members of the Fashion Group did not see themselves as part of the women's movement—which by the 1930s lost much of its popular appeal and influence—they, like Roosevelt, saw opportunity and empowerment for women in fashion. Group members harnessed their professional status as experts not only to advance their own careers and influence, but also to expand cultural ideas of womanhood. Thus, they helped to incorporate feminist ideas and rhetoric into mainstream culture. The organization and its activities offered them a framework to promote ideas of gender equality outside of the political realm, especially with regard to education and the workplace. As Kenneth Collins—the vice president of Macy's—admitted, the Fashion Group was "one of the first organization of women who actually are in the stream of events, and are really carving out their own careers and having a tremendous influence on the business of this country." He credited the founding of the

Group to the changing status of women and their growing presence in the public sphere, commenting that "the formation of the Fashion Group was in some sense a part of a scheme of this whole business of the emancipation of women."[13] Believing in women's ability and right to thrive in the fashion industry and the market in general, members championed a liberal vision influenced by the popularization of feminist ideas a decade prior. Yet, if in the 1920s this vision was connected to women's position as consumers, the Fashion Group positioned women's work, and their status as producers of fashion, at the center.

Indeed, fashion offered women professional possibilities not available to them in any other field. Although in the early part of the twentieth century women were discouraged from pursuing careers in design—due to the assumption that they would abandon the profession in favor of marriage and children—by the 1930s this assumption reversed. Fashion became an appropriate employment avenue for women because it adhered to gendered notions regarding the feminine realm. The women who comprised this cadre of American designers in the 1930s were the first generation who came to the profession with formal training and degrees in design, turning fashion into a skilled professional trade.[14] Considered more qualified to work in fashion due to their feminine sense of style, women managed to achieve positions of power within the industry in ways that were rarely accessible in more male-dominated fields. By 1940, nearly 84 percent of female executives in the United States (218 out of 260) held positions in a fashion-related field, using the industry to advance and legitimize their career aspirations.[15]

Harnessing their status as specialists in observing and translating "the changing desires of American women into clothes for American realities," the Fashion Group's mission was to promote American design and women's influence in the industry.[16] Since its beginning, the Fashion Group directed its efforts both outward, to the general public, and inward, to women working in the fashion field. Publicly, it endeavored to elevate the domestic fashion industry, turning the United States, and New York in particular, into a prominent fashion center, on par with Paris. Already before World War I, calls for greater independence of American fashion were evident among proponents within the industry, leading to campaigns that urged consumers to buy local designs. These campaigns argued that, unlike in the French fashion world, where clothes appealed to the elite woman of leisure, the domestic fashion industry understood better the modern American woman, especially those working in offices and factories.[17] "The average American woman is the best-dressed average woman in the world," declared fashion designer Nettie Rosenstein, crediting the strength of the ready-made industry to successfully "make any little manicurist in a $16.50 dress look just about as well as any little heiress in a $250 model."[18] Fashion Group members capitalized on this perspective, pushing to the forefront the idea that American-designed fashion better suited the modern American woman because it was made by American women. "Machine production is in masses and should be for masses," argued the Group member and designer Elizabeth Hawes. According to her, American design was both a democratic and an empowering force, providing women with a sartorial means to claim their freedom and independence. "[Clothes] must be conceived in relation to the actual lives of the people who are going to wear it and not in relation to a group of women who lead lives of leisure," she maintained.[19]

Yet, as much as the Fashion Group emphasized the importance of American design, its main focus was to create a networking opportunity and a supportive community where women could not only make their voice heard, but also to shift the gender balance that favored men in the industry. These women aimed to claim fashion as a professional field that demanded skills and knowledge, not simply a preference or love of beautiful clothes.[20] Members envisioned the Fashion Group as a forum where they could "dignify and clarify the position of women" whose business was to "interpret and promote good taste and good fashion." According to the organization's constitution, its main mission was to "advance the principles of applied art in industry" by encouraging the cooperation of those working in the business, as well as "other women who are desirous of entering these professions or who are just beginning work in them."[21]

To achieve this end, the organization formed as a distinct group by and for women, with membership restricted to women. The Fashion Group was thus an amalgam of a professional society and a women's club, which historically was a political space for women's activism. However, instead of focusing their effort on politics, members used their positions to advance women in the fashion field through education, career development, and training. The Fashion Group founded a placement bureau "to help women of the right educational background and experience to enter any of the various fashion fields." It also established a fund to help sick and unemployed members, and initiated an educational committee that was responsible for disseminating information and advising schools and colleges on professional standards.[22]

The professional background of the members dictated the interests and focus of the Fashion Group. Although it was based in New York City and the majority of the membership was drawn from the city's busting fashion industries, the organization was always national and even international in scope. In 1932, the first regional branch was formed in Cleveland, and by 1940, it had branches across the country in Chicago, St. Louis, Los Angeles, Philadelphia, and Washington, D.C. The first international branch was founded in Paris in 1956, followed by branches in Montreal, Melbourne, and Mexico City.[23] The Fashion Group's monthly meetings and publications aimed to keep members informed of the major trends in the business and provided a place to discuss important industry issues. Yet these meetings also addressed contemporary social, political, and cultural matters not directly related to fashion. The organization, perhaps due to Eleanor Roosevelt's influence, did not shy away from issues of labor and unionization of the garment industry. On June 1933, for example, union activists and government representatives discussed the problem of sweatshop labor in the Fashion Group's monthly meeting.[24]

However, the main focus of the Fashion Group was not garment workers but professional women in the fashion industry. Indeed, the Fashion Group was founded as an elite professional organization, which, as with other female professional networks at the time, sought first and foremost to empower women like them.[25] In order to join, members had to have "a cultural and educational background to fit her for a position of responsibility in directing public taste," plus a minimum of three years of experience in the industry. Potential members also had to be proposed and supported by five existing members, thus situating the organization as a forum for networking, an avenue that was often closed to professional women in more masculine professions.[26] This membership process, however, also determined the class and racial component of the group. All members were White, gainfully employed women, who had already made a name for themselves in fashion circles. Although the Fashion Group did not have a formal policy to bar Blacks, membership based on personal endorsements and the segregated nature of the fashion industry and media, led to their de facto absence. Only in 1955, twenty-five years after the founding of the Fashion Group, was the first African American member, Mrs. Artie Bell of Washington, D.C., admitted to the organization.[27]

Excluded from the Fashion Group, African American female designers nonetheless carved themselves a professional space in the industry. New York, the nation's fashion capital, became a center for African American professional designers who found Harlem's middle class as well as its growing entertainment scene in the interwar period a great potential source of profits. Designer Zelda Wynn Valdes, for example, was popular among Black performers, gaining publicity after designing dresses for the wedding of jazz singer Maria Hawkins Ellington and Nat King Cole in 1948. She became known for designing glamorous outfits both for on and off stage for Ella Fitzgerald and Dorothy Dandridge, who were among her most loyal clients.[28] Whereas the bulk of the clientele for Black designers usually came from the Black community, designers such as Ann Lowe, who designed the dress Jacqueline Bouvier wore to her wedding to John F. Kennedy, achieved national fame and acquired a long list of White customers.[29] Selling both custom-made and ready-to-wear dresses, Black women designers like Wynn and Lowe served as important financial pillars of their communities and played a pivotal role in bringing fashion within African American women's reach. Wynn open her first business in 1935 in White Plains, New York, and in 1948 opened a store on Broadway in New York City, which became an important fashion resource for the local community.[30]

These designers also saw the importance of creating their own professional and support networks, which they perceived as useful in promoting Black design. In 1949, with the support of Mary McLeod Bethune and the National Council of Negro Women (NCNW), a group of designers led by Jeanette Welch Brown found the National Association of Fashion and Accessory Designers (NAFAD), a mirror organization to the Fashion Group. Frustrated from being ignored by the mainstream industry, the decision to form NAFAD came in 1948 after Wynn integrated a fashion show in celebration of New York City's golden jubilee. Despite the initial exclusion of Black designers, show organizers agreed that Wynn's design, together with leather goods accessories by Helen Cornele Cuyjet, would represent Harlem in the event, showcasing African American design to White audience.[31] Acknowledging the need of creating a more permanent organization to represent Black designers' interests, Wynn—who was one of NAFAD's chief organizers—pushed for action.

NAFAD was created as a professional organization that would use its members' influence and connections in the industry to increase the visibility of Black design and designers. Its mission was to "foster complete integration of its membership in all phases of the fashion industry through the extension of educational and economic opportunities . . ., the dissemination of pertinent information, the offering of local and national scholarship, and the display of fashion in good taste." As part of this mission, NAFAD organized conferences and meetings in which prominent people from the industry, many of them were members of the Fashion Group, came and talked to members. In addition, NAFAD also published a monthly newsletter, built a showroom for retail buyers, and sought affiliation with the Costume Institute of the Metropolitan Museum of Art so members could use its collections for inspirations to their designs.[32] Like the Fashion Group, NAFAD was led by women and had branches all over the country, although its affiliation with NCNW meant that its headquarters was in Washington, D.C., and not in New York City, where most designers resided.

While advocating for racial equality and better opportunities for African Americans in the fashion industry became more crucial to NAFAD than gender equality, both NAFAD and the Fashion Group saw their purpose to be turning the business into an empowering realm for women. Both organizations sought to fulfill the need for professional networks, especially for women, that could serve as a space to advocate for social change. And although the racist structures of the industry prevented NAFAD's members from gaining the public attention that the Fashion Group attracted, the two organizations collaborated and helped to make Black designers' presence more visible.[33] Indeed, both organizations fought to increase the reputation of American design by cultivating a cadre of talented women who could gain an influential role in shaping the business. Whether Black or White, they utilized the opportunities that the fashion industry provided women to carve spaces of independence and power, creating a platform from which they could advocate both for women and for fashion.

The American Female Designer and the Rise of the Career Woman

In their efforts to advance women in the business of fashion, organizations like the Fashion Group and NAFAD concentrated their activities on promoting the domestic fashion industry and turning it into a useful space for women's empowerment. Luckily for them, the economic and social realities of the Great Depression and World War II provided unique circumstances that positioned fashion as a fertile ground to shape and expand gendered ideas regarding women's roles in society. The crisis of the Great Depression became the catalyst for boosting the domestic ready-made industry. Like other sectors of the economy, fashion and retail suffered from the economic downturn, as consumption of clothing, accessories, and jewelry plummeted from $11.2 billion in 1929 to $5.4 billion in 1933. Moreover, during 1931 and 1932, a wave of strikes in the garment trade pushed many businesses into bankruptcy and further destabilized the industry. Responding to this reality and to shifts in consumers' spending habits, the ready-made industry made structural changes, such as increasing output and lowering prices, which ultimately kept it viable. Clothing consumption throughout the decade remained at around 12 percent, despite the economic depression.[34]

As part of the structural changes that manufacturers established, the industry began to look toward domestic talent rather than to France as a source of inspiration. This move stemmed from economic considerations, since many U.S. manufacturers that had depended on the counterfeit business of copying French designs could no longer afford to maintain their Paris offices or to send buyers and copiers to the seasonal exhibitions.[35] Moreover, the decision to concentrate on ready-made production and wholesale trade made retailers less reliant on buying Paris originals that were expensive to import and appealed to a shrinking consumer base. Yet, the industry did not present its shift to American design as an economic decision but instead appealed to consumers' national pride. Retailers tried to convince consumers that buying from domestic manufacturers was good citizenship and a tribute to the nation's resilience. As an ad for Lonsdale Sport Clothes declared, "Buy America!," casting the purchase of clothes as a patriotic act. "Let American women know that by insisting on American garments they are increasing the employment of American citizens," the ad claimed, "now is the time when pride in American designing and American industry should be brought home to American women—as a definite and patriotic means of bettering American business."[36]

By the 1940s, calls for supporting American design shifted from focusing on economic recovery to framing fashion as part of good citizens' war duties, reaching a culmination after June 1940 when France surrendered to the Nazi forces. The occupation of Paris put an end to Americans' presence in the French capital, forcing the American fashion industry to rely almost exclusively on domestic talent. Over the course of a few months, promoting American fashion became more than just fostering patriotic sentiments—it turned into a matter of necessity. Although some questioned domestic designers' ability to continue operating without Parisian influence and inspiration, the Fashion Group was among the ones that saw the forced separation as an opportunity to strengthen the U.S. industry and to boost their organization.[37]

In September 1940, the Fashion Group organized a New York alternative to the Paris openings, showcasing American-made collections. In 1941, it merged the January season opening with the Fashion Group's tenth anniversary celebration under the banner "New York's Fashion Futures."[38] The show was themed around New York City and celebrated American innovation and the rise of New York as a fashion capital, but also, and no less important, it celebrated on-the-move American women. "The fashions will be conceived by Americans for the American woman's mode of living, her activities, her needs, her physical type, her very thinking," announced George A. Sloan, the city's commerce commissioner. Scenes depicted "daytime clothes for every occasion" set in realistic settings such as LaGuardia Airport, Central Park, and the Sixth Avenue Subway, which appealed to "busy career girls."[39] The event was a power demonstration for the Fashion Group's members and a testament to their influence on the industry.[40] It anchored American-designed clothing as the ultimate expression of democracy, pride, and freedom at a time of war, creating a coherent look that was associated with the modern American woman that the Fashion Group promoted. Indeed, by associating feminine modernity with American values, events like Fashion Futures contributed to the mainstreaming of the career woman as a role model and added another layer to the Fashion Group's mission to advance women in the business.

For Fashion Group members, highlighting the creativity of American-made fashions was intertwined with the promotion of the female American designer as the harbinger of innovation.[41] According to Mary Lewis, a Fashion Group member and an executive for the department store Best & Co., the only way to make American design appealing to customers was by emphasizing designers' individual personalities.[42] Unlike the French couture industry, which was based on a few known designers of custom-made fashion, most costume designers in the United States worked for the ready-made industry and had been relatively anonymous prior to the 1930s. Seeking to change this reality, women in the industry banded together to create the female American designer as a new role model of modern femininity. Only in this way they believed, they could make the domestic fashion industry competitive with the French one. "We believe that there must be clothes which are intrinsically American and that only the American designer can create them," Dorothy Shaver asserted.[43]

Back in 1932, Shaver—then the new vice president of Lord & Taylor—orchestrated an "American Fashions for American Women" campaign, marketing American designers in an attempt to boost sales. In its first year, the store featured the work of Elizabeth Hawes, Annette Simpson, and Edith Marie Reuss. Subsequent years introduced Clare Potter, Claire McCardell, Muriel King, and Bonnie Cashin. Making these names known to the public for the very first time, the "American Fashions" campaign sought to create a cult of personality around American fashion designers, amplifying the message that these fashions were made by and for women (figure 4.1).[44] An ad announcing the campaign declared "LORD & TAYLOR recognizes a new trend towards clothes of, by, and for the American women," assuring readers that "in presenting these collections we believe that you will discover a new satisfaction in buying, and wearing clothes that *understand* you."[45] This appeal to consumers formed a connection between the designer and the clothes she made, but it also created a sense of female solidarity between those who made clothes and those who bought them. Following Shaver's campaign success in Lord & Taylor, other retailers began marketing American fashions to their female consumers. Franklin Simon introduced a new campaign under the title "American Genius," and Bergdorf Goodman offered its first all-American collection in 1940.[46]

The fashion press, albeit more reluctantly than retailers, also joined the effort to promote American design. In February 1938, after years of boasting almost exclusively Parisian design, *Vogue* published its first "Americana Issue," featuring American design on its pages for the first time.[47] *Harper's Bazaar*, partly out of necessity, presented in September 1940 its first issue without any fashions from Paris. The editorial complemented Seventh Avenue American designers' innovativeness, asserting that it was them "who have made it possible for everywoman in America to dress with style."[48] However, it was the popular press, most notably Virginia Pope at the *New York Times* and Sally Kirkland at *Life* magazine—both Fashion Group members—that spearheaded the rising status and public recognition of American design. Through favorable articles on American couturiers, they facilitated the entrance of their designs into the cultural mainstream while also turning fashion into a news worthy topic.[49]

Pope was one of the first reporters to write about the wholesale market, forging relationships with manufacturers and retailers, not just couture designers. "I was trying to promote the American designer," she recalled in an interview. "We did write about French designers, and mention their names, but we ignored the Americans.... So, I think it was in 1939, 1940, I went to Lester Markel [*New York Times* editor], and I said I would like to do a series of stories about top New York designers, mentioning their names, what they were doing, and so forth. I got *The Times'* permission to do that."[50] Pope's articles portrayed female designers as the embodiment of femininity, originality, practicality, and above all Americanism. In a 1944 series, Pope presented designers like Clare Potter and Adele Simpson as the true representatives of the modern woman—both in spirit and in style—connecting their biographies, and especially their nationality, with their design philosophy.[51]

Indeed, the designer, rather than the clothes she made, received the most attention. Describing her as "under thirty, or very little about it, and usually ... pretty, well-educated, poised, sophisticated, intelligent, chic," articles heralded the American female designer as the embodiment of a new generation of women. "She knows exactly what the American woman will wear, because

FIGURE 4.1: Department stores, particularly Lord & Taylor under the management of Dorothy Shaver, were instrumental in promoting female American designers in the interwar period, marketing their clothes as designed by and for the modern American woman. (Fashions of Lord & Taylor, window display featuring American designers, 1933 Worsinger photo, X2010.11.4555, Museum of the City of New York)

... she is the American woman," the journalist Selma Robinson argued. Being portrayed as an authoritative creator of clothing styles and trends, the female designer not only reflected but also shaped the ideal modern woman through the clothes she made. "Only an American can understand how a business woman can require a dress that will be suitable for a busy morning at the office, a hasty lunch at the drug store, and unexpected tea date and an informal dinner-theater engagement... [that] look exactly right for each occasion."[52] In addition to touting designers' talent, articles also featured their photographs as a way to elevate their celebrity status. In carefully curated poses, as if they were fashion models, photographs of designers such as Elizabeth Hawes, Muriel King, and Clare Potter presented a new fashionable ideal that emphasized their status as career women and offered an inspiration to women who sought to achieve fame and economic stability (figure 4.2).[53]

Whereas the segregation of the printed media meant that most of the attention in the popular press was directed toward White designers, the Black press celebrated the achievements of African American designers, covering them and their fashion shows extensively. The Black press also provided a platform for designers to advertise their business, further advancing their public visibility.[54] NAFAD in particular played an important role in increasing designers' name recognition among the Black community. NAFAD members used their connections with Black publishers to publicize the organization's fashion shows and members' designs, giving attention not only to the clothes but also to the women who made them. Articles about NAFAD and its activities often included photographs of models wearing African American designs, with credit to the designers. Some articles also included photographs of "designers at work"—which, as in the White press, raised their celebrity status.[55]

Although career women, and fashion designers in particular, were only a minority among working women, they represented a subtle shift in ideas of femininity in the interwar period. Indeed, the female designer became the ultimate role model and a consumer of a style that fitted the "bright, resourceful, daring, and unprejudiced young woman," incorporating a strong and independent mind with feminine beauty.[56] The association of high fashion with femininity that designers embodied through their image and work turned the career woman from a threat into a positive and fashionable figure. Yet, in presenting the female designer as a desirable role model for the average consumer, magazines did not just popularize fashion design as a career for women, they popularized careers in general. Paid labor was recognized not only as a temporary stage in women's life or as a marker of working-class status but as a respectable path for the middle-class woman. In a 1934 *Vogue* spread titled "Beauty and Four Women," the "Business Woman" and the woman on a "Limited Income" joined the "Leisured Lady" and the "Globe-Trotter" as archetypes of beauty, modernity, and progress.[57] No longer a curiosity, the pursuit of a business career became a legitimate, even desired, aspect of womanhood for both Whites and Blacks.

Magazines appealed directly to the young working woman, giving her advice on how to pick the right colleges, to apply for a job, to handle office etiquette, and of course, how to maintain a suitable wardrobe.[58] In 1936, for example, the *Pictorial Review* published a spread titled the "The Busy Woman's

FIGURE 4.2: In the 1930s and 1940s, the female fashion designer was a new role model for the modern career woman, promoting in the process American design. ("American Designers," *Good Housekeeping*, September 1938, Hearst Magazines Inc., photography by Martin Munkácsi © Estate of Martin Munkácsi, Courtesy Howard Greenberg Gallery, New York. Image published with permission of ProQuest LLC. Further reproduction is prohibited without permission.)

Wardrobe Does 24 Hours Duty," giving women sartorial solutions for working, shopping, and meeting friends.[59] Department stores also began featuring suitable work attire in their windows, quite literally selling the notion of career-oriented femininity as a desirable aspect.[60] By 1941, new magazines appeared that catered specifically to working women, symbolizing their increasing importance in mainstream culture. *Charm* positioned itself as the "Magazine for the Business Girl," while in 1943, *Glamor of Hollywood*—which was founded in 1939—changed its name to *Glamour*, with the subtitle "For the Girl with a Job." The cover that August featured a young model in a red dress suit by the American brand Swansdown, holding a newspaper in her red-gloved hand, as

CHAPTER FOUR

FIGURE 4.3: The rise of the female fashion designer helped legitimatize careers for women, turning the young working girl into a cultural icon celebrated in the press and in Hollywood. (*Glamour*, August 1943 cover, by Gjon Mili, Glamour © Condé Nast)

a black bag swung from her shoulder (figure 4.3).[61] Photographed from below and against an empty blue background to enhance her height and presence, the model did not look directly at the camera and seems to be in motion. This position conveys a message of power and determination, situating the White working girl as the ideal American woman. Highlighting femininity, fashion, and wage work, magazines like *Glamour* and *Charm* popularized a consumerist version of empowerment and success that the female designer represented, and made it accessible to larger audiences through the clothes she made.

The Black press also looked favorably on the working woman, and like its White counterparts provided fashion and beauty advice about what to wear on the job. Although work was a necessity for most African American women, girls were encouraged to seek a professional career rather than settle for domestic work.[62] Unlike previous decades in which the Black press encouraged women to become mothers and caregivers, in the 1930s and 1940s the same newspapers heralded the Black career woman as a role model of racial uplift and middle-class respectability. "The Business women," the African American career woman Helen Woodward argued in the *Chicago Defender*, "has had a certain kind of special training which makes her a better wife than the girl who has never worked outside her home." Woodward ran a column titled "The Woman Who Makes Good," in which she extended practical advice for working women on etiquette, balancing family and a career, and potential careers options.[63]

Indeed, by the 1940s, careers for women were not only desired but encouraged, and the female designer stood as the epitome of the professional young woman. Through the clothes she designed and wore, it was the female designer, with her unique design language, that stood for American modernity and sophisticated femininity. No longer seen as a threat, or as unfeminine, the fashionable career woman was now celebrated and adored.

Hollywood and the Glamorization of the Fashion Designer

The printed press was not the only media heralding the career woman and her fashions. During the 1930s and 1940s, Katharine Hepburn, Greta Garbo, Joan Crawford, Marlene Dietrich, and Bette Davis were among the female Hollywood actors to rise as new fashion icons both on and off screen. Through their clothing and the roles they played, Hollywood's female heroines provided a commercialized fantasy of the career woman or the business girl, espousing a new beauty ideal that was based on "practical glamour" and sexual appeal. In the film *Fashions of 1934*, for example, Bette Davis portrays a young fashion designer who appears alternately in practical suits and luxurious evening dresses.[64] This new representation was geared toward the female fan base that comprised the majority of moviegoers, for whom Hollywood was striving to project not romantic naïveté but independent sophistication and resilience.[65] Dressed in luxurious bias-cut satin dresses, furs, and bold diamond jewelry, these female actors also wore slacks, simple dress suits, and functional sportswear, bringing their own fashionable tastes and preferences to the screen.

In particular, these female actors played an active role in promoting the American female designer, further aligning themselves with a new ethos of femininity that applauded freedom, mobility, youth, and individuality. Hepburn endorsed Clare Potter, both in the pages of *Vogue* and in the Lord & Taylor window display, where her image was featured with Potter's designs. Hepburn also influenced Columbia Pictures to hire Muriel King to be in charge of designing the star's wardrobe.[66] Similarly, Crawford advertised Jo Copeland's designs in *Harper's Bazaar*.[67] By lionizing the simple and modern sportswear styles that these designers created, Hepburn and other stars created an approachable image with which other women could identify. Ironically, it was the exotic appeal of Swedish Garbo and German Dietrich that became the epitome of American glamour. Yet, their success, as well as of other U.S.-born female actors, offered a new way to imagine the modern American woman as a career professional who was also a fashionable beauty.[68]

While only a few could emulate these stars' lifestyle, by the mid-1930s, both movies' plotlines and heroines' fashions began to increasingly resemble their viewers. Movies featured stories of working girls with dreams of love, marriage, self-fulfillment, and financial success, and movie stars like Crawford—who came from a working-class background—helped legitimize the working girl dressing on a budget. "The general story trend in the industry is leaning towards a more legitimate, less madcap theme," argued Paramount Pictures chief costume designer Edith Head. "Our screen heroines are now normal, average, every-day girls and women instead of overdramatized, synthetic sirens."[69] As more women gained prominent designing positions in the major studios, they pushed for simpler, modern styles that fitted with their ideas of the stylish career woman living a mobile life. Hollywood female designers used stars' appearance on screen to redefine glamour by creating visual associations between fashionability and women's power. In these films, heroines' clothing conveyed their ability to act with authority and compete successfully with men, especially in a workplace or urban environment, while also looking fashionably feminine.[70] Yet, Head and other designers did not view their role as limited to only styling female actors. By dressing Hollywood's stars in outfits most women could affordably adapt for themselves, designers aspired to provide fashionable solutions to millions of women who sought to look glamorous without compromising their independence or pocketbooks.[71]

Hollywood's growing popularity among the masses turned its thriving apparel industry into an influential cultural trendsetter, comparable to New

York. Specializing in casual wear, California designers, and most notably Hollywood's female designers, offered their interpretation of the modern American woman that further aided the national industry's turn from Paris and the creation of a unique American look.[72] Constantly moving between film costume design and working for retail manufacturers, Hollywood costume designers brought their glamorous styles within ordinary women's reach. Bonnie Cashin's designs for film, for example, were almost all adapted for retail sale, and she used film settings to test her ideas and see how they would play in a mass market.[73]

The ready-made industry readily capitalized on Hollywood's appeal by manufacturing inexpensive copies of the gowns seen on the screen. A dress that Adrian designed for Joan Crawford's character in the 1932 film *Letty Lynton* became a hit. Only a few months after the film was released, Macy's sold over fifty thousand copies of the gown, and by 1933 versions of it appeared in the Sears catalog ranging from $1.29 to $6 (around $25 to $120 today).[74] Butterick and Vogue were among the pattern companies to offer movie-inspired outfits for the home sewer. In 1931, the fan magazine *Photoplay* introduced Hollywood Fashion, a chain of clothing retailing franchises that offered affordable fashion inspired by movies.[75]

Yet, the rise of Hollywood as a fashion harbinger was not limited only to the popularity of female actors on the screen. Costume designers, most notably Edith Head, Irene Gibbons, and Helen Rose, also became familiar names, signaling the growing recognition that fashion designers received. Autographed dresses by Edith Head were advertised by the Eighth Avenue retailer Gelitsman, Chopp & Sadowsky, promising their clients that each model was an "authentic original Edith Head [design]."[76] Moreover, the introduction of the Academy Award for Best Costume Design in 1949 further solidified the status of these designers as celebrities. Recognized by their talent, Hollywood's female designers became a role model for young women who sought a career in the movie industry but lacked acting talent. Becoming a chief costume designer for one of the studios, like Head was in Paramount and Rose in MGM, demonstrated how women could secure positions of power and shape the industry from within.[77]

The cooperation between Hollywood, designers, and the ready-made industry gave rise to a new film genre in the 1930s: the fashion film. These movies focused on women who worked in the fashion business as models, designers, or in department stores, which further legitimized the career woman and her styles. While these films tended to ignore the poor garment workers who comprised the bulk of female employees in the industry, they helped to create fashion as a glamorous and positive workplace, framing it as a realm where women could gain independence, social and economic mobility, and even fame. Films such as *Street of Women* (1932), *Fashions of 1934* (1934) and *Roberta* (1935) glorified the status of the female designer and acknowledged her centrality to the industry.[78] In the mid-1940s, as Head's influence became ever so powerful, Paramount planned a biopic on her life, though the project never came to fruition.[79] The fashion film, however, did not just glorify careers in fashion. In many of these films, promotional fashion shows were inserted into the plotline as an advertising tool for the national ready-made industry. Sometimes, as in the 1939 film *The Women*, the fashion show segment was filmed in color to enhance the clothes' appeal to viewers and potential consumers.[80] Thus, by including fashion shows segments in the films, and by offering viewers cheap imitations of stars' costumes through ready-made patterns and reproductions, Hollywood became the most successful global ambassador of the American fashion industry. As millions in the United States and around the world saw their favorite stars wearing American-designed fashion, their clothes, and more importantly the casual style that Hollywood promoted, received their public legitimacy.

The growing name recognition and popularity of fashion designers in the 1930s and 1940s—enhanced and abetted by the press and Hollywood—changed the nature of the industry and its status on the global stage. Female American designers, whether they worked in New York, Chicago, St. Louis, or Hollywood, were no longer the forgotten stepdaughters of fashion. Offering a real alternative to French fashions, now they were the ones who defined the American Look, and in so doing also the modern American woman and her meaning. "We [designers] specialize in what we like best, in what we do best, and in what satisfies us most deeply," designer Claire McCardell claimed. "For me," she added, "It is American—what looks like and feels like America. It's Freedom. It's democracy. It's casualness, It's good health. Clothes can say all that."[81] As sportswear in the 1930s and 1940s would become the epitome of Americanness, the women behind their design would also come to represent an American ideal.

Sportswear and the Feminist Aesthetics of the American Look

Female fashion designers brought with them not only a new appreciation of the career woman but also a new aesthetic language and philosophy that heralded the independent on-the-go woman who refused to be hindered by dress. Designers such as Claire McCardell, Bonnie Cashin, Vera Maxwell, Clare Potter, and Elizabeth Hawes popularized sportswear—the new category for casual, daytime clothing that were based on comfort, unfettered movement, functionality, and accessibility, yet presented a feminine silhouette and look.[82] "I like comfort in the rain, in the sun, for active sports, comfort for sitting still and looking pretty. The color and line of a costume should flow naturally with the body," wrote McCardell in explaining her design philosophy.[83] Continuing trends for simplicity and utility that were so suitable for mass production, sportswear included dresses, suits, knits, and separates appropriate for a range of activities and times of day that appealed to diverse social groups at different income levels. These clothes were made of simple, cheap, and durable fabrics that could be mass-produced at different price points.[84] "I believe that clothes are for real live women, not for pedestals. They are made to be worn, to be lived in. Not to walk around on models with perfect figures," argued McCardell.[85]

Moving away from the connotation of elite leisure and free time, sportswear became associated with working women who sought both practical and beautiful clothes. Indeed, sportswear's main feature was its utility and casualness that suited the body and lifestyle of the modern American woman epitomized by the career woman and the college girl.[86] While the universal flat and boyish image of the flapper was abandoned in favor of a return to a more mature feminine ideal that emphasized women's curves and natural waistline, sportswear retained the liberating connotations that the flapper styles entailed. It signified the progression of feminist ideas such as freedom, independence, and individuality into the realm of fashion, offering designers a framework to construct femininity through mass culture.[87] According to designer Bonnie Cashin, sportswear captured a new awareness that "more than ever, today's living calls for non-restriction and simplicity, because we're busy; for mobility, because we are always on the go; for the 'quality of the lasting seam,' because if we believe in it—we love it and live it." Designed for a specific "kind-of-girl-for-a-certain-kind-of-living," sportswear offered a material expression to a new role model of femininity that took her right to freedom as a given.[88] "Fashion does not demand a submissive spirit—in fact it asks for a certain independence," McCardell defined the function of clothes to the person who wore them.[89]

Yet, sportswear designers did not only translate feminist ideas into a clothing aesthetic, but also turned them into a mainstay of American culture. "There are certain fashions that are America's own," declared *Vogue*, casting sportswear as classic style garments that Americans "design better, make better, wear better than anyone else."[90] By 1945, sportswear would define what Dorothy Shaver coined as the "American Look," signaling how much these styles became entrenched in mainstream discourse. According to Shaver, the look was "the epitome of everything American. It is young; it is feminine; it emphasizes the American figure, always considered the finest in the world. It is without artifice, designed for the active, vigorous life lived by American women."[91] This idealized vision of fashion imagined all American women as a unified group who shared not only American values of democracy and freedom but also the same lifestyles, needs, and desires. Glossing over racial, ethnic, and class differences, advocates of the American Look positioned sportswear and fashionability as an attainable ideal.[92] "I belong to a mass-production country where any of us, all of us, deserve the right to good fashion and where fashion must be made available to all," stated Claire McCardell, lauding the American Look she helped to create.[93] However, despite the democratic tone and national identity that the American Look conveyed, it was the White, middle-class woman who became the epitome of modern American femininity in this period. Although the simplicity and affordability of sportswear made them accessible to non-White and working-class women, many sportswear designers—who were White and middle-class—tended to imagine their clients as a reflection of themselves.[94]

Indeed, while Black designers like Zelda Wynn Valdes advertised themselves as specialists in "Evening Gowns, Afternoon, and Sportswear," they geared their designs toward the spectacular and the celebratory, not the everyday casual styles of sportswear.[95] As eveningwear demanded more skill and commanded a higher price than sportswear, it benefited Black designers to position themselves as high-fashion professionals. It was also easier for NAFAD to raise the visibility and name recognition of Black couture designers than those who worked for the wholesale ready-made industry, and oftentimes remained anonymous. Yet, if Black couture designers such as Wynn refrained from being identified with the sportswear revolution, and White designers at best ignored the African American market, other Black designers stepped up to meet consumers' demand. At the second annual *New York Amsterdam Star-News* fashion show in 1942, Ruth Ellis of the ArLene Shop and Vidal Inc.—two of the community's top designers—displayed a variety of slack suits, swimwear, and play clothes alongside more glamorous evening gowns by Wynn and Jane Brooks.[96]

To some degree, sportswear styles stemmed from the economic conditions of the Great Depression and the war years, which contributed to a new appreciation of simplicity and thrift. As sportswear was geared toward mass production, many of the style elements and innovations derived from the industry's own interests and calculations. The need to cut manufacturing costs, for example, brought the use of the zipper, which was cheaper to produce and apply than hand-sewn buttons or snaps. Additionally, belts, which became a staple of sportswear, were implemented by manufacturers as a way to address the challenge of fitting standardized sizes to the specific body type of the individual wearer.[97] Designer Elizabeth Hawes complained about this fixture, arguing that her dresses did not require additional accessories and looked right fitted at the waist. But she complied with the industry's demand for belts when she designed for mass production, understanding that it is not "that the public were fanatical on the matter of belts. The public merely wanted to give a semblance of fit.... As no two size twelve women have the same waist measure, the simple way out of the whole difficulty is to hitch in the extra inches with the belt."[98] Moreover, the 1930s also saw the rise in use of much simpler, sturdier, and cheaper fabrics such as corduroy and knits instead of the delicate and ornamented silks that were popular in the 1920s. The introduction of Lastex in the early 1930s, an artificial elastic fiber that was often woven into wools and other knits, as well as the invention of nylon in 1939, both improved the quality of ready-made clothing and increased their appeal as a viable option for the middle-class consumer.

The L-85 regulation introduced by the War Production Board in 1942 restricted the use of fabrics, clothing, and accessories, thereby also shaping sportswear fashions. The regulation was intended to ensure "that clothes which women already owned would not go out [of] fashion," as well as reduced the yardage used by clothing. The severest restrictions of L-85 concerned wool clothing: the maximum length for jackets was 25 inches, and skirts had to be no more than 28 inches in length, with a circumference of no more than 72 inches.[99] Rather than fight the regulations, the ready-made industry eagerly joined the war effort. Claire McCardell, for example, bypassed the restriction of three pairs of leather shoes per year by introducing a version of printed ballet flats, which were not rationed because they were considered a dancer's tool. The style became a classic almost immediately, showing the innovativeness of the industry to deal with war shortages.[100] In general, contemporaries noticed, the regulation did not bring fashion to halt but rather helped American design develop its own uniqueness. "The designers who have been led, or pushed, by L-85 are making this spring American clothes which make women, in our opinion, look prettier than they have in a long time," claimed Jessica Daves, the managing editor of *Vogue*.[101]

Yet more than a response to economic and national needs, sportswear designers developed the style as the manifestation of their design philosophy that sought to empower women—especially working women with active lifestyles—by prioritizing their needs. As a design philosophy, sportswear espoused simplicity, practicality, and comfort, allowing women physical movement. Although the clothes changed according to trends in colors or silhouettes, the ideas behind them and the overall design language remained remarkably stable over decades.[102] "Sport clothes... are comfortable, practical, easy to wear—qualities which do not preclude the decorative element," argued Elizabeth Hawes. "They express the mentality of the women who wear them. They are suited to the lives the women are choosing to lead."[103] Seeing clothes as a democratic measure, Hawes sought to make her designs accessible to all, arguing that fashionability was not a right reserved only to those who could afford it. "There are hundreds of thousands of women who appreciate and are quite ready today to buy beautiful clothes if only they had the money to pay for them. It is [the designer's] job to create such clothes for the price the majority of women can afford to pay," she claimed.[104]

Designers saw their role as creators of clothes that would provide affordable sartorial solutions and allow women to take control over how they look. Bonnie Cashin believed that the role of the industrial designer was to employ "a flexible, creative skill to meet specific product needs wherever and however they develop."[105] Designers implemented pockets, trousers, and easily laundered materials in their designs. However, they did not think that comfort or utility should come at the expense of feminine appearance and a fashionable taste. Whereas some sportswear elements were inspired by menswear, the goal was not to imitate men's clothes but to create feminine styles that could be sensibly worn in work settings, not just in the home. "I'd always wondered why women's clothes had to be delicate—why they couldn't be practical and sturdy as well as feminine," McCardell said. Like Hawes, she aimed her designs to be both casual and easy fitting, yet also elegant and imaginative so that women could shape them according to their own preference, not the dictates of others.[106]

One of McCardell's most successful designs—her 1938 monastic dress—epitomized this philosophy (figure 4.4). This full dress, cut like a tent (or a monk's robe) with a hem reaching just below the knee, could be worn full, swinging from the shoulders, or secured by a big belt at the waist. The simple design, devoid of any detail or ornament, was adaptable to a range of body types, giving the wearer some control over the look and fit of the dress.[107] This control, permitted by the use of the belt, enabled women to translate ideas of self-determination and independence into a tangible outfit and a mate-

FIGURE 4.4: Claire McCardell's "monastic" dress, 1949, epitomized the goal of sportswear not only to supply the wearer with comfort and a sense of mobility but allowed her to take control over her appearance and image by using accessories such as belts. (Los Angeles County Museum of Art, Gift of Dr. Marva Spelman. Digital Image © 2020 Museum Associates/LACMA. Licensed by Art Resource, NY.)

rial experience. First marketed by Best & Co. as the Nada Frock, the design became an overnight success. It was copied and recopied at every imaginable price and version. The dress became a staple in McCardell's collections for decades, causing some contemporaries to declare it as the hallmark of American design: "American women might just be ready for something so incredibly easy to wear and so refreshingly different.... Here, women seemed instinctively to realize, was an American dress."[108]

Sportswear was not so much an invention of a new style language as a culmination of earlier trends that began with the Gibson Girl ensemble of the late 1890s and the shift toward functionality in fashion. Like the ensemble fashions and the loose-cut dresses of the early twentieth century, sportswear designers in the 1930s and 1940s embraced the long-sought feminist ideas of comfort and ease in fashion as the expression of women's freedom. Moreover, the all-American Gibson Girl, who was associated with ideas of freedom, mobility, and modernity, became the perfect precursor for the modern woman in the mid-twentieth century who wore sportswear as a marker of her identity.[109] Sportswear designers popularized the idea of "separates" and the interchangeable wardrobe, consisting of five or six items that could be worn in different combinations, and allowed women to create a versatile appearance on a limited budget. Despite initial reluctance from buyers, female shoppers found the mix-and-match system the perfect answer to their needs. In 1944, *Harper's Bazaar* featured McCardell's six-piece separates system, which included a suit, long skirt, pants, a bareback halter blouse, and a knotted-front blouse. Described as a great solution for a weekend retreat or a busy day on the town, McCardell's separates were marketed as the ultimate solution for the modern woman.[110] Bonnie Cashin was also a big advocate of separates, arguing it was not just a "pleasant game" of experiment in color and arrangement, but more importantly suitable to women's modern lifestyle: "this type of dressing I find is very sympathetic to the timeless wardrobe idea—and best of all it's the simpliest [sic] solution to my favorite sport—travel!"[111]

By 1950, Cashin would coin the term "layering" to describe her ensemble designs, dropping "a bombshell" on the fashion world. While the idea of dressing with one item over another was not new, nesting clothes as a modular system, where each piece could work as an ensemble, alone, and in different combinations, was revolutionary in high fashion. Recognized for the innovativeness of the layered look, Cashin would become the first designer to win both the Neiman Marcus Fashion Award and the Coty American Fashion Critics' Awards—the industry's most prestigious awards—in the same year.

Layering was a practical solution for changes in weather throughout the day. Cashin's collections were designed to work from 0 to 65 degrees Fahrenheit, believing that "summer, spring, fall, and winter do not describe a style of clothing—but temperatures and activities do." Yet the motivation behind layering was to enable a mobile life to the woman who was out and about, and to let her control the way she looked.[112] Layering and interchangeable wardrobe offered women the possibility to become their own designers by mixing and matching colors, fabrics, and accessories.

In addition to the ensemble, the shirtwaist dress was another popular design that referenced the old feminist ideas of the New Woman, and translated the 1890s trend into a mid-century one- or two-piece dress for women. Articles and editorials celebrated the shirtwaist dress as the modern incarnation of the versatile 1890s shirtwaist, promoting it as "an all-American classic" and as the "summer uniform of the land," suitable both for daywear and eveningwear.[113] As an ad for the department store Best & Co. from 1939 argued, "not since the era of the romantic Gibson Girl have blouses been so attractive, so becoming, so important in the fashion picture."[114] *Women's Wear Daily* also reported on the Gibson Girl craze, noting how the style became a best seller, especially among college girls.[115] The reference to the Gibson Girl's shirtwaist alluded to the longevity and resonance of expressing feminist ideas through fashion. Just as the shirtwaist of the 1890s represented Americanness and female determination, these same ideas were relevant a generation later when the shirtwaist dress marked another stage in the long legacy of women fighting for better fashions.

Together with the revival of the shirtwaist, sportswear brought a new appreciation of so-called mannish styles, borrowing elements from masculine clothes such as broad shoulders, boxy jackets, coats, hats, tailored suits, and trousers. "There is a large portion of the feminine population of these United States which has a special predilection for tailored, yes, strictly tailored, clothes," declared *Women's Wear Daily*, situating the trend as part of a long history of women's adopting mannish dress.[116] The mannish tailored suit consisting of a manly jacket and a skirt was heralded as the perfect fashionable and economic solution for the working woman who needed to appear professional in the office and to balance between "looking like a man" and being too feminine to gain respect. According to fashion reporter Virginia Pope, while the masculine lines of the suit accentuated women's boyish figure, they did not diminish the feminine charm of the wearer, as the suit still featured feminine elements such as full sleeves and a low-cut front. Becoming a staple of women's wardrobes by the mid-1930s, the mannish tailored suit allowed women to reclaim it as a symbol of power without sacrificing feminine appeal.[117]

The popularization of the mannish look was facilitated mainly by Hollywood stars like Garbo, Hepburn, and Dietrich, who turned the trouser suit not only into acceptable attire, but elevated it to a glamorous one. Loose slacks, also known as "pajama pants," and even shorts for women gained acceptance as resort wear in the late 1920s, becoming associated with the leisure and sport culture of California. Still, it was Hollywood female actors who brought trousers from the beach and the home into the streets. "While slacks have been popular at the beach clubs, on yachts, and to a limited extent for home wear for the past two years, they have only recently invaded the streets and become general for almost all types of informal wear," *Women's Wear Daily* credited Hollywood in starting the trend.[118] Dietrich and Garbo openly promoted women's adoption of menswear, and were regularly reported shopping for suits among male tailors. Garbo in particular took pride in having fought for the right of women to wear trousers. Hepburn similarly celebrated a carefree approach to formality and etiquette and often framed her wearing slacks as a feminist choice.[119]

Whereas wearing trouser suits à la Dietrich was often too extreme for the ordinary woman, the fashion press and the industry embraced Dietrich's style, marketing it as desirable casual wear that every woman could adopt.[120] A *Vogue* feature of the actor wearing her famous trouser suit posited: "Spectacularly tailored slacks are [Dietrich's] passion in clothes.... Her suit of black alpaca shrewdly understates her glamour, but has the force of an exclamation-point ... her hands ... are the hands of a competent woman, a good cook, a cool, canny executive." By positioning Dietrich both as a canny executive and a good cook, *Vogue* signaled readers that they too could be like the glamorous Hollywood star.[121] Unlike in earlier years, when the woman in pants was the epitome of the threat to gender hierarchies, Dietrich's stardom mitigated fears about gender transgression. Her masculine suit was presented as an appealing feminine attire, not as a peril to be avoided. Moreover, unlike the woman's rights advocates of the nineteenth century, Dietrich did not present her choice of trousers as an action against fashion, instead framing it as a conscious fashionable choice to enhance her sensuality. "I am sincere in my preference for men's clothes," she noted, "I do not wear them to be sensational ... I think I am much more alluring in these clothes." While Dietrich confessed that in "wearing such clothes ... there is a sense of perfect freedom and comfort," a statement that alluded to the feminist messages behind them, the reporter did not describe her "one-woman dress reform movement" as problematic, but rather emphasized Dietrich's irresistible beauty and appeal.[122]

As the popularity of pants as a Hollywood fad grew throughout the 1930s and 1940s, they became an appropriate casual wear for women.[123] Retailers' growing attention to the collegiate market, and especially to college women's demand for casual styles also facilitated the entrance of slacks into the mainstream.[124] However, it was not Hollywood but World War II that brought the wearing of pants to the masses. "It took a world war to get women out of corsets. It will probably take another to get them into trousers," Elizabeth Hawes predicted in 1939.[125] The need for appropriate workwear for women in factories and the war industries drove the military and the ready-made industry to invest in the marketing of slacks, overalls, and denim jeans, also called dungarees. The war also provided college students, who fought to wear slacks and jeans on campus with the public legitimization to do it, at least for class and in the dorms.[126]

Designers' philosophy on putting the working woman at the center, and that clothing should serve the wearer's needs, found expression also in their designs for women war workers and soldiers. Sportswear designers from Muriel King, Elizabeth Haws, and Claire McCardell to more upscale designers such as Adrian and Mainbucher joined the war effort and designed uniforms and work clothes for the millions of mobilized women. Dorothy Shaver also enlisted to the war effort when she was appointed as consultant to the Office of the Quartermaster General to oversee the research, development, and redesign of women's uniforms.[127] King, for example, created an outfit for women working in aircraft factories. In order to ensure the best suitable design, King met with Boeing workers in Washington State and Southern California to understand their needs. The result was a tailored slack made of a special fabric called aeronese, which was water- and dirt-resistant, machine washable, and with the durability of denim but with "the feel and appearance of a fine sportswear fabric." The pants were cut without any loose ends or cuffs to adhere to safety regulations, and also featured large pockets and stitched-down pleats for "an extra slendering appearance." The slack went together with a shirt and cap. For the total price of only $16.85 (around $250 today), King offered the everyday woman a bargain for a top designer outfit.[128]

The war aesthetic of slacks and boxy tailored suits moved beyond the realm of war factories to enter the realm of high fashion. In 1944, *Harper's Bazaar* featured Clare Potter's velveteen overall slack "cut precisely like a mechanic's suit." In the spread, titled "At Home in Pants," the magazine not only situated the overall as a high-fashion item but also alluded to the extent to which trousers had become acceptable for casual wear.[129] Although Potter's overall was marketed as an attire suited for the home, which reduced the radical potential that wearing pants in public entailed, their association with the role of the mechanic gave the war worker a clout of fashionability and legitimacy. Indeed, the war worker became another feminine role model for designers, further legitimizing the presence of women in the workplace and a new feminine ideal that extolled independence and self-determination.[130] As casual, practical, and durable clothing became more and more fashionable, the working woman who was wearing them also became a fashionable idea.

The wage-working woman captured the imagination of designers as they created clothes to suit women's new status. However, designers like Claire McCardell did not neglect the women who worked at home, seeing their domestic job also as worthy for practical and becoming apparel. In 1941, McCardell introduced the "kitchen dinner dress," an evening dress with a matching removable apron so women could host guests while taking care of the cooking without changing outfits. A year later, *Harper's Bazaar*'s editors Carmel Snow and Diana Vreeland asked her to design a house dress that would appeal to busy housewives who were left without servants. The result was what would become one of McCardell's biggest hits: the "Pop-Over" dress.[131] Made of denim with wide rolled-up sleeves, dropped shoulders, and a quilted pocket big enough "for matches, cigarettes, the morning mail, and the duster," the pop-over dress also came with a matching mitten and cost a mere $6.95 (around $100 today). Appearing in the November 1942 issue under the title "I'm Doing My Work," the pop-over was framed not as a dress for the bored, privileged housewife but as a work outfit that was part of women's contribution to the war effort. The color scheme of red, white, and blue of the original design also contributed to framing the dress as a "war work outfit" for the homemaker (figure 4.5).[132] The dress became an overnight hit and was made and remade in other fabrics and colors. Staying true to her belief that women deserve to look and feel attractive, even as homemakers, McCardell made the pop-over a permanent part of her collection for the next sixteen years. She believed that clothes should always be born out of necessity and that their design should be determined by women's way of life more than anything else. And in order to achieve this purpose, McCardell offered women solutions for work and home, understanding the importance of both to women's lives.

Whether it was the professional career woman, the white-collar secretary, the war worker, the military woman, or the housewife, sportswear brought women's work—both in and outside the home—into the cultural main-

FIGURE 4.5: With "the Pop-over dress," Claire McCardell had designed what became a staple in women's wardrobes. Sportswear designers did not only herald the career woman but sought to supply the homemaker with comfortable and functional clothes, believing that they too deserved good fashion. (*Harper's Bazaar*, November 1942, Hearst Magazines Inc., photograph by Louise Dahl-Wolfe © Center for Creative Photography, Arizona Board of Regents. Image published with permission of ProQuest LLC. Further reproduction is prohibited without permission.)

stream. By the end of World War II, the ubiquity of sportswear offered women practical sartorial solutions. But it also, and more importantly, popularized a new type of woman and consumer. "Today, the woman who works... can be counted on to be the one consistent, dependable consumer," argued Helen Valentine, the editor in chief of *Charm* magazine. The rise of this "beautiful, wonderfully powerful" market, Valentine continued, pushed retailers, designers, magazine editors, advertisers, and the entire fashion industry to cater to their needs.[133] Women used their clothing to express feminist ideas of decades prior, championing ideas of comfort, mobility, independence, and freedom. They asserted their right not only to be an equal part of the public sphere but also to feel comfortable and beautiful in it. Indeed, for Dorothy Shaver and her fellow Fashion Group members, sportswear was nothing short of a revolution. "The ability to create beautiful clothes is a rare talent in itself, but to create beautiful clothes that capture the essence of a whole social revolution is rather overwhelming," she argued. "All of us who are here today personally have been involved in that revolution. As women, our lives are radically changed because of it."[134] As they sought to fashion the modern woman in a way that would serve her needs and lifestyle, Shaver and her designer friends turned clothing into a powerful means to express the modern woman's values and ideas.

The Status of Sportswear after the War

The end of the war and the liberation of Europe revived the connections between the American fashion industry and Paris, igniting debates about whether the French capital would regain its fashion supremacy, as in the prewar years. In 1944, the Fashion Group had discussed what the future might hold for French fashion. Predicting that while Paris would eventually return to its prewar status, "for all our sakes," it would need to share its fashion leadership with other centers, most notably the United States. "It will be Paris plus America rather than Paris versus America," argued Mildred Smolze, the dress editor of Tobé. "It will certainly be our own fault if we lose the fashion leadership we have established in the past few years. We should hold it—and we believe we will."[135] With the help and support of U.S. retailers, buyers, and organizations like the Fashion Group, many were confident that the styles that appealed to so many women during the war period would continue to define women's fashion tastes after it. In fact, some were certain that the women who found war fashions both practical and becoming would stick with them and refuse to go back to more restrictive styles.[136]

Yet, as the winds of war quelled and the world rearranged itself according to the Cold War order, a backlash against women's achievements in the war also began to take form. As many scholars have noted, the postwar period and the conservative 1950s espoused a renewed ideology of domesticity and femininity that pushed women back into the traditional roles of the housewife and mother. Magazines devoted renewed attention to domestic issues, shifting the focus from the working and single girl to providing advice on cooking, keeping a house, and raising children.[137] This conservative antifeminist backlash permeated all aspects of popular culture, including fashion. In 1947, the young designer Christian Dior amazed the fashion world with his first independent collection, revolutionizing almost single-handedly fashion styles and reclaiming the prominence of French design. The collection was characterized by a return to a Victorian feminine ideal of an hourglass silhouette, a molded torso with a wasp waist, emphasized hips, and a very full and longer skirt padded with petticoats. Coined the New Look, Dior's designs offered a construction of the female body that was completely different from its predecessors and stood as the antithesis to sportswear aesthetics and the woman who wore them. The New Look circumscribed mobility and was difficult to put on and to wear, depriving women of their independence to move freely. Moreover, due to the increase in the amount of fabric and the inclusion of petticoats, stiffeners, and other assorted layers, costs were much higher than for the mass-made sportswear suitable for any purse.[138] Despite the restrictive elements of the New Look, the fashion industry immediately acclaimed the collection, causing *Harper's Bazaar* to declare the new silhouette as "the essence of femininity," furthering the notion that Dior's New Look, not the American Look, defined fashion in the 1940s.[139]

Although Dior's New Look was a fashionable and commercial success, histories of fashion tend to overestimate its reception among American women.[140] As the Fashion Group predicted, women were no longer prepared to relinquish their comfort for foreign fashion dictates. As in the late 1920s, when women banded together to protest the return of long skirts, American women in the late 1940s and early 1950s were also reluctant to give up the freedoms that sportswear styles had provided them. Revolt against the New Look centered in Texas, where women banded together to form "Little Below the Knee" clubs to protest Dior's style, declaring "the Alamo fell, but our hemlines will not."[141] At Berkeley, California, wives of GI students, calling themselves WOWS—Women's Organization to War on Styles, organized a protest against the New Look, carrying signs that declared "Don't Let Down the Slip" and "United We Stand, Divided They Fall."[142] These protesters framed their resistance in political terms, arguing that the long skirt of the New Look was an attack on their freedom and democracy. Some argued it was not the length of the skirt that posed a problem as much as its width, which due to its volume curtailed free movement and posed a real health hazard. Others complained that the New Look put a financial burden on women during the postwar economic downturn.[143]

Designers also joined protesters. Bonnie Cashin, who was in Paris at the time, lamented that the New Look distorted the female form and ignored women's modern needs. "You can't stuff a dress weighting twenty pounds into an overnight bag," she complained.[144] Jo Copeland announced in 1947 she would no longer travel to Paris for inspiration. And Sophie Gimbel, the house designer of Saks Fifth Avenue, directly challenged Dior's influence on high fashion when she displayed her 1947 collection without any sign of the "fantastic extremes that had given the New Look its painful expression." The collection featured more than 125 models with shoulders slightly padded; daytime hemlines, although slightly lower than before the war, "were still a long way from the ankles." Believing that women would stick to the sportswear styles, Gimbel questioned Dior's success. "Our girls have beautiful figures. Do you think they'll want to spoil them with padded hips? Even if they do like this tight waistline, how many are willing to go through the agony to get it? I put on one of those new corsets and after 15 minutes I had to take it off. I've never been so uncomfortable in my life."[145] For the American women who had become used to the freedoms sportswear provided, the New Look was a step backward they were unwilling to take.

In the face of opposition, Dior himself accommodated his designs to the U.S. market. In later collections, he reduced the fullness of the skirts and even added pockets. His American dresses also weighed less and had fewer hooks and eyes so they were easier to don. In 1948, Dior shortened the skirt from twelve inches to fourteen inches from the floor, and in 1949 he abandoned the corset.[146] By 1950, Dior dropped the New Look in favor of slimmer silhouette and shorter skirts.[147] These accommodations, and the eventual abandonment of the New Look, attested to the power of women consumers who demanded comfortable clothing for themselves. As in the 1920s, however, women did not fight just to keep their skirts' hemlines short but for the ideas and values sportswear fashion represented. The success of sportswear designers to keep the feminist ideas of freedom, mobility, independence, and comfort relevant in the 1930s and 1940s, in a time when the feminist movement itself was less visible, laid the groundwork for women's resistance to the New Look in the postwar period.

Even those who favored the fuller styles that began to reappear after the war preferred not to adopt the New Look, instead choosing a modernized version of the Gibson Girl outfit, which was marketed as a more accessible alternative to the French design. During 1947-48, the Gibson Girl ensemble of a shirtwaist and a full skirt gained popularity among big retailers who marketed the outfit as a modern—and American—take on the New Look.[148] Although by the end of the 1940s the original Gibson Girl was not seen as an icon of independence and freedom, her modern reincarnation had a narrower and shorter skirt than the original and thus was more functional and casual in appearance. Furthermore, the Gibson Girl style of the late 1940s and early 1950s, despite representing a move away from sportswear, still maintained its connotation with youthfulness and college education, encouraging young girls to pursue their intellectual aspirations, not to stay at home.[149]

Women's resistance to Dior attested to the continuous appeal of sportswear style as the epitome of American freedom. As millions of college students redefined fashion trends and opted for more casual styles, they drove the mainstreaming of sportswear and its prevalence in women's wardrobes. Some of these students opted for the romantic styles of the Gibson Girl, but many more preferred a more casual look. In particular, students in the 1950s and 1960s pushed to wear pants and blue jeans on campus, challenging their institutions' dress codes and gaining control over their student culture.[150] The rise of the Beat subculture in the late 1950s also brought an appreciation for casual styles. Beat fashions of loose turtleneck sweaters, capri pants (preferably in black), wrap skirts, leotards, and flat shoes were grounded in the aesthetic language of sportswear that had gained popularity in the 1940s. Associated with a youthful rebellion against conformity, by 1957, much thanks to Hollywood and the press, they became part of the mainstream. Beat fashions like the ones Audrey Hepburn wore in *Funny Face* (1957) were quickly commercialized by the ready-made industry, which marketed them to college students across the country.[151]

Not only Hollywood, but also television and the rising consumer culture, popularized sportswear as a suitable style for the suburban housewife. Although the 1950s espoused a dressier and more tailored look, the suburban lifestyle of shopping and child rearing also opened up a space for casual clothes. Straight dresses and the sheath silhouette replaced the New Look by the late 1950s, while styles for leisure wear became even looser. Indeed, distinctions between day and evening wear became much more evident in the 1950s. Eveningwear, as well as the increasingly popular cocktail dress, celebrated luxurious femininity, defined by elaborate sleeveless dresses with full skirts. However, the daytime wardrobe often was comprised of casual ensembles of blouses in pastel colors and fitted, narrow pants, topped with a cardigan or short jacket.[152] Continuing the trend for feminine fashionability, the 1950s mostly extended the fashion language that the wartime period established.

Thus, although Paris regained its fashion leadership after the war, the popularity of American sportswear did not wane, but in fact only increased. The domestic ready-made industry proved its vitality and independence as sportswear became a staple of American women's everyday lives, providing them with suitable fashions for their new suburban environments.[153] With the notable exception of Elizabeth Hawes, most sportswear designers remained successful during the postwar years, some even reaching the height of their careers in the 1950s and 1960s. Bonnie Cashin, for example, after years of working for the retailer Adler and Adler, founded in 1952 her own company: Bonnie Cashin Designs Inc. The company not only became an ongoing commercial success but also was responsible for Cashin's most innovative award-winning designs, making hers one of the most noted names in fashion. Indeed, the success of sportswear constructed fashion as an arena where women could keep engaging with the feminist ideas that underlined their appearance and with their struggle to expand their rights, whether sartorially or otherwise.

The Feminist Effects of Sportswear

In 1942, as part of the *New York Times*' annual fashion show, "Fashions of the Times," designers were asked to imagine both fashions suitable for wartime and those that would be possible once war rations disappeared. As expected, the "Fashions of Today" segment showed the innovativeness of sportswear to create functional clothes that achieved "smartness and elegance." Yet, the "Fashions of Tomorrow" did not offer a sharp break in design from the wartime models. Designed for the "symbolic girl of the future," a sportswear outfit by Bonnie Cashin featured a "tunic suit for play and work," which embodied the feminist essence of the American Look, "permitting [the girl of the future] plenty of freedom of action."[154] As Cashin's "girl of the future" design predicted, the feminist aesthetics that defined sportswear style in the 1930s and 1940s continued to shape women's lives and the American ready-to-wear market long after the war and for decades to come. And with the ongoing popularity of sportswear, the feminist ideas behind it would also continue to be popular, despite the backlash to the movement in the 1950s.

In 1955, sportswear would receive its ultimate acceptance into the mainstream when Claire McCardell, the designer most associated with the American Look, was featured on the cover of *Time* magazine.[155] That same year, she also drew the attention of a young journalist named Betty Friedan. Celebrating McCardell as "the Gal Who Defied Dior," Friedan understood the power of clothing to advance social change, especially when they were made with the American woman and her active lifestyle in mind. Friedan believed that McCardell's success lay in the fact that "she's always had a lot of faith in 'Mrs. Jones.' . . . [she] keeps making dresses women can fit to their own figures . . . so that 'Mrs. Jones' will be free to express herself."[156] When in 1963 Friedan articulated the "feminine mystique" for millions of women like "Mrs. Jones," the legacy of designers like McCardell would not be lost on her.[157] Like McCardell, Friedan also had faith in Mrs. Jones and in her ability to change her life and to demand her freedom, in the realm of fashion or otherwise. And like McCardell, Friedan also believed that clothing could be both feminine and comfortable, providing women with freedom instead of hampering it. Moreover, both Friedan and McCardell believed that women should have the choice to dress in a way that expressed their identities.

Indeed, the popularity of sportswear kept the ideas behind it part of the mainstream discourse. For McCardell and her colleagues, the idea behind the American Look was to create beautiful clothes that women would enjoy wearing; that would be comfortable and easy to take care of; that would be suitable for home, work, or on the weekend. They did not see feminist ideas of freedom and independence as abstract but sought to turn them into an everyday practice. The success of sportswear to become a staple in women's wardrobes pointed to the success and longevity of the ideas it celebrated, even in periods of social backlash that sought to deprive women of these freedoms. As women again would demand their rights to choose their own style of dress in the 1960s and 1970s, the values of freedom, comfort, and utility that made sportswear so popular would guide them as well.

CHAPTER FIVE

This Is What a Feminist Looks Like

Fashion in the Era of Women's Liberation

On September 1968, over a hundred women gathered on the boardwalk of Atlantic City to protest the Miss America Pageant and what they conceived as its oppressive message to women. Organized by the feminist group New York Radical Women (NYRW), the demonstration included protesters parading signs that compared women's bodies to cattle, and staging a guerilla theater skit in which they crowned a live sheep as "Miss America." Protesters also threw girdles, high heels, hair curlers, bras, *Playboy* magazines, and other "instruments of female torture" into a "Freedom Trash Can." In a well-prepared ten-point statement they gave reporters, NYRW explained their agenda against the "Degrading Mindless-Boob-Girlies Symbol" and the "Consumer Con-Game," which forced "women in our society ... to compete for male approval, enslaved by ludicrous 'beauty' standards [they] are conditioned to take seriously." Unwilling to succumb to gender expectations of "looking and acting like a lady" that magazines and pageants such as Miss America perpetuated, NYRW called on women to resist cultural practices and beauty methods that reduced women to sexual objects only meant to please men.[1]

As many scholars have noted, the No More Miss America demonstration symbolized the "mythological birth" of the U.S. women's movement in the late 1960s. It brought women's liberation to the center of national public attention and consolidated the image of "the feminist" for generations to come.[2] Although no bras were burned during the event, the media, which covered the protest extensively, was quick to describe protesters as angry, masculine-looking, radical "bra-burners," an image that became a code name for feminists who challenged gender hierarchies and norms, both in their looks and in their demands.[3] Indeed, almost instantaneously the bra burner became the most potent image of feminists in the late twentieth century and beyond. Yet, what the media coverage (and many of the scholarly accounts) missed about the No More Miss America protest was that as much as it was against the popular fashion and beauty standards, protesters were not interested in forgoing these standards completely. "Our purpose was not to put down Miss America but to attack the male chauvinism, commercialization of beauty, racism and oppression of women symbolized by the Pageant," argued Judith Duffett, one of the organizers.[4] Acknowledging that clothing could empower women if they had control over their appearance, NYRW feminists did not reject dealing with fashion or appearance, but protested against a fashion industry that prevented women from enacting their independence.[5] In fact, these feminists were much more pro-fashion than the media gave them credit for. Despite the fact that the protest included the trashing of girdles, makeup, and other fashion items, photographs from the demonstration show that many of the protesters embraced the prevailing fashion trends, appearing in miniskirts, long hair, and feminine shoes, albeit mostly with flat heels (figure 5.1).[6]

The prevalence and endurance of the "bra-burner" myth led many to characterize feminism in the 1960s and 1970s as antifashionable and as hostile to all matters of adornment practices. However, while some feminists repudiated entirely the concept of fashion, the majority saw clothing as an important vehicle for expressing their identities and promoting their politics. Like the generation of early twentieth-century feminists who came before them, many feminists in the late 1960s and 1970s did not view fashion as alien to their struggle or as only a tool of oppression. For them, clothes became a central element in shaping feminist ideology and gender politics, and they turned fashion, and even fashionability, into an important site of political expression.

Feminists were not the only ones to utilize fashion as part of their politics during this period. Activists in various movements—New Left, counterculture, antiwar, civil rights, and Black Power—employed dress, hair, and beauty practices in their political activism, shaping the cultural, social, and political debates of the period.[7] And, as activists in other movements had done, women's liberationists adopted the popular youth fashions of the time: blue jeans, army-surplus jackets, miniskirts, turtlenecks, Oriental- and African-inspired styles, T-shirts, and button-down work shirts. Whereas these styles

FIGURE 5.1: No More Miss America protest, Atlantic City, 1968. While feminists protested the commercial beauty culture that prescribed submissive roles to women, they did not reject feminine fashions and adopted popular styles as part of their political identity. (© Beverly Grant, photographer)

functioned differently for each movement, women's liberationists imbued these clothes with feminist meanings, using them to express and advance their political agendas.[8]

However, feminism has never been contained within a coherent single movement, but was an umbrella term that encompassed various groups and ideas, oftentimes with tensions between them.[9] Liberal, radical, women of color, lesbian, and working-class feminists worked for different goals and with different emphases. Sometimes they formed broad coalitions, with overlaps in methods and activists, and sometimes they adopted more combative and separatist approaches toward both society at large and other feminist groups.[10] The diversity of feminist organizations, methods, and causes also created a vast array of images, looks, and fashions. Some feminists emphasized their feminine sensuality, celebrating women's power to assert themselves as sexual beings. Others abandoned gendered fashion attributes, adopting instead androgynous looks that expressed their gender critique of society and the capitalistic consumer market. Black feminists, many of them activists in civil rights and Black Power movements, also created their own version of feminist looks. They incorporated African motifs into their dress and adopted natural hairstyles as a symbol of racial pride. Whereas feminists often disagreed over the proper strategy and image activists should adopt, this variety of looks and images presented a more complex and nuanced approach to fashion than in the media and public discourse, which often flattened the diversity of visual and fashionable expressions that feminists adopted.[11]

Feminists also differed in the ways they used fashion. For some, dress was a way to express their identities and political commitment to the movement, while others used it as a tactic to gain public attention and support. Yet, one's style and attitude toward fashion did not align along neat distinctions between liberal and radical. Some feminists used fashion and beauty practices to challenge gender, racial, and class hierarchies, asserting a new understanding regarding the meanings of womanhood and femininity. Others sought not to eliminate gender differences but to expand women's choices regarding their appearance and mode of dress. However, regardless of their position, as feminists cultivated personal styles that suited the various political agendas they pursued, they did not reject fashion but turned it into an empowering force.

This chapter delineates the various approaches and fashionable expressions that feminists employed during the late 1960s and 1970s, thus challenging the myth that all feminists in this period were antifashion. It analyzes the debates among feminists over the role of fashion in shaping ideas regarding women's liberation, femininity, and gender roles, in order to revise our understanding of the ways in which fashion worked within the movement and in influencing public discourse and opinion. Clothing and appearance provided a route through which women could both show solidarity with the struggle and shape what feminism meant in the era of women's liberation. Yet, more than breaking with their mothers' generation—as many feminists believed they were doing—their engagement with fashion proved to be a continuation of much of what came before the resurgence of the movement in the late 1960s.

As in the previous generation, the styles that feminists adopted in the 1960s and 1970s did not remain an alternative subculture but entered the fashionable mainstream. Some feminists lamented the commercialization of their looks, arguing that the market diluted the political message that stood behind them. Yet, the popularization of these styles offered more women a way to identify with the movement and its feminist ideology, without necessarily identifying with its activism. Indeed, as blue jeans, pantsuits, miniskirts, and unisex attire became popular fashions, so too did the ideas they represented. Through fashion, a broadening base of women adopted the feminist message of choice and empowerment, and enacted their rights to gain control over their appearance and their lives. These women incorporated feminist arguments in their fight for the freedom to wear miniskirts and pants, seeing them as a symbol of their liberation. In their efforts, they made fashion a central site not only of feminist politics, but also of what it meant to be a liberated woman in society in a time of great social change.

Feminist Attitudes toward Fashion

The question of "what a feminist looks like" and whether there is or should be a unified feminist look became an important part of feminist politics in the late 1960s and early 1970s. As in the generation before them, feminists were quick to make the connection between appearance and women's status in society, seeing fashion not as a frivolous issue, but as central to their struggle for equality. For mainstream liberal feminists, represented by Betty Friedan and the National Organization for Women (NOW), fashion and appearance were part of their efforts to achieve full legal and economic equality. "As I become more myself and freer, I dress in a way that reflects that. I like clothes, I like color," stated Friedan.[12] Promoting the concept of "choice feminism," NOW feminists argued that just as women should have the choice of sexual partners, marriage, motherhood, or a career, they should have the choice to present themselves in the way that most suited their personal style and individual lives.[13]

Although NOW feminists were more skeptical toward the fashion industry than their suffragist foremothers, they also viewed fashion as an important political tool in the efforts to win hearts and minds for the feminist cause. Understanding the power of fashion to convey political messages, Friedan encouraged members to pay close attention to their outfits, and emphasized the importance of presenting a respectable, feminine appearance, especially when dealing with the media. Friedan herself—who was forty-five when she cofounded NOW in 1966—tended to appear in matronly tailored dress suits, full makeup, and jewelry that not only reflected her mature taste but also conveyed a nonthreatening look that did not challenge gender norms. In fact, Friedan's appearance was not so different from that of conservative women such as Phyllis Schlafly and Anita Bryant, who also adopted the respectable feminine style of tailored dress suits and carefully done hair and makeup. Both Schlafly and Friedan understood the power of femininity in shaping public discourse and they both harnessed fashion to construct their image as politically active women. However, Friedan used feminine attire to promote a message of gender equality, employing it as a tactical tool to garner public support. Schlafly, on the other hand, weaponized her feminine appearance to condemn feminism and especially radical feminists' critique of gender roles.[14]

Other leaders of NOW, such as Shirley Chisholm and Bella Abzug, presented a more colorful appearance than Friedan, favoring bold colors and prints, striking hats, accessories, and large jewelry. Yet they too did not challenge gender notions of feminine appearance, understanding their political utility. Abzug confessed that her penchant for wearing hats stemmed from her desire to be taken seriously as a woman. "By wearing a hat, I was able to show everyone that I was there on serious business. In 1970, when I first ran for office, I was always pointed out as 'the lady in the hat.' I became recognizable that way."[15] Chisholm, like Abzug, saw in fashion a useful way to draw public attention to her feminist message. However, she cultivated her image not only as a feminist but also as a Black woman and a politician, offering a modern interpretation of Black femininity. Chisholm's unique style of bold prints and colors did not abandon practices of beautification or breach the boundaries of respectability, but celebrated a fashionable role model for Black activists that symbolized her independent taste and her overall image of "unbought and unbossed."

Gloria Steinem, always aware of her public image, also presented a similar approach to Friedan and other NOW leaders, stressing the need for feminists to carefully fashion their appearance in order to gain political influence. "Clothing should be totally aesthetic or practical in a just society," she argued, "but at the moment and for some time to come, it has tactical implications." Steinem admitted that "in a political sense, it is better to send a woman in a print dress and pearls, rather than a woman in blue jeans, to a meeting of the Democratic National Committee. Even if they say the same things, the woman in the dress has more of a chance for acceptance and therefore is more subversive."[16]

In general, liberal feminists adhered to trends in mainstream fashions, but many young activists, emerging from "consciousness-raising" groups organized by New Left activists, became frustrated by Friedan's leadership in NOW as well as by her attitude toward fashion. These young feminists pushed for a more radical change to the status quo than Friedan was willing to accept. They introduced the now-familiar concept of "the personal is political," arguing that feminist efforts should not only focus on legal equality and political representation, but also on the private aspects of life such as marriage, sexual relationships, and abortion. According to activists, these issues that were previously seen as private have also shaped women's status in society and thus entailed political import. As they shifted their attention toward these issues, culture and appearance became a significant aspect of radical feminists' "personal politics" agenda.[17]

Seeing fashion and appearance as more than just a political tactic, these feminists found clothing central to their identities as feminists and to finding sisterhood with other activists. Consciousness-raising groups included discussions about the role of fashion and beauty culture in women's lives. For these participants, finding a space to share their frustration with the need to uphold social norms of beauty on the one hand, and receive affirmation from fellow sisters for their decision to deviate from fashion norms on the other, became crucial to their process of becoming feminists.[18]

Radical feminist critique, which was grounded in Marxist theory and was inspired by the New Left, targeted its arguments against consumer capitalism and its effects on women. This critique was bound up with an anticonsumerist approach that criticized the fashion industry and its endless pursuit for profits, oftentimes with disregard to women's needs, health, or interests. According to these feminists, the fashion industry placed enormous economic and mental burdens on women to alter their appearance according to whimsical changes in styles, thereby contributing to their oppression.[19] "Clothing is a political statement," one feminist claimed. "We have thrown off our former mindless and painful conformity to fashion. We show what women's liberation is all about: The individuality of women showing through in every facet of life."[20]

These women's liberationists made a distinction between clothing, which they found central to their identities, and fashion, which they identified with the industry and interpreted as oppressive force. They did not dismiss the political value of appearance but sought to negate the influence of the industry on women's lives by creating an alternative to the mainstream styles. "The problem is not current fashion per se; it's the rigidity with which it is prescribed by the fashion industry," argued a feminist named Toby Silvey. Echoing previous arguments of feminists from the 1910s, this feminist did not reject the idea that fashion could be beautiful or empowering, but argued that it was the idea of "choice," especially in matters of dress that was crucial to expressing a feminist identity. "We are not liberated unless we can choose freely between a hair shirt and a sequined dress," she maintained.[21]

Indeed, for many radical feminists, fashionable appearance did not necessarily stand in contrast with women's liberation. "Contrary to the variety of popular images, Women's Liberation is not a movement of hardened and coldly unfeeling females, shouting slogans, hating men, and scorning 'unliberated' sisters. . . . Women do not have to leave their husbands and lovers, abandon their children, throw away their make-up, burn their bras . . . or sleep with each other in order to be part of the movement," one feminist claimed.[22] Pam Kearon from the radical group the Feminists argued that "people like to look nice for other people. It's just not true that we want to look like ugly freaks." Although they condemned seductiveness, or the need to beautify oneself to please men, feminists such as Kearon still valued the pleasure that came from fashion and beauty.[23] For these women's liberationists, looking attractive while wearing clothes they felt good and empowered in was an important aspect of their politics. They refused to turn themselves into sexual objects, however feminists were not willing to give up so easily the joy that dressing up gave them. "I'd like to dress up and look sexy," one feminist from San Francisco proclaimed. "But I want men to see me as a human being first and a potential sex partner second."[24] These feminists justified their choice in adopting a fashionable feminine appearance not as a tactical maneuver to avoid damaging stereotypes of the "bra-burning feminist" but as the true fulfillment of women's liberation. They wanted to be recognized for their humanity, but they were not willing to cast off their femininity.

Similarly, Black activists also viewed fashion as an empowering source of pleasure and an important feminist tool. The feminist lawyer and activist Florynce "Flo" Kennedy—who worked outside of NOW but joined with the organization on certain actions—saw fashion, and especially the adoption of soul style, as "a validation of our power, even if it is only style-deep." Although Kennedy adopted a more masculine look, using cowboy hats and pants, she did not challenge gender norms as much as norms of female propriety, especially when they pertained to Black womanhood. "I don't take diction from the pig-o-cratic style setters who say I should dress like a middle-aged colored lady. My politics don't depend on whether my tits are in or out of a bra," she argued.[25]

Many Black women also did not share radical feminists' critique of the beauty and fashion industries as exploitive, but celebrated Black models breaking into *Vogue* and *Glamour* as major victories and as a symbol of the growing acceptance of Black beauty in mainstream culture. Indeed, in 1968, alongside the No More Miss America protest, another protest in the form of the first Miss Black America Pageant also took place. Challenging Miss America Pageant's racism and its segregated nature, the Miss Black America Pageant embraced beauty culture and femininity as a means of resistance. Unlike the No More Miss America demonstration, Black protesters did not criticize the fashion industry but sought to gain an equal standing in it.[26] As clothing and appearance were important means for African American women to claim access to the privileges of respectable femininity, they were more reluctant to relinquish their gains. In a society that often portrayed Black women as animalistic or masculine, forgoing femininity and fashionability did not seem so empowering for Black feminists.

Feminists such as Germaine Greer, and most notably Gloria Steinem, became the ultimate examples that one did not have to reject fashionability to claim a feminist identity. Championing a youthful, sexy, feminine look, that was often contrasted with depictions of "angry" activists, Greer and Steinem became the symbol of a feminist "radical chic" that offered a nonthreatening version of feminism.[27] They refused to adopt a separatist view that marked all men as the enemy and rebuffed the idea that a woman had to make herself unattractive in order to avoid being a sexual object. "I don't go for that whole pants-and-battle-dress routine. It just puts men off, and there's already been too much defensiveness in the movement," argued Greer.[28] Indeed, even when Steinem changed her style from miniskirts to jeans and T-shirt as she became more radicalized regarding the movement and its causes, she did not abandon her feminine look. She refused to forgo her pro-fashion attitude and the pleasure she received from dressing up.[29] As one reporter commented, in her "hip-hugging raspberry Levies, 2-inches wedgies and tight poor-boy T-shirt . . . long, blond-streaked hair falling just so about each breast and her cheerleader-pretty face made wiser by the addition of blue-tinted glasses," Steinem was "a chic apotheosis of with-it cool."[30] As her popularity grew in the 1970s, Steinem became not only the unofficial face and spokesperson of the movement but also a fashion icon of the new feminine ideal. Between 1971 and 1974, she appeared on the covers of *People*, *McCall's*, *Newsweek*, *Redbook*, and *New Woman*. *McCall's* named her "Woman of the Year," while *Newsweek* defined her as "The New Woman."[31] Steinem also received favorable interviews in *Vogue* and the *New York Times*, which glorified her as the epitome of the modern liberated woman.[32]

Through their appearance, Greer and Steinem offered a model through which women could claim their affiliation with the movement but not desert heterosexuality or adornment practices. Steinem's signature look of long hair with highlighted stripes parted in the middle and a pair of aviation glasses became a fashion trend among young White women who identified with Steinem but also with the political message she promoted.[33] Yet, Greer's and Steinem's beauty (and race) also shielded them to a certain extent from attacks by critics who used the androgynous look of women's liberationists to frame them, and the movement as a whole, as a group of frustrated women who could not find suitable husbands. Even as they advocated radical views about marriage, child-rearing, and work, Steinem's and Greer's feminine appearance helped to legitimize these ideas. In its profile on Greer, *Life* depicted her not as a crazy radical but as an appealing woman, offering flattering images that positioned her as a "saucy feminist even men like."[34]

However, this image that Steinem and Greer presented appealed mainly to White, middle-class, college-educated women. For White working-class women working in offices and the retail world, Helen Gurley Brown, *Cosmopolitan* editor and the author of the 1962 bestseller *Sex and the Single Girl*, was much more inspiring as a feminist role model. Brown's pro-commercial, pro-fashion, feminine style appealed to many working-class women who were happy to join the sexual revolution and aspired to achieve professional and economic independence, though they were less comfortable with radical feminism. Brown advocated the wearing of minis, makeup, and other sexy clothes that celebrated women's femininity instead of subduing it, seeing it as important part of the liberated working-woman identity.[35] Yet for Brown, wearing feminine clothes that emphasized one's sexuality was not just a means to an end but an enjoyable practice that was important for individual self-fulfillment and the building of self-esteem. "There's no reason you can't be a strong feminist and look sensational," she argued.[36] Brown became a fierce and unapologetic voice for sexuality and hyper-femininity, insisting that beauty and fashion practices were not antithetical with women's liberation but were in fact integral to it.

Brown's approach was often criticized by radical feminists, including Steinem, who saw in the image of the Cosmo Girl an unreal fantasy that further oppressed women by turning them into sex objects. Yet, as a *New York Times Magazine* reporter noticed, Steinem and Brown did not represent two opposite camps of feminism and antifeminism, but "Two Faces of the Same Eve."[37] In fact, in many aspects, Steinem, who pursued her career seriously and represented a liberated approach to her sexuality and relationship with men, was the perfect emblem of the Cosmo Girl Brown promoted.[38] The differences between Steinem and the Cosmo Girl were thus more in style than in substance. The feature cover of the *New York Times Magazine* showed a split image of the same model. On the left she was dressed as a version of Gloria Steinem, with aviator glasses, turtleneck, and waist belt, and on the right as a sexy Cosmo Girl with deep cleavage that revealed her braless bosom, heavy makeup, and glittery outfit (figure 5.2). Both images portrayed a beautiful, fashionable woman who did not eschew beauty standards and gender norms but interpreted them with a different emphasis. And both images offered the media a fashionable image of "the feminist" that women could identify with.

To be sure, some feminists did reject entirely the concept of fashion and beauty. "Find what is comfortable and wear it," argued an editorial by the radical feminist group Cell 16. "Stop following fashions, looking at fashion magazines, shopping," it exclaimed. Founded by Roxanne Dunbar, the group viewed the notion of "creating 'our image' through the way we dress," as nothing but exploitation.[39] As women were only being judged by their appearance, they argued, Cell 16 feminists sought to discard all forms of adornment and decorative elements as a way to challenge the notion that women are reduced to their appearance. Seeing self-expression through clothes as a form of neurotic disorder, these feminists hoped that women would not define themselves through their looks but through their actions and other attributes such as brains, personality, and character. If women would abandon fashion completely, Cell 16 argued, they would also begin to move beyond the need to uphold unrealistic ideals of beauty that were only setting them back. For Cell 16 members, adherence to fashion only kept women in bondage—psychological, economic, and physical.[40]

Other radical feminists also rejected fashion. Andrea Dworkin, for example, saw fashion and beauty practices not only as a waste of time and an affront on women's liberation, but also as a form of bodily torture. Dworkin argued that the emphasis on fashion caused women to internalize the message that enduring pain was necessary in order to be considered a "beautiful woman."[41] Others found that dealing with fashion only deterred them from the struggle and from developing their full potential as human beings. "I used to spend hours putting on make-up, which I now use more productively to read feminist and revolutionary literature," a feminist named Ann confessed, justifying her decision to avoid beauty culture entirely.[42]

However, if Cell 16 members found clothing and beauty practices a waste of time and mental power, many feminists did not agree with Dunbar's extremist approach, and instead looked to create a compelling political statement through their clothes.[43] "Many women are just beginning to realize that, in the act of liberating themselves, somewhere along the way, they lost the aes-

FIGURE 5.2: "Two Faces of the Same Eve: Ms. Versus Cosmo," *New York Times Magazine* cover, August 1974. Despite stereotypes regarding the bra-burning feminist that circulated in the media, feminists represented a pro-fashion approach that sought to celebrate women's sexuality, not subdue it. (The New York Times. © 1974 The New York Times Company. All rights reserved. Used under license.)

thetic pleasure of putting together colors and textures or the selfish sensuality of wearing something soft and clinging," argued an article in *Ms.* magazine. "The Women's Movement revolves around the importance of giving people options. Unless we all want to end up in uniform... perhaps style needs to operate on the same premise," the article concluded.[44] For feminists who embraced fashion, clothing was not an enemy to fight against, but a source of empowerment. "The clothes I wear help me to know my own power," argued lesbian feminist Liza Cowan.[45]

As feminists grappled with questions of fashion, appearance, femininity, and beauty practices, they did not present a monolithic approach but a range of attitudes and looks. This diversity offered a more complex picture of feminism's relationship with fashion in the 1960s and 1970s that in turn shaped, and broadened, public opinion regarding feminism and feminists. Indeed, despite media portrayals of feminists as drab, masculine-looking, and angry, the public—much due to the popularity of feminine-looking feminists like Steinem—formed a more nuanced opinion regarding feminists and their appearance.[46] In a 1970 opinion poll for the Virginia Slims company, only 12 percent of the 2,972 women polled associated "women's liberation" with a "bunch of frustrated, insecure, angry hysterical, masculine-type women group."[47]

Moreover, although fashion could be a source of tension, both among feminists themselves and between feminists and nonfeminists, it could also offer a bridge and a way to form solidarity between groups. This was evident in one of the most iconic photographs of the feminist movement, featuring Dorothy Pitman-Hughes and Gloria Steinem (figure 5.3).[48] In this black-and-white photograph, the two women—wearing snug-fitting, long-sleeved turtlenecks—face the camera in a position of protest, raising their fists in the Black Panther salute in a show of solidarity for women's rights.[49] Despite their identical clothes, Pitman-Hughes and Steinem did not portray an identical appearance, but instead presented a feminist image with different emphases and interpretations. But more importantly, they were not depicted as threatening but as fashionable models of a new feminist consciousness. The photo, which appeared in *Esquire* magazine in October 1971 as part of a profile on Steinem, offered a powerful response to the stereotype of the radical feminist. Earlier that year, in an article titled "The Feminine Mistake," the magazine published an illustration of a defiant angry-looking woman, wearing a semitransparent short dress that revealed her braless nipples, with a "WITCH" button pinned to her dress, and a burning bra dangling from her upraised, fisted hand.[50] Providing a sharp contrast to this image, and using the documentary power of the camera, the photograph of Steinem and Pitman-Hughes presented

This Is What a Feminist Looks Like

FIGURE 5.3: Dan Wynn's iconic photograph of Gloria Steinem and Dorothy Pitman-Hughes showed how feminists used fashion not only to express their identities but also to convey political messages. Although there was not a unified feminist style that all feminists adopted, clothing served as a way to create a group consciousness and express solidarity with other struggles. (© Dan Wynn Archive and Farmani Group, Co LTD)

tangible proof that the bra-burning feminist image the media perpetuated was indeed just a myth. In real life, Steinem and Pitman-Hughes showed that what a feminist looks like could be both powerful and fashionable. Yet they also showed that fashion was a crucial realm where feminist messages and politics would play out.

CHAPTER FIVE

Feminist Fashions and Construction of "the Feminist" Image

Feminists' various approaches to fashion and beauty practices affected the styles they adopted and adapted. Whereas some stuck to the popular fashions in their attempt to present a respectable appearance, other sought to create an alternative to the mainstream styles that would express their politics, yet without compromising on the pleasure of dressing up. "I am confident that there will begin to evolve a true Dyke fashion," argued Liza Cowan. "I have no idea what these clothes will look like, but I do know that they will be liberating, physically and psychologically, and they will be beautiful."[51] For lesbian feminists and women's liberationists like Cowan, this search for alternative style was not a meaningless endeavor but an important political act of resistance and self-determination.

In their attempts to create alternatives to the fashion industry and consumer capitalism, some feminists opted for secondhand clothing, while others encouraged women to create their own clothes, seeing it as an empowering activity and a feminist practice. "We have got to start making and designing clothes for ourselves," Cowan argued. "If you know how to sew, you might make your own clothes and teach your friends to sew too. . . . Don't let men get rich (richer) with our money and ideas."[52] Other liberal feminists encouraged women to change the industry from within. Acknowledging that fashion was a big business, one member urged her NOW sisters to take over the industry, arguing that it was a venue where women could gain influence, as it was already deemed a female field. Echoing the mission of the Fashion Group, this feminist also sought to make women a powerful voice in the industry. "Why not feminist designers owning feminist factories making a great deal of money from women who would be glad to buy and wear un-sexist clothes?" she asked. Instead of rejecting the industry all together, this feminist sought to build it as a feminist realm, where women's creativity, power, and solidarity could come into play.[53]

Some feminists answered this call by establishing their own businesses, seeing it as a way to gain control over their images without succumbing to capitalist interests that were often determined by men. A mail-order company named Liberation Enterprises, for example, founded in 1972 by NOW members Rose Fontanella and Stephanie Marcus, sold a variety of clothes, jewelry, and paraphernalia with feminist messages. Creating clothes with feminist themes or slogans offered a business venue for feminists but also popularized and rallied support for the movement. According to the founders, these items gave "women the opportunity to express the spirit of the women's movement" and served as "consciousness-raisers, by making the feminist spirit more visible." Using fashion as a form of political statement by literally wearing their feminism on their bodies, women could convey their support. Yet, more importantly, these feminist businesses offered women a way to harness their financial power in service of their politics.[54]

Black women, while not necessarily driven by anticonsumerism, also saw in designing African-inspired garments a source of pride and creativity, as well as a form of feminist and race resistance. Indeed, the creation of soul style was largely a "do-it-yourself endeavor" due to many women's lack of access to more upscale Black boutiques that sold custom-made designs of African-inspired dashikis, caftans, boubous, *lapas* (wrappers) and *geles* (head wraps). College students who looked to adopt soul styles usually mixed and matched items found in thrift stores that looked or felt "African" or, if they had sewing skills, resorted to buying African textiles and making their own clothes.[55] Wearing self-made designs enabled Black women to identify with their cultural heroes and assert their pride in Black femininity. It also symbolized an act of resistance against the White fashion industry, which often ignored the Black consumer market. However, although soul style contained racial critique on the mainstream White fashion industry, it was not seen as a critique of capitalism, nor as a separatist move to create alternative styles. In fact, the Black community encouraged young women to become professionals in the fashion field, celebrating in the Black press the success of Black designers in the mainstream fashion industry and the commercialization of African-inspired styles.[56]

Whether they designed their clothes or acquired them secondhand, feminists were interested in creating a style that would be a visual statement of their politics and their solidarity with one another. "I've learned out of boredom that clothing can be used by and for me to express myself in a non-oppressive way. I don't have to be a sex symbol or a male replica to wear clothing that is an extension of myself," argued a feminist named Anne Thompson.[57] However, feminists never detailed what un-sexist clothes would look like or what exactly a "feminist style" entailed. Some feminists suggested creating a "feminist uniform" that would express sartorially the wearer's politics without the need to adhere to consumerist or social pressures. The outfit was conceived as "an attractive, up to date dress . . . made in three colors; in cotton for summer and wool for winter." Like other forms of feminist activism, the proposed uniform was meant to become an arena of consciousness-raising and feminist practice. By wearing the same dress each day, proponents argued, feminists could show their solidarity with the struggle. The greatest benefit of the uniform, however, was its ability to create a community in which feminists could recognize one another and claim their affiliation with the movement. A unified "feminist look" could create sisterhood between women, promoters of the feminist uniform argued, as it would eliminate competition among women over appearance that the male chauvinist culture perpetuated.[58]

Uniform advocates paid attention not only to the aesthetic value of the dress but also to the economic and social implications of clothing as a product of human labor. The feminist uniform, advocates suggested, would be "made by the 'Poor People's Corporation' so that we would be giving our money to a co-operative rather than a profit-making corporation." Adopting a feminist uniform was also a useful way to resist a consumerist ideology that demanded versatile wardrobes and the social pressures of changing one's outfit constantly. Instead of adjusting one's clothing to the social environment and physical activities they required, a woman could wear her functional feminist uniform throughout the day.[59] Some reacted positively to the idea, making suggestions to improve the design by adding pockets, opting for culottes (trousers) instead of a dress, and creating sleeveless versions for summer. Yet others rejected the idea of an official uniform, claiming it will only substitute one oppression with another.[60]

For many lesbian feminists, adopting so-called dyke fashions—often consisting of work shirts and pants—became the style of choice. By discarding feminine fashions such as skirts, makeup, and high heels, these feminists created a style that symbolized their rejection of gender binaries and expressed their lesbian identity.[61] As the manifest "The Woman-Identified Woman" by the feminist group Radicalesbians argued, "as long as we cling to the idea of 'being a woman,' we will sense some conflict with ... that sense of a whole person.... [We need] to accept that being 'feminine' and being a whole person are irreconcilable."[62] By removing feminine attributes from their appearance, lesbian feminists sought to challenge heterosexual social norms that prescribed separate roles to men and women.[63] "We're breaking down the old butch-femme roles which mimic heterosexual society," explained a San Francisco lesbian named Susan Walsh. "We're getting through all those layers and becoming real."[64] As they cultivated a more androgynous or masculine appearance, these feminists also challenged what it meant to be a woman, arguing that biological differences between men and women were not innate but socially and culturally constructed.

Short hair also served as an important symbolic gesture of gender nonconformity and androgyny. "Long hair is a patriarchal symbol of femininity," claimed Liza Cowan.[65] The act of cutting one's hair was for many radical feminists a political act of liberation. During the 1969 Congress to Unite Women in New York City, Cell 16 members took the stage and ceremonially cut off each other's hair, chanting slogans, and calling the audience to follow suit.[66] By cutting one's hair, these radical feminists not only showed their commitment to the cause, protesting against male-defined standard of beauty, but also formed a sense of community among activists. The collective haircutting events went beyond Cell 16's actions and became popular among other feminist groups, serving as a symbolic rite of passage into the movement. A woman from Iowa City described such an experience, seeing it as a pivotal moment in her evolution as a feminist. From having her hair down to her waist, this woman shortened her hair to below her ears, refusing, at first, she said, to let go her perception of being feminine and attractive. Yet, after attending a feminist conference and going through further consciousness-raising, she decided to join her friends and cut her hair extremely short. "Now my hair does not cover my ears, it does not swing in my face, it doesn't swing at all," she commented. Although she lost her hair, this woman felt more empowered, confessing that the act taught her to see how seriously she was actually taking herself.[67]

Hair also played an important role in the politicization of Black women and their cultivation of an activist identity. By the beginning of the 1960s, young Black women—many of them active in Student Nonviolent Coordinating Committee (SNCC)—started to wear their hair in natural styles. As they began organizing in rural areas in the South and consequently faced arrests, these female activists found that regular visits to the hair salon were not only unattainable but also futile. Maintaining what was then considered a respectable appearance as a political strategy, which for Black women meant straight and pressed hair, no longer proved useful in avoiding the sexual and racial violence many civil rights activists endured.[68] Yet, activists also justified their adoption of natural styles, most notably the Afro, in ideological terms, using the style to challenge racist beauty standards and creating a sense of solidarity and community among activists. For them, the decision to wear an Afro was an expression of their political and feminist identity. The Afro allowed them to celebrate their culture and African heritage and to reclaim Blackness as a source of pride.[69]

In addition, some activists used the Afro to promote a feminist critique that connected White racism to consumer capitalism. Like White radical feminists, these Black activists denounced the commercial beauty industry, which according to them not only perpetuated White beauty ideals but turned all women, both Black and White, into sexual objects. "I'm protesting against the black Anglo-Saxon and the white man," argued Lee McDaniel, an activist and a fashion designer of African-inspired clothing. "I'm tired of going through all these changes trying to look like Doris Day and Elizabeth Taylor. I'm not going to measure myself by their yardstick any longer!" she exclaimed.[70] Wearing the Afro became a public act of defiance not only toward White beauty standards, but also against understandings of femininity within Black communities, which perceived straightened hair as the hallmark of beauty. Asserting that "Black is Beautiful" through the celebration of natural hairstyles, these Black women expanded the definition of beauty to include a more diverse and inclusive types of Black femininity.[71]

Despite the preference to gender-bending or androgynous styles among radical feminists, the spectrum of gender appearances was broad among women's liberationists, allowing each woman to create her own interpretation of how a woman (and a feminist) should look like. "Fashions this fall are swinging with the vicissitudes of that oh-so-elusive sexual identity, from the butch look to the femme and everything is between," commented one feminist on the variety of "feminist fashions."[72] A photograph of the editorial board of *Women: A Journal of Liberation* demonstrates the range of images feminists employed (figure 5.4).[73] The women posed for an article that dealt with the issue of androgyny, with the photograph capturing the different negotiations each woman chose regarding her self-presentation. Although none presented a hyper-feminine appearance, their fashions presented a range of gender attributes between masculine and feminine. All eight women are wearing pants, and either turtlenecks or polo shirts. Half have short hair, while the other half sport longer styles. Two wear visible jewelry and makeup. Seeking to break gender definitions, not only dichotomies, fashion served as a way for these women to express a more complex understanding of androgyny. "I am not masculine or feminine, or masculine and feminine; I am a person with myriad characteristics," one of them stated.[74] Claiming androgyny enabled these women to find pleasure in the ability to play with their appearance, changing between styles and identities. "I wear jeans and yellow ruffled dresses, too. . . . It's an unconscious harmony—the balancing of that part of me that needs the ruffles and security and tradition with that part of me so desirous of jeans and responsibility and independence," another wrote. "Should I classify and catalogue my needs under the rubric 'Feminine—Masculine' and regard them as 'natural' dissonance to be individually assaulted, compromised, and bastardized into an artificial image? No," she asserted confidently.[75]

FIGURE 5.4: Whereas many lesbian feminists tended to adopt more unisex, androgynous styles, the spectrum of appearances remained broad, as demonstrated in this 1974 photo of the editorial board of the feminist journal *Women*. (*Women: A Journal of Liberation* Records, Sophia Smith Collection, Smith College, Northampton, Mass.)

Whereas the adoption of unisex or androgynous styles offered freedom to many feminists, it also became a contested issue in the movement. For NOW leaders in particular, the rejection of feminine styles and attributes of many on the feminist Left was a cause of concern. Betty Friedan was especially bothered by the appearance of lesbian feminists, famously describing them as a "lavender menace." Seeing the importance of presenting a feminine appearance as a tactical move to gain public support, and perhaps feeling uncomfortable personally with gender nonconforming styles, Friedan criticized the need of radical feminists to "make yourself ugly" in order to feel liberated. Yet, more than a personal preference, Friedan was concerned about the impact that adopting androgynous styles would have on the movement.

She complained that the "sexual shock tactics and man-hating, down-with motherhood stance" of many women's liberationists only alienated more conservative women from the feminist cause.[76] Moreover, like the suffragists a generation prior, Friedan believed that presenting a respectable appearance was the surest way to avoid accusations that feminists were ugly or masculine. Hence, she saw young activists' choice to eschew mainstream feminine styles as a liability to the organization. Fearing that these activists' appearance would mark all feminists as "men haters," thus inflaming hostility toward the movement, Friedan sought to minimize their influence and visibility in the media.[77]

Friedan was not completely wrong in her analysis. When Phyllis Schlafly's STOP ERA campaign would start to gain popularity in the mid-1970s, it harnessed radical feminists' appearance, especially those who favored unisex styles, to point to what the group characterized as the "dangers of feminism." Schlafly and her anti-ERA supporters adopted a hyper-feminine appearance, often wearing pink dresses as part of their political strategy, trying to claim feminine fashionability as a conservative trait.[78] As youthful and more casual styles became popular, Schlafly and her supporters continued to cling to the boxy and more formal silhouette of the early 1960s and scorned feminists' increasing tendency to adopt denim and pants into their wardrobe.[79]

Working-class and minority women, who could not adopt radical styles as easily as their White middle-class sisters, also chafed at the androgynous styles. Although some feminists justified their adoption of denim and work boots as a statement of solidarity with the working class, they ignored the millions of women working as secretaries, waitresses, flight attendants, and teachers. For these women, abandoning skirts, heels, and makeup in favor of more androgynous alternative styles posed the risk of losing one's job, which many of them could not take.[80] As one woman confessed, she could not get a job without wearing makeup or a miniskirt. After trying to interview with knee-length skirts and no makeup, and without securing a job, she returned to her miniskirt and "landed one right away."[81] Some radical feminist groups also showed hostility to activists who refused to abandon their feminine appearance, blaming them for betraying the feminist cause or accusing them of succumbing to conformity and false consciousness.[82] Ignoring the economic reality of many working women, as well as denying the pleasure and the empowering feeling many women felt when they dressed up in skirts and makeup exacerbated class and racial tensions among feminists and led some to feel excluded from the movement.

Some Black women also found the pressure to conform with radical styles alienating. Florynce Kennedy pointed to "the fact that middle-class white women need to reject the tailored well-dress image shoved down their throats and often find jeans as the panacea, doesn't mean that working-class or black or Spanish women too, will find in jeans a symbolic end to oppression." For women who have had to wear "shapeless hand-me-downs for the majority of their lives," Kennedy claimed, indulging in feminine fashions was a declaration of independence.[83] Moreover, not all Black women felt comfortable with the Afro, seeing it as "too masculine" and as a threat to feminine beauty. "I go along with being black, thinking black, and living black, but I don't go along with the new 'Afro' hair style on our women," one *Ebony* reader wrote. "Disagree all you want, but think. The men look great and masculine in their Afro hair styles—our women look great and masculine too," she argued.[84] While in general many championed Black-is-Beautiful sentiments and adopted African-inspired clothing and natural hairstyles, for many Black women, even for those who embraced feminism, maintaining femininity was no less important.

Even among White radical circles, non-feminine clothes were a cause of tension. Some lesbian feminists felt uncomfortable with the androgynous styles, finding them too masculine. "I refuse to look to the dull dead male and his dull dead clothes for inspiration," one lesbian feminist complained about work shirts and suits. "I'm a gay *woman*, free and beautiful to myself.... *I can be free, and strong, and work and play in anything*—closed or open fabric, dress or pants."[85] Although some lesbian feminists welcomed the comfort and freedom of movement that characterized menswear, and were especially pleased to avoid the harassment that went along with the presentation of feminine appearance, they were also tired of blue jeans and suits. Instead, they sought to create a style in which they "could feel comfortable and confident wearing" but would not look like men's clothes.[86] "I don't like to see a woman who wants to look like a man," argued Dixie McMills, a lesbian postal worker. "I hate Frisco jeans and I hate capri outfits too. A woman looks best as herself without trying to look like some dumb man," she argued.[87]

The question of how to create a feminist style that would not be an imitation of menswear yet would also not perpetuate patriarchal ideas about women's roles in society became pertinent in feminist circles in the mid-1970s. Clothing and appearance offered a material route to engage with feminist ideas in everyday life, and thus feminists were invested in finding a style that would best suit their politics and identities. They adapted existing styles to their own use, either by repurposing work clothes, by claiming masculine fashions as suitable for women, and by expanding the boundaries of sexual propriety. Even those who rejected mainstream feminine appearance did not place themselves outside the world of fashion. Clothing were a powerful political statement, and they utilized it to promote their agendas.

However, while some fashions, such as blue jeans and short or natural hair, were popular among many feminists, there was not one style that activists adopted, or agreed it best represented them and their politics. "We are everywhere, and we dress every way," argued feminist Maureen Turner in a *Boston Globe* article.[88] Even though there was not one feminist style that feminists could agree on, feminists and their clothing indeed seemed ubiquitous by the 1970s. The ready-made industry adopted (or co-opted, as some feminists would argue) some of the styles feminists wore, marketing them as the latest fashion trends. Yet, when these styles became popular, the ideas of freedom, choice, and empowerment that stood behind them also received popular acceptance.

The Popularization of Feminist Styles and the Commercialization of Feminism

Feminists' utilization of fashion constituted feminism not only as an ideology or political activism, but also as a cultural style and an everyday practice manifested through clothes. For feminists, fashion was a tool through which they could understand themselves and the world around them, form solidarities with one another, and promote change. Yet ironically, the alternative styles that women's liberationists and Black feminists promoted extended beyond activist circles and were adopted by the mainstream market. Despite some feminists' critique on the exploitive and racist nature of the fashion industry, retailers and the media embraced these feminist styles and marketed them to the general public. In that process, these styles lost their radical message, turning instead into fashion statements. However, if some feminists lamented the commercialization of their fashions, others saw it as the cultural success of the movement, pointing to the influence of feminism on public opinion.

The most notable contribution of feminists to mainstream fashion was the popularization of "unisex styles" and the androgynous look that appealed to many lesbian feminists. Retail designers and manufacturers responded to the growing demand of young women who searched for clothes that provided both comfort and freedom, recognizing the potential for profits.[89] They created women's lines for masculine items such as pants and jackets, while marketing identical shirts suitable both for men and women. "In our sportswear-oriented world, young people are too busy trying to capture and control today's spirit to be bothered by thoughts of looking particularly like a man or a woman," explained designer Ed Baynard to *Women's Wear Daily*.[90] In addition, department stores began to include menswear in women's departments and created "unisex boutiques" that included both male and female changing rooms.[91] Unisex fashions were marketed as the image of the "new genderation" of young people who asserted a "new freedom in dressing . . . doing your own thing . . . wearing what you want when you want," and as a symbol of the true integration between men's and women's fashions (figure 5.5).[92] However, rather than a true integration, or the masculinization of women's clothes, the unisex style was part of a continuing process in which menswear became more feminized, or no longer considered solely masculine. Indeed, although some items—most notably pants for women—became conventional mainstream fashion, there was never an attempt to create truly genderless styles. Masculine items were adjusted to fit women's bodies, and despite their name, were never meant for both genders.[93]

Moreover, when radical feminists promoted the unisex styles, they did so as part of their challenge to gender differences and their effort to upset the very structure of society. When the industry promoted them, they looked to expand their profits, not to make a political statement. The industry promoted unisex items mostly to women. It did not seek to popularize feminine styles like skirts for men, and thus limited the revolutionary potential unisex styles could have had on society. While ads alluded to a growing recognition of the changing expectations of women, they also turned feminism into a commodity focused on individual freedom of choice, undermining the larger social and political message that androgynous fashions entailed.[94]

The unisex look included a range of items and accessories, yet blue jeans became one of the most popular items, worn by all ages and genders alike. Seen as too casual and inappropriate in the 1950s, by the 1960s—much thanks to college students and the counterculture—jeans became popular everyday wear. Fashion magazines appealed to the growing student market and promoted casual wear and comfort to which jeans was essential component. The influence of Hollywood stars such as James Dean and Marlon Brando, as well as their association with rock and roll, also turned jeans into the uniform of youth.[95] The greatest appeal of jeans was their durability and price, two qualities that feminists valued. Yet, while one could buy a pair of Levi's or Lees for $10 to $15 (about $45-$70 today), by the mid-1970s, couture designers such as Valentino, Yves St. Laurent, and most notably Calvin Klein rebranded jeans as couture wear and as a sexy clothing item.[96] No longer the symbol of

CHAPTER FIVE

FIGURE 5.5: The mainstream market quickly adopted feminists' styles, offering commodified versions of them to the general public. Yet, as these fashions became popular, they enabled women to engage with the ideas that stood behind these styles, popularizing feminism in the process. ("The New Genderation," *Women's Wear Daily*, August 23, 1968. Image published with permission of ProQuest LLC. Further reproduction is prohibited without permission.)

rebellion against traditional gender and class prescriptions, jeans became the embodiment of sexual seduction and the capitalist market, turning full circle to join the mini as a symbol of the sexual revolution.

The publication of *Cheap Chic* (1975) and *The Woman's Dress for Success Book* (1977), two what-to-wear guides demonstrated the extent to which the market was able to incorporate feminist messages into a consumerist agenda. Written by two journalists, Caterine Milinaire and Carol Troy, *Cheap Chic* adopted the feminists' do-it-yourself approach and called for body acceptance and pleasure in fashioning a personal style. "Nobody knows better than you what you should wear or how you should look," the authors instructed readers. "Find the clothes that suit you best, that make you feel comfortable, confident, sexy, good looking and happy," they advised, arguing that one does not have to spend a lot of money or follow ridiculous trends to be in fashion.[97]

John T. Molloy's *Dress for Success* took a more utilitarian and didactic approach. Recognizing the growing presence of women in the workforce in influential positions, the book provided practical sartorial advice to the career woman in the masculine professional workplace. Molloy popularized the "success suit" outfit: a blazer-style jacket and a skirt hemmed just below the knee in a dark color that conveyed power and authority.[98] Although Molloy himself discouraged women from wearing a pantsuit to the office, revealing a more conservative approach regarding women's appearance than feminists, his book ultimately helped in legitimizing women's professional wear that included pants.[99] Both books championed fashion as an empowering force for women, and helped mainstream feminist ideas regarding careers and personal choice. However, none of these books advocated or supported the more radical gender critique of feminists in this period, and certainly did not help in legitimizing the movement or its demands. Molloy's book in particular did not seek to promote feminism, but instead sought to maintain the power relationships between the genders in the workplace.

The fashion industry also coopted the bra-less fashions and the so-called "natural look" of hippies and feminists into the mainstream market. High-fashion magazines, as well as more conservative ones such as the *Ladies' Home Journal*, recommended that women "rely more on nature, less on hardware" when it came to bras. And department stores displayed fashions meant to be worn without a bra, giving mannequins nipples for the first time.[100] Ignoring the irony that feminists were depicted as bra burners, and that discarding bras and corsets were a long-time symbol of feminist resistance, the mainstream fashion industry celebrated the new age of "bosom-baring" fashions not as a symbol of women's liberation but as the latest manifestation of the "natural" trend, emptying it of any radical meanings.[101]

Another natural look that became commercialized in the 1970s was the Afro, which transformed from a radical political statement into a fashionable style. The Afro became a national sensation after the FBI targeted activist-scholar Angela Davis and placed her on its Most Wanted Fugitives list, circulating images of her wearing a halo-shaped Afro, an African dashiki, and see-through sunglasses.[102] The large Afro became so identified with Davis that it became a trademark not only of her activism, but also of a new image of Black beauty, as media portrayals of Davis focused not only on her political views but most notably on her looks.[103] Beauticians, wig makers, and the public framed Davis's appearance as both radical and glamorous, and turned her look into a model for other women who identified with her political message, yet not necessarily with her actions. By adopting the Afro, Black women could engage with Black Power through appearance, showing their solidarity with the cause.[104]

However, as the decade progressed, instead of being a symbol of radicalism and a rejection of the White beauty industry and standards, the Afro became yet another hairstyle that required maintenance through hair products and salon visits.[105] Black beauticians and Black-owned beauty companies marketed their products using themes of racial pride and Black beauty, but those were devoid of direct political reference and instead portrayed the natural style as one choice of many.[106] Moreover, the popularization of Afro wigs by the late 1960s provided women the option of adopting the Afro not as a political choice to go natural, but as a hairstyle that could be changed depending on the circumstances. "You can change your hair style as easily as you change your mind," one ad promised.[107]

If Davis lamented the reduction of her politics to a simple hairdo, her feelings were also shared by other feminists who resented the market's co-option of feminist styles.[108] These feminists argued that the main problem with the commercialization of these fashions was in the subtraction of their political meaning. As one feminist complained: "The establishment . . . spread the anti-establishment group's words/ideas, dress, etc., around society so successfully that you can't tell who's who anymore in clothes; and through misuse and overuse the words and clothes lose their original anti-establishment meaning. . . . The clothes are sold in Bloomingdales, and are no longer threatening or signify anything but the latest fashion." Turning the "liberated woman" and even the "radical feminist" into an advertising strategy did not indicate that the market had embraced these ideas, this feminist argued. On the contrary, it was through the commercialization of "the feminist" image that the market continued in its oppression of women. "THE PATRIARCHY IS MAKING MONEY OFF THE MOVEMENT, AND THAT IS PRECISELY WHY WE ARE ALLOWED TO EXIST," she exclaimed.[109] As this feminist and others noted, the commercialization of feminist fashions did not signal the movement's success and public legitimization. At best, it reduced feminism to a consumer product, and at worst, it actually contributed to the growing backlash against feminists.

Indeed, feminist fashions were mainstreamed *despite* feminists' attempts to create an alternative to capitalism. Whereas most feminists did not reject fashionability as a concept, they were less invested than previous generations were in making feminism fashionable. They sought to create styles that would be both comfortable and appealing, seeing clothes as a tangible way to express their politics and to put feminism into practice. Yet, they remained ambivalent toward the commercial success of their ideas. However, despite this ambivalence, it is important to remember that the popularization of feminist fashions—even among women who did not belong to radical feminist groups—offered a tangible way to complicate the popular image of "the feminist" and to shape the meaning of the liberated woman. These women, who gladly adopted unisex styles, Afros, and minis, did not interpret liberation as a critique of patriarchal conventions, whether of femininity, beauty, or capitalism, as many radical feminists did. For them, liberation was about choice and empowerment, claiming their right to shape their own image. And as feminist fashions increasingly became mainstream, it was this message of choice that resonated, not more radical claims for equality.

The Battle of the Hemlines: The Mini-Midi Debate

If many radical feminists chose to adopt a more unisex or androgynous appearance as a way to challenge conventions of gender, other women found the celebration of women's sexuality more appealing. They found the adoption of a hyper-feminine, hyper-sexual appearance more suitable to express their identities as liberated women. The miniskirt, despite not being a fashion that began in feminist circles, became—perhaps more than any other clothing item of the period—a potent symbol for the changing cultural attitudes toward women's sexuality and the growing influence of youth as a market. First introduced in 1965 in Britain by the designer Mary Quant and popularized by the model Twiggy, this high-thigh style became popular in the United States in the late 1960s. High school and college students, many of whom were also active in New Left and civil rights movements, adopted the skirt as part of their political identity. Indeed, although couture designers included the mini in their collections and supported this style, it sprang from the streets as young women began rebelling against fashion dictates that demanded comportment and the respectability of ladyhood.[110] "This generation stepped out and away and did things their way," noted *Vogue*'s editor Diana Vreeland, who did not seem concerned about the decreasing influence of Paris designers and fashion professionals like herself. "No one is obliged to wear anything she doesn't want to, and one can go as far as she wants. She can wear absolutely anything that is wildly becoming."[111] Vreeland in general supported the mini, seeing it as a positive fashion development. Predicting that "the mini-skirt will become more and more miniscule," Vreeland suggested to "not worry about it. ... Let us just enjoy what suits us. It's part of fashion. Part of our freedom."[112]

The ready-made industry was more ambivalent regarding the mini than Vreeland.[113] Still, as the popularity of the mini grew almost instantaneously among the teenager market, retailers responded quickly to consumer demand, albeit often by adding an inch or two to the European versions. By 1967, the style became ubiquitous, spreading beyond teenagers to become a popular trend. "Virtually women of all ages want shorter skirts than in past seasons," a retail executive confessed. The mini's popularity crossed ages, classes, races, regions, and partisan lines. "Girls on the New Left wear them. Young Republican women wear them. Matrons wear them. If they're rebelling, they're in the majority already, so they've won the battle," commented Martin Marty, a University of Chicago professor.[114]

Women could choose to wear their minis in a wide variety of designs and lengths, ranging from the micro-mini, mid-thigh, to the more modest one or two inches above the knee, making the trend impossible for retailers to resist.[115] However, not everyone welcomed the shorter minis. Some women complained about the impracticability of wearing a very short skirt, finding it difficult to sit or cross their legs without risking unwanted underwear exposure. One woman confessed that she could not wear her favorite mini cocktail dress to dates, as it was too short to sit down in it. The fashion designer Anne Klein also admitted that "now I never budge without a scarf, which I try to drape across my knees without looking as if I were setting a table."[116] Yet, other women found the shorter, thigh-length mini fun and liberating. "I wear my skirts about three inches above my knees. I feel attractive, young, and free in this dress length," one woman wrote to *Women's Wear Daily*.[117] Ultimately, the question of length was often determined by one's age and class status. The older one became, the longer was her hem. "I've shortened my skirts about an inch since last summer, but I won't go above the top of the knee—that's enough if you're over 25," confessed one woman to the *New York Times*.[118] Elite matrons and professional women were also less likely to adopt the shorter mini, preferring knee-length skirts.

Although women differed in their preference of mini length, they imbued the skirt with political meanings, seeing it as a symbol of liberation, of their ability to choose, and of being independent women. Associated with youth, freedom, and sexuality, many viewed the mini as a mark of the "new freedom," connecting it not only to general rebellious attitudes that defined the 1960s, but to the women's movement and its politics specifically. One teenager associated the mini with the "new feminine drive for full freedom and equality," calling her skirt "my independence flag."[119] Together with the birth-control pill, miniskirts became the epitome of the sexual revolution that provided women with unprecedented freedom to assert themselves as sexual beings, equal to men.[120] However, it was this revived understanding of female sexuality with which the mini was most identified, not with concrete demands for gender equality that feminist activists called for.

The sexualized nature of the miniskirt stirred the most public debate and concerns. Many of the arguments for and against the mini sounded very familiar, invoking much of the 1920s debates over the flapper and her short skirts. Miniskirts were blamed for corrupting the morality of youth, for deteriorating women's health, and for destroying women's feminine charms or respectability.[121] Some argued that the skirt was unfeminine because of its lack of modesty. However, unlike the boyish connotations of the flapper, the unfeminine aspects of the mini were not related to its association with masculinity or gender-bending appearance. It was the mini's hypersexuality that conservatives interpreted as unfeminine and as a threat on the family and social system.[122] High schools and colleges across the country banned the miniskirt, arguing it led to a "distraction" among fellow students, and Republican lawmakers in California barred legislative employees from wearing miniskirts, which they deemed an impropriety for public workers.[123] Whereas by the early 1970s the public grew accustomed to knee-length or just-above-the knee hemlines, the very short and hypersexualized micro-mini was more controversial. Although some businessmen "relished" the view of a secretary bending over to reach the bottom drawer of a filing cabinet, others felt uncomfortable with the "for-goodness'-sake-don't-bend-over style" and banned them from the office.[124] Although it was often one's age and professional status, not their politics, that determined their attitude toward the mini, the skirt nonetheless became part of the political culture of the period.

The importance of the mini as a political symbol of sexual liberation and youth reached its visual apex in 1970, when the industry pushed for longer hemlines. Marketed as "midi" or "longette" (to give it a French flair), the campaign for this mid-calf skirt was led mainly by *Women's Wear Daily*. It was justified as a means of boosting the industry in difficult economic times. According to manufacturers' logic, the change in styles would force women to change their wardrobe and thus to spend more money in department stores.[125] Whereas women were not oblivious to the economic interests behind the shift in styles, they interpreted the move as an attack on their personal freedom.

CHAPTER FIVE

As in previous times when women resisted changes in skirt lengths, the battle over the mini became a political site, as women organized to fight the longer hemlines and to protect what they constituted as their right to choose.

The detest for the midi crossed age, class, and racial lines.[126] Women complained that the midi made them look "old, or ugly, or dumpy, or sawed-off—or all of these," and demanded that department stores "keep the mini on the market."[127] According to a poll by *Chicago Today*, out of the 14,770 responders, the anti-midi sentiment ran four to one among the women. A Louis Harris Company poll also showed similar results, when 59 percent of the women responders favored the mini compared to only 32 percent who favored the midi. And in a survey for the *New York Amsterdam News*, the majority polled voted wholeheartedly for the mini.[128]

Some women engaged in direct action to resist the midi trend. Like the generation before them who fought against the lengthening of skirts in the late 1920s, women all across the country circulated petitions and organized protests. In an open letter to the *Pittsburgh Courier*, one such protester assured that "the American women is too individualistic to give up her diversified wardrobe.... The midi (mid-calf) will be seen on Main Street, USA, but, make no mistake, the above-the-knee look is not out!"[129] Some took their protest into the streets, picketing in front of stores that promoted the midis by staging "clip-ins," in which they publicly cut midis with scissors. While these tactics—which were similar to those radical feminists used—drew media attention, anti-midi activists found that organizing boycotts proved most effective.[130] "Our best weapon is to stay away from the stores," argued Mrs. Michael Deem, the thirty-three-year-old cofounder of FADD (Fight Against Dictating Designers). Juli Hunter from POOFF (Perseveration of Our Femininity and Finances) also supported a boycott, arguing that "if we boycott the midi and just don't buy, the store will have to give us what we want."[131]

The response was swift, widespread, and well-organized. Inspired by the more militant feminist protests of the era and adopting many of their arguments, protest groups such as POOFF, FADD, GAMS (Girls/Guys Against More Skirts), and the Madison Avenue Women's League for Preservation of the Right to Select Our Own Skirt Lengths framed their campaigns as part of the rise of women's consciousness and their ongoing battle for rights. "You forget you are dealing with a new generation that no longer accepts the pronouncement of the fashion industry—or anyone—as dictates," one of FADD's leaders cautioned.[132] Another activist echoed this sentiment, announcing that "the time has passed when women were powder puffs and pushovers." Refusing to adopt the midi, she reminded the reporter that "we belong to a generation that isn't going to be pushed into wearing something we don't want to wear simply because it's new."[133] For these activists, a woman's right to choose her appearance, free from the dictates of the fashion industry, was the meaning of women's liberation.

In general, these women did not identify as feminists or declare an affiliation with NOW or other known feminist groups at the time. Particularly, mini advocates tried to distance themselves from the popular image of radical feminists, which they feared would hurt their cause. "We were not originally a war-like group," one of POOFF's leaders explained. "When we organized and incorporated POOFF ... we very carefully said we're not against anything. We were merely for women being allowed to dress in a manner most flattering to them as individuals."[134] Yet, when POOFF members used arguments of individual choice and their right for sartorial freedom, they echoed the main of feminist activists' messages. In demanding their right to wear what they please, and by utilizing protest methods like demonstrations, boycotts, parades, and even legal measures, they also turned their battle into a realm of feminist activism. "A lot of people might say we're a frivolous lot to spend our time on something like this when there are much more important issues to worry about. Granted, clothes are not the most important thing in the world," Juli Hunter commented. She justified her decision for the protest: "But suddenly someone is interfering with our lives. And they're trying to make fools of us. There are millions of women who can't afford to change their fashion every whipstitch. And yet many of these ladies *want* to be fashionable. Who looks out for them?"[135] For Hunter and her fellow mini supporters, demanding their right to dress as they pleased, as well as to claim their status as fashionable women, were parts of a broader discourse of women's rights that feminism promoted and legitimized. Even if the only issue these women took on was their right for sartorial freedom, in their actions they expanded the range of topics that feminism addressed.

Contemporaries also identified the feminist aspects of the protest. Some retailers admitted that the issue was not about skirt length but represented a broader debate about women's social status. "It seems to me that your fight is more than just for length," a Saks Fifth Avenue designer replied to a POOFF activist. He defined the struggle as being about "a way of life. You want to be able to choose."[136] Indeed, although pro-mini advocates did not join the movement, and as already noted not every woman felt comfortable identifying as a feminist, the underlying message of power and choice appealed to them. Pro-mini advocates found new ways to engage with feminism, which was based on sartorial expression. Yet, through their struggle, these women not only turned fashion into a suitable arena to fight for women's freedom and rights, but also facilitated the feminist idea of choice spreading to the general public.

If POOFF was not a feminist organization per se, its battle was taken up by the movement. Self-proclaimed feminists and activists also addressed the mini-midi debate, treating the issue as part of their agenda. NOW activists, for example, commented that "thanks to the atmosphere of freedom that has started surrounding women more and more, due to the movement, they have actively resisted being strait-jacketed just to be 'fashionable.'" Seeing this debate not as a frivolous issue that meant to distract women from promoting equality, but as another issue feminists should rally against, NOW feminists also put out a call to resist the midi.[137] For them, the mini-midi debate served as a recruiting opportunity, drawing more women to the feminist cause. NOW activists hoped that by rallying women to fight for their sartorial right to choose, they would introduce activism into other realms of women's lives. Even the radical feminist newspaper *Off Our Backs* addressed the issue, advising its readers to boycott the midi in order to "prove to the industry that perhaps fashions can no longer be dictated to women."[138]

By late 1970, it was clear that the majority of women voted with their purses against the midi. Yet, as in the late 1920s, what could be seen as the big battle of the hemlines ended with a compromise rather than a victory for either side. Despite designers' and *Women's Wear Daily*'s efforts to push the midi as the only fashionable option for women, the mini did not disappear, although some hemlines did fall. Most women refused the midi, choosing knee-length or just hovering-the-knee lengths.[139] Although it is tempting to dismiss the mini-midi debate as another example of the cooption of the feminist agenda into commercial interests, its influence reached beyond the fashion industry. As women asserted their right to choose the length of their skirts and to independently shape their bodies and appearance, they also legitimized the feminist concept of choice in the popular mainstream.[140] Moreover, the feminine and sexual associations of the mini also complicated the popular misconception that a true feminist cannot endorse fashion and beauty, or that feminine clothing always stands in the way of women's liberation. Through their support of the mini, women could show solidarity with ideas of freedom and choice that feminists promoted.

Furthermore, although the hemline debate ended in a compromise, its unintended consequence was to popularize, and more importantly to legitimize, pants for women, especially in the workplace. Amid the controversy over skirts' length, more and more women began to see pants as more flattering, practical, and modest than either the mini or the midi. As a consequence, they bought pantsuits, which became a new symbol for women's empowerment and economic independence.[141] Defining it as the "real revolution in fashion," the *Los Angeles Times* announced that the fall of 1970, instead of being characterized by the hemline war, "will be the greatest season for pants ever."[142] Contemporaries were also quick to associate wearing a pantsuit or a pair of trousers with the feminist struggle, connecting it to women's demands to gain influence and status in the workplace as career professionals.[143] For some, the demand to wear pants provided an entrance to the movement, as they expanded their battles over fashion to other realms of life. A union organizer for the Distributive Workers of America, for example, credited her feminist politicization to an office fight over secretaries' right to wear pants for work. Mobilized by their success, these women also pursued other "subversive ideas of 'feminism,'" such as an end to sex discrimination at work, the right to be treated with respect, and an increase in wages.[144]

Whereas not all women who wore pants to work affiliated themselves with the movement as this union organizer did, "it became," as the feminist activist Susan Brownmiller argued, "a feminist statement to wear pants."[145] Just like the mini, pants challenged traditional notions of femininity and asserted a new presence in the public sphere. Yet, if the problem with the mini was its overt sexuality, critics of pants found their masculine association to be the most threatening aspect to society.[146] Some argued that pants could be feminine just like skirts and dresses, especially when they were paired with soft, ruffled blouses or long tunics. However, women's decision to adopt pants as part of their working wardrobe was viewed not as a mere fashion decision but as a reflection of a larger social change.[147] "There is a question as to whether . . . sex differentiation by clothing will continue in the world of the future, especially in view of the change which is now taking place in the power and position of women," an article in the *New York Times* warned of the dangers of women wearing pants. "The trend towards similarity in dress reflects the end of the patriarchal system."[148]

While jeans became acceptable leisurewear for both genders, tailored pants were more controversial because they were associated not only with women's appearance but with their changing status in the workforce. Indeed, the mini-midi debate and women's adoption of pants demonstrated the political importance of fashion: it could express power and be a liberating force, not just a tool of women's oppression. Marking another episode in the long struggle of women in the twentieth century to gain sartorial freedom for their legs (and bodies in general), the mini-midi debate of 1970 and its aftermaths further politicized fashion as a useful site for activism.

Fashion as a Feminist Practice

The politics of style and self-presentation became central to how feminists and the public interpreted the meaning of women's liberation in the 1960s and 1970s. For some, clothing and appearance served as a visual and material means to resist the fashion and beauty industries, and to challenge gender, race, and class norms and hierarchies. For others, fashion was a way to celebrate women's bodies, sexuality, and freedom of choice. Yet, although fashion was oftentimes a contested site of struggle for feminists and nonfeminists alike, for the women who chose to express their politics and their identities through the clothes they wore, fashion became both a feminist symbol and a political practice. Although the popularization and commercialization of feminist fashions subdued some of the radical message these clothing carried, they also helped turn feminist ideas of freedom and choice into a palpable, popular, and fashionable ideology.

Fashion would continue to be an important part of how feminists viewed and expressed their politics and identities. When a new generation of feminists appeared on the national stage in the 1990s, they would also engage with the question of "what a feminist looks like," continuing the long relationship feminism had with fashion. Just as their forebearers, they did not reject fashion and beauty practices but saw them as a path for liberation and self-expression. These "lipstick feminists" or "Girlies," as they would come to be known, asserted their right to wear fashionable, feminine clothes while still maintaining their political commitment to ideas of gender equality. They sought to reclaim fashion not only as a realm of power but also as a realm of pleasure, arguing for a more inclusive and expansive vision of feminist styles.[149] In their efforts to create an image that would express their identities and politics, the debates over fashion from the era of women's liberation would reverberate once again. These debates began not in the 1960s and the 1970s but the early twentieth century, when women sought to express their freedom through their clothes, proving that fashion was a feminist issue all along.

EPILOGUE

The Fashionable Legacies of American Feminism

In 2006, the outspoken feminist magazine *BUST* dedicated its entire August/September issue to fashion. "The culture of clothing has been central to women's lives for centuries, and we think it's as important to find out what could be right with it as it is to pinpoint what's wrong," editor Debbie Stoller told readers. Rather than just criticize fashion, Stoller decided to focus on the aspects of clothing that feminists like her could embrace: an expression of fun, pleasure, and empowerment.[1] This approach, which adopted a pro-market, commercialized viewpoint, characterized many young feminists coming of age in the 1990s and 2000s. These Girlie feminists—as some called themselves—reclaimed girl culture, beauty practices, and femininity as spaces of pleasure and feminist consciousness. They viewed fashion as liberating and empowering feminist praxis and rejected the notion that celebrating femininity and sexuality is participating in one's own oppression.[2]

Although some interpreted Girlie feminists' pro-fashion attitudes as a generational revolt against more purist critique of their predecessors, this book points to how *BUST* editors were in fact part of a long feminist tradition. In a sense, Girlie feminists did not need to reclaim fashion as a feminist form of expression, because it has already been an important element of feminism's history and culture.[3] And indeed, the articles in the issue acknowledged this legacy, highlighting the significance of fashion and its role in empowering women, and connected the current fashion scene with a broader feminist history.[4] The most explicit tribute to the previous generations, however, was a fashion spread titled "Our Outfits, Ourselves," a clear reference to the 1960s seminal collaborative feminist book, *Our Bodies, Ourselves*. The spread featured six "looks inspired by fashionable feminists," displaying modern stylistic interpretations of the clothes of Elizabeth Cady Stanton, Angela Davis, Bella Abzug, Gloria Steinem, Camille Paglia, and Kathleen Hanna. Representing diverse races, ethnicities, religions, and sexual orientations, as well as every "wave" of feminist activism, each image was accompanied by a representative quote as well as a description on how to achieve these feminists' looks, including prices. However, the spread did not provide a chronological narrative of fashionable development, instead portraying the diversity of feminist expressions through clothes.[5]

Urging readers to "Be a feminist, or just dress like one," the spread not only claimed these feminists as fashionable icons but also pointed to the constitutive force of fashion in shaping feminist identities.[6] Through the imitation of the ways these feminists looked, the spread offered readers tangible means to identify with the message they promoted. Indeed, for the editors, the point was not to re-create these feminists' image by using authentic historical costumes that framed their styles as part of a distant past. Rather, in presenting a modern interpretation of these styles, they connected these feminists' philosophies with a fashionable appearance, thus asserting the continuous fashionability of feminism, as well as the relevancy of clothes in shaping public attitudes toward the movement. Yet, the fact that the only representative from the "first wave" was Elizabeth Cady Stanton suggested that the editors looked mainly to "second-wave" feminists for fashionable inspiration. In their choice to ignore the early and mid-twentieth century, *BUST* further drove these fashionable legacies into oblivion and erased their contribution to feminist politics. Just like scholarly understandings of feminism, *BUST* framed fashionability within the boundaries of the waves, favoring the second wave as a model to follow.[7]

However, as the chapters in this book reveal, the fashionable politics of American feminism were shaped throughout the long twentieth century. Women adopted and adapted clothing styles to redefine and expand what feminism meant to them, and in the process also what it meant in popular culture. Far from being a frivolous distraction, fashion became the means through which various women articulated their claims for gender and racial equality, and shaped their identities as modern women. These women—whether they were Gibson Girls, Rainy Daisies, suffragists, bohemian feminists, flappers, fashion designers, Hollywood stars, or radical women's liberationists—demonstrated not only that fashion and feminism could coexist, but that fashion could serve as an effective realm for conveying feminist messages. By using clothes in political ways, these women asserted their sexual freedom, their economic independence, and their racial equality. Yet, even those who wore their clothes "just because" they were fashionable helped to popularize the ideas that these clothes carried. Through fashion, these women facilitated the mainstreaming of feminist ideas in popular culture, even if only in their commercialized version. And as ideas of freedom, independence, and equality became increasingly part of the fashionable discourse, so did feminism.

As this book demonstrates, feminist ideas have been making their way into the fashionable mainstream throughout the twentieth century, beginning with the Gibson Girl's shirtwaist, through the American Look of the interwar period, and the unisex fashions of the 1970s. And while popular myths regarding feminists as antifashionable continue to endure in our culture, feminism has been gradually embraced as a fashionable concept both by the fashion world and the general public. Couture designers from Carl Lagerfeld at Chanel to Maria Grazia Chiuri at Dior utilize feminism to make fashionable statements that do not reject ideas of femininity and beauty but claim them as a source of power.[8] When Chiuri became in July 2016 Dior's first woman chief designer, she featured in her debut collection a T-shirt bearing the title of Chimamanda Ngozi Adichie's famous essay, "We Should All Be Feminists." Signaling a new era for the brand not known for its feminist attitudes, Chiuri's T-shirt sent a strong message regarding the agenda she sought to promote. But perhaps more importantly, the shirt turned feminism into a popular fashionable statement

Indeed, although Chiuri's T-shirt debut predated the 2016 presidential elections, its feminist message received much more visibility and urgency by the time the outfit reached the stores in May 2017. Celebrities—most notably Rihanna—wore it to convey their political views and to advance a feminist agenda.[9] And while with its $710 price tag the shirt could have never become a mass fashion, it was part of a growing trend after the elections in which women devised new models of political engagement through their clothes. If celebrities such as Rihanna turned the Dior T-shirt into a rallying cry of feminist resistance, many other millions used their pink pussyhats to express their outrage and make their voices heard against the misogyny and racism of the Trump administration. Sending a powerful visual message of unity, protest, and power, the pussyhat became for a short while a popular fashionable statement, symbolizing women's resistance in the current political climate.[10] "Wearing pink together is a powerful statement that we are unapologetically feminine and we unapologetically stand for women's rights!" declared the Pussyhat Project's website.[11] As they claimed fashion as a feminist means of power and pleasure, these women—like their predecessors—asserted fashion's relevancy to struggles for gender equality and social justice, creatively shaping a new feminist presence in the public sphere.

The political usefulness of fashion also received renewed attention from women politicians who made it part of their political vocabulary. They do not view fashion as oppressive, belittling, or just superficial, but instead harness feminism's fashionable legacies to promote their cause and to shape public images and opinions. Unlike the Girlie feminists from *BUST*, however, these politicians look to early twentieth-century suffragists for inspiration, finding the color white useful to convey feminist pride and power. For them, the clothes they wear are not just accessories in their campaigns but an integral part of their message. "I wore all-white today to honor the women who paved the path before me, and for all the women yet to come," Representative Alexandria Ocasio-Cortez tweeted when she was sworn into Congress in 2018. Referring to the suffragists as her influence, as well as to other pathbreaking women who came before her, she asserted the new role of fashion in the political realm. "From suffragettes to Shirley Chisholm, I wouldn't be here if it wasn't for the mothers of the movement."[12] By invoking the fashionable language of the suffragists, women politicians position themselves within a long tradition of fashionable feminism, bridging these seemingly separate fields.[13] They are treating fashion and appearance not as an oppressive tool to be ignored or resisted but as a liberating force through which they could reclaim their voice and power.[14]

As fashion serves both as a mirror of social changes and as a medium through which people generate and make meaning of these changes, its political power is unlikely to fade away anytime soon. Indeed, as a *Washington Post* reporter commented in 2019, "fashion is increasingly being used as an exclamation point at the end of a pointed statement."[15] However, more than a reaction to the current political moment, the current fashionable politics are part of a long history of women's engagement with clothes to express feminist ideas. In order to fully understand the impact of fashion statements like the ones we see today, it is important to look at the long history of the feminist uses of fashion that this book delineates. This broader context, which threads together the fashionable practices of women in the past with those of the present, points to the longevity and persistence of the notion that fashion can be an empowering, liberating, and enjoyable force in the lives of women. As we pay more attention to the joyful aspects of feminism, we can also reimagine it not only as a constant struggle but also as an appealing everyday practice and a constructive force.

Fashion styles, like politics, have changed throughout the period this book covers, and they continue to change. Yet, the multiple and complex ways in which the women in this book engaged with fashion are still very much relevant to current feminist battles. Women today, as in previous generations, try to navigate the oppressive messages that consumer and popular culture send regarding their bodies, their look, and their behaviors. But they also seek to enjoy the pleasures and liberating sensations that wearing a short skirt or a sexy dress provide them. Fashion for them is an accessible medium through which they can express their claims and their identities. Furthermore, as this book shows, there is not a clear distinction between fashion and political agency. Fashion can be a useful vehicle for articulating feminist ideas and attitudes, and feminism can promote fashionability. Of course, "dress[ing] like a feminist" as the *BUST* editors suggested, or donning a T-shirt with a feminist slogan, does not necessarily make one a feminist.[16] And while fashion statements can be powerful, they are not always the most meaningful way to advance women's rights. Yet, we should not dismiss ways in which fashion can open a space for activism and resistance. Whether it is by legitimizing feminist ideas in mainstream culture, or by creating a common identity among activists, the way we dress matters.

In fashion, the trajectory and emphasis are often forward. However, by "looking back" at the fashionable politics of American feminism, we can begin to uncover the links between today's feminism and its past. Moreover, acknowledging this fashionable feminist past allows us to point to the continuities between feminist generations, as well as to revisit models of political activism. By shifting our attention to not only the content of feminist ideas, but also to how they were fashioned and delivered, we are able not only to better understand feminism's history, but also to form a framework for present and future action.

Notes

Abbreviations

FGI   Fashion Group International Records, Manuscripts and Archives Division, New York Public Library. Astor, Lenox and Tilden Foundations

MFR   Federated Department Stores' Records of Marshall Field & Company, Chicago History Museum

NAFAD   National Association of Fashion and Accessory Designers Inc. Records, National Archives for Black Women's History, National Park Service Museum Resource Center

SL   Arthur and Elizabeth Schlesinger Library, Radcliffe Institute for Advanced Study, Harvard University

SSC   Sophia Smith Collection, Smith College

Introduction

1. "The New Costume for the Ladies," *Lily* (1851), in Daniel Leonhard Purdy, ed., *The Rise of Fashion: A Reader* (Minneapolis: University of Minnesota Press, 2004), 109–13.

2. Elizabeth Cady Stanton, Susan Brownell Anthony, and Matilda Joslyn Gage, *History of Women Suffrage*, vol. 1, *1848–1861*, 2d ed. (Rochester, NY: Charles Mann, 1881, 1889), 470–71.

3. While feminism as an ideology that strives for women's equality and rights existed before the term "feminism" appeared around 1911–12, it would be anachronistic to

define nineteenth-century woman's rights advocates as feminists, despite their feminist ideas and politics. Thus, I use "feminism" and "feminists" to refer to twentieth-century ideas and reformers, while for nineteenth-century reformers I use the term "woman's rights advocates."

4. Carol Mattingly, *Appropriat[ing] Dress: Women's Rhetorical Style in Nineteenth-Century America* (Carbondale: Southern Illinois University Press, 2002), 4–8.

5. Since the French Revolution, trousers became the mark of masculine dress in the West, and thus contemporaries saw women wearing them a direct attack on male privilege. While women adopted masculine articles into their dress all throughout the nineteenth century, daily use of the bloomer made it so controversial. Jill Fields, *An Intimate Affair: Women, Lingerie, and Sexuality* (Berkeley: University of California Press, 2007), 25–26; Patricia Campbell Warner, *When the Girls Came Out to Play: The Birth of American Sportswear* (Amherst: University of Massachusetts Press, 2006), 149–57; Diana Crane, *Fashion and Its Social Agendas: Class, Gender, and Identity in Clothing* (Chicago: Chicago University Press, 2000), 112.

6. Stanton, Anthony, and Gage, *History of Women Suffrage*, 470.

7. For more on the bloomer incident and the debates that followed it, see Mattingly, *Appropriat[ing] Dress*; Gayle Fischer, *Pantaloons and Power: A Nineteenth-Century Dress Reform in the United States* (Kent, OH: Kent State University Press, 2001); Robert Riegel, "Women's Clothes and Women's Rights," *American Quarterly* 15, no. 3 (1963): 390–401; Lois Banner, *American Beauty* (Chicago: Chicago University Press, 1983), 86–105; Patricia A. Cunningham, *Reforming Women's Fashion, 1850–1920: Politics, Health, and Art* (Kent, OH: Kent State University Press, 2003), 38–48.

8. The late twentieth-century image of the radical feminist as a bra burner—an angry, masculine-looking, antifashionable woman—bore a striking resemblance to the bloomer of the nineteenth century. See chapter 5 for further discussion.

9. Cheryl Buckley and Hilary Fawcett, *Fashioning the Feminine: Representation and Women's Fashion from the Fin de Siècle to the Present* (London: I. B. Tauris, 2002), 9.

10. Simone de Beauvoir, *The Second Sex*, translated by Constance Borde and Sheila Malovany-Chevallier, with an introduction by Judith Thurman (New York: Vintage Books, 2011), originally published: Paris: Éditions Gallimard, 1949; Naomi Wolf, *The Beauty Myth: How Images of Beauty Are Used Against Women* (New York: W. Morrow, 1991); Andi Zeisler, *We Were Feminists Once: From Riot Grrrl to CoverGirl®, The Buying and Selling of a Political Movement* (New York: PublicAffairs, 2016). For a more complex analysis of this strand of feminist critique, see Astrid Henry, "Fashioning a Feminist Style, Or, How I Learned to Dress from Reading Feminist Theory," in *Fashion Talks: Undressing the Power of Style*, ed. Shira Tarrant and Marjorie Jolles (Albany: State University of New York, 2012), 13–32.

11. Buckley and Fawcett, *Fashioning the Feminine*, 8.

12. Kathy Peiss cautions against narrow reading of radical styles or subculture aesthetics purely as politics. Focusing on the example of the Zoot Suit, she argues that while clothes can be a statement of resistance to the mainstream culture, they often

articulate a range of social meanings that are not limited to politics of opposition. Peiss, *Zoot Suit: The Enigmatic Career of an Extreme Style* (Philadelphia: University of Pennsylvania Press, 2011), 8–9, 13.

13. Mattingly, *Appropriat[ing] Dress*; Nan Enstad, *Ladies of Labor, Girls of Adventure: Working Women, Popular Culture, and Labor Politics at the Turn of the Twentieth Century* (New York: Columbia University Press, 1999); Tanisha C. Ford, *Liberated Threads: Black Women, Style, and the Global Politics of Soul* (Chapel Hill: University of North Carolina Press, 2015); Betty Luther Hillman, *Dressing for the Culture Wars: Style and the Politics of Self-Presentation in the 1960s and 1970s* (Lincoln: University of Nebraska Press, 2015); Peiss, *Zoot Suit*.

14. Ilya Parkins and Elizabeth M. Sheehan, introduction, in *Cultures of Femininity in Modern Fashion*, ed. Ilya Parkins and Elizabeth M. Sheehan (Durham: University of New Hampshire Press, 2011), 1–3; Buckley and Fawcett, *Fashioning the Feminine*, 4–9.

15. Roland Barthes, *The Fashion System* (New York: Hill and Wang, 1983).

16. I take my definition of "fashion" from the work of Malcolm Bernard and Joanne Entwistle who see fashion as a social practice and a system that both affirms and constitutes meanings and identities. Malcolm Barnard, *Fashion as Communication*, 2d ed. (New York: Routledge, 2002), 11–12, 102–3; Joanne Entwistle, *The Fashioned Body: Fashion, Dress, and Modern Social Theory* (Cambridge, UK: Polity Press, 2015), 47–49.

17. I define "style" as a manner of dress or an assortment of garments that reflect specific aesthetic logic and meaning. A style can be an expression of individual taste as well as a group effort, yet it represents a more constant element than fashion.

18. Barnard, *Fashion as Communication*, 12; Entwistle, *Fashioned Body*, 49, 80–81.

19. Martha Weinman Lear, "The Second Feminist Wave," *New York Times*, March 10, 1968, 24–25, 50–62.

20. Lisa Tetrault's excellent account of the myth of Seneca Falls challenges the periodization of the "first wave" and its major narrative. Tetrault, *The Myth of Seneca Falls: Memory and the Women's Suffrage Movement, 1848–1898* (Chapel Hill: University of North Carolina Press, 2014).

21. There are debates on if and when a third wave (and even a fourth) emerged, but some scholars identify the 1990s as the resurgence of a third wave of feminism which focused on culture and was more intersectional in its character than previous waves. Yet, since the entire periodization of waves have come under scrutiny in recent years, we need to ask ourselves whether should we keep the designation of the Third Wave at all.

22. Linda Nicholson, "Feminism in 'Waves': Useful Metaphor or Not?," *New Politics* 12, no. 4 (Winter 2010), http://newpol.org/content/feminism-waves-useful-metaphor-or-not; Kathleen A. Laughlin et al., "Is It Time to Jump Ship? Historians Rethink the Waves Metaphor," *Feminist Formations* 22, no. 1 (Spring 2010): 76–135. Some scholars suggest replacing the metaphor of oceanic waves with radio waves, arguing that it

better captures the plurality of feminist attitudes and activism by considering different lengths and frequencies of movements as well as the simultaneous existence and overlapping of multiple movements across time and space. See Edna Kaeh Garrison, "Are We on a Wavelength Yet? On Feminist Oceanography, Radios and Third Wave Feminism," in *Different Wavelengths: Studies of the Contemporary Women's Movement*, ed. Jo Reger (New York: Routledge, 2005), 237–56; and also Nancy Hewitt, *No Permanent Waves: Recasting Histories of U.S, Feminism* (New Brunswick, NJ: Rutgers University Press, 2010).

23. This corpus is vast and growing, but herewith a few examples: Leila Rupp and Verta Taylor, *Survival in the Doldrums: The American Women's Rights Movement, 1945 to the 1960s* (New York: Oxford University Press, 1987); Joanne Meyerowitz, ed., *Not June Cleaver: Women and Gender in Postwar America, 1945–1960* (Philadelphia: Temple University Press, 1994); Annelise Orleck, *Common Sense and Little Fire: Women and Working-Class Politics in the United States 1900–1965* (Chapel Hill: University of North Carolina Press, 1995); Beverly Guy-Sheftall, *Words of Fire: An Anthology of African American Feminist Thought* (New York: New Press, 1995); Kate Weigand, *Red Feminism: American Communism and the Making of Women's Liberation* (Baltimore: Johns Hopkins University Press, 2001); Barbara Ransby, *Ella Baker and the Black Freedom Movement: A Radical Democratic Vision* (Chapel Hill: University of North Carolina Press, 2002); Dorothy Sue Cobble, *The Other Women's Movement: Workplace Justice and Social Rights in Modern America* (Princeton, NJ: Princeton University Press, 2004); Landon R. Y. Storrs, "Left-Feminism, the Consumer Movement, and Red Scare Politics in the United States, 1935–1960," *Journal of Women's Studies* 18, no. 3 (2006): 40–67; Kathleen A. Laughlin and Jacqueline L. Castledine, eds., *Breaking the Wave: Women, Their Organizations, and Feminism, 1945–1985* (New York: Routledge, 2011); Stephanie Gilmore, *Groundswell: Grassroots Feminist Activism in Postwar America* (New York: Routledge, 2013); Ashley D. Farmer, *Remaking Black Power: How Black Women Transformed an Era* (Chapel Hill: University of North Carolina Press, 2017); Jessica Wilkerson, *To Live Here, You Have to Fight: How Women Led Appalachian Movements for Social Justice* (Urbana: University of Illinois Press, 2019).

24. Studies that underline the fashion politics of feminism tend to focus either on nineteenth-century dress reform and the bloomer or on the 1960s and 1970s women's liberation movement, thus obscuring the continuities between these two moments. See, for example, Fischer, *Pantaloons and Power*; Cunningham, *Reforming Women's Fashion*; Hillman, *Dressing for the Cultural Wars*; Jo B. Paoletti, *Sex and Unisex: Fashion, Feminism, and the Sexual Revolution* (Bloomington: Indiana University Press, 2015). A notable exception is Linda M. Scott, *Fresh Lipstick: Redressing Fashion and Feminism* (New York: Palgrave MacMillan, 2005), that examines the entire period from the nineteenth century to the present, but its analysis does not address the waves metaphor or aim to challenge it.

25. Kathy Peiss, *Hope in a Jar: The Making of America's Beauty Culture* (New York: Owl Books, 1998), 6.

26. In fact, since feminists and proponents of women's rights oftentimes appropriated the mainstream styles, there was not much stylistic difference between them and their opponents, who also adopted the prevalent fashions.

27. Barnard, *Fashion as Communication*, 29–31.

Chapter 1. Fashioning the New Woman

1. Carolyn Kitch, *The Girl on the Magazine Cover: The Origins of Visual Stereotypes in American Mass Media* (Chapel Hill: University of North Carolina Press, 2001), 37–39.

2. Charlotte Perkins Gilman, *Women and Economics: A Study of the Economic Relation between Men and Women as a Factor in Social Evolution* (Boston: Small, Maynard, and Company, 1898), 148–49.

3. Scholars identify the New Woman as either a political figure, focusing on her activism in social movements and reform, or as a literary figure that was part of a broader cultural change that manifested itself in artistic forms and popular culture. Nancy F. Cott, *The Grounding of Modern Feminism* (New Haven, CT: Yale University Press, 1987); Jean Matthews, *The Rise of the New Woman: The Woman's Movement in America, 1875–1930* (Chicago: Ivan R. Dee, 2003); Marjorie Spruill Wheeler, *New Women of the New South: The Leaders of the Woman Suffrage Movement in the Southern States* (New York: Oxford University Press, 1993); Ellen Wiley Todd, *The "New Woman" Revised: Painting and Gender Politics on Fourteenth Street* (Berkeley: University of California Press, 1993); Martha H. Patterson, *Beyond the Gibson Girl: Reimagining the American New Woman, 1895–1915* (Urbana: University of Illinois Press, 2005); Martha Banta, *Imaging American Women: Ideas and Ideals in Cultural History* (New York: Columbia University Press, 1987); Kitch, *Girl on the Magazine Cover*; Patricia Marks, *Bicycles, Bangs, and Bloomers: The New Woman in the Popular Press* (Lexington: University Press of Kentucky, 1990). In recent years, scholars have also pointed to the global aspects of the New Woman. See in particular, Elizabeth Otto and Vanessa Rocco, eds., *The New Woman International: Representations in Photography and Film from the 1870s to the 1960s* (Ann Arbor: University of Michigan Press, 2011); Ann Heilmann and Margaret Beetham, eds., *New Woman Hybridities: Femininity, Feminism, and International Consumer Culture, 1880–1930* (New York: Routledge, 2004).

4. Martha H. Patterson, *The American New Woman Revisited: A Reader, 1894–1930* (New Brunswick, NJ: Rutgers University Press, 2008), 1–25.

5. Maria Elena Buszek, *Pin-Up Grrrls: Feminism, Sexuality, Popular Culture* (Durham, NC: Duke University Press, 2006), 34–35. For further discussion on the True Woman, see Barbara Welter, "The Cult of True Womanhood: 1820–1860," *American Quarterly* 18, no. 2 (1966): 151–74.

Notes to Chapter 1

6. Caroline Rennolds Milbank, *New York Fashions: The Evolution of American Style* (New York: Harry N. Abrams, 1996), 48.

7. Ibid.; Daniel James Cole and Nancy Deihl, *The History of Modern Fashion* (London: Laurence King, 2015), 62.

8. Edward Marshall, "The Gibson Girl Analyzed by Her Originator," *New York Times*, November 20, 1910, SM6.

9. For more on the other "Girls," see "The American Girl" and "Dangerous Women and the Crisis of Masculinity" in Kitch, *Girl on the Magazine Cover*, 37–74.

10. Robert Bridges, "Charles Dana Gibson," *Collier's Weekly*, October 15, 1904, 12.

11. Ellen Gruber Garvey, *The Adman in the Parlor: Magazines and the Gendering of Consumer Culture, 1880s to 1910s* (New York: Oxford University Press, 1996), 9, 11.

12. Kitch, *Girl on the Magazine Cover*, 37–39; Lois W. Banner, *American Beauty* (Chicago: Chicago University Press, 1983), 156–58.

13. Patterson, *Beyond the Gibson Girl*, 37–39; Banner, *American Beauty*, 169.

14. Kitch, *Girl on the Magazine Cover*, 44; Banner, *American Beauty*, 165–66; Buszek, *Pin-Up Grrrls*, 87–88.

15. Cole and Deihl, *History of Modern Fashion*, 61–63; Charles Dana Gibson, "School Days" (illustration), *Scribner's Magazine*, November 1899, 673.

16. Lynn D. Gordon, "The Gibson Girl Goes to College: Popular Culture and Women's Height Education in the Progressive Era, 1890–1920," *American Quarterly* 39, no. 2 (1987): 214

17. Kitch, *Girl on the Magazine Cover*, 44; Buszek, *Pin-Up Grrrls*, 96.

18. Margret A. Lowe, *Looking Good: College Women and Body Image, 1875–1930* (Baltimore: Johns Hopkins University Press, 2003), 4, 164.

19. "Group of Students at Radcliffe, including Maud Wood Park; Inez Haynes Irwin; and Beulah Dix," 1898, folder PA2–19, Maud Wood Park Papers (Woman's Rights Collection), SL.

20. "Untitled Photograph," folder PD.2, Doris Stevens Papers, SL.

21. "Our Sweet College Graduates of 1895," *New York World*, June 22, 1895, 4.

22. John D'Emilio and Estelle B. Freedman, *Intimate Matters: A History of Sexuality in America*, 3d ed. (Chicago: Chicago University Press, 2012), 190; Gordon, "Gibson Girl Goes to College," 223.

23. Mary Trigg, *Feminism as Life's Work: Four American Women through Two World Wars* (New Brunswick, NJ: Rutgers University Press, 2014), 32–33.

24. Inez Haynes Irwin, *Adventures of Yesterday*, reel 974–75, no. 17, Papers of Inez Haynes Gillmore, 1872–1945, SL.

25. Inez Haynes Irwin, *Angles and Amazons: A Hundred Years of American Women* (New York: Doubleday, 1934), 267–74.

26. Robert Grant "Charles Dana Gibson: The Artist and His Art," *Collier's Weekly*, November 29, 1902, 8; Caroline Ticknor, "The Steel-Engraving Lady and the Gibson Girl," *Atlantic Monthly Magazine*, July 1901, 105–8.

27. Banner, *American Beauty*, 154; Buszek, *Pin-Up Grrrls*, 92.

28. Paterson, *Beyond the Gibson Girl*, 45–47.

29. Treva B. Lindsey, *Colored No More: Reinventing Black Womanhood in Washington, D.C.* (Urbana: University of Illinois Press, 2017), 55–57.

30. Evelyn Brooks Higginbotham, *Righteous Discontent: The Women's Movement in the Black Baptist Church, 1880–1920* (Cambridge, MA: Harvard University Press, 1993), 185–92; Victoria Wolcott, *Remaking Respectability: African American Women in Interwar Detroit* (Chapel Hill: University of North Carolina Press, 2000), 4–7, 18–20, 38–39, 56–59, 63; Michele Mitchell, *Righteous Propagation: African Americans and the Politics of Racial Destiny after Reconstruction* (Chapel Hill: University of North Carolina Press, 2004), 10, 84–85; Anne Stavney, "'Mothers of Tomorrow': The New Negro Renaissance and the Politics of Maternal Representation," *African American Review* 32, no. 4 (1998): 537.

31. Emma Azalia Hackley, *The Colored Girl Beautiful* (Kansas City, MO: Burton Publishing Company, 1916), 75.

32. Mary Church Terrell, "What the Colored Women's League Will Do," *Afro-American Journal of Fashion*, May–June 1893, reel 6, Records of the National Association of Colored Women's Clubs 1895–1992 (microform), consulting editor, Lillian Serece Williams; associate editor, Randolph Boehm (Bethesda, MD: University Publications of America, 1993).

33. Noliwe Rooks, *Ladies' Pages: African American Women's Magazines and the Culture That Made Them* (New Brunswick, NJ: Rutgers University Press, 2004) 49–52.

34. John H. Adams Jr., "Rough Sketches: A Study of the Features of the New Negro Woman," *Voice of the Negro*, August 1904, 324–25.

35. Lowe, *Looking Good*, 80–81; Rooks, *Ladies' Pages*, 49.

36. W. E. B. Du Bois, collector, and Thomas E. Askew, photographer, *Four African American women seated on steps of building at Atlanta University, Georgia*, Atlanta, Georgia, 1899 [or 1900] photograph, Library of Congress, https://www.loc.gov/item/95507126/, accessed January 13, 2021.

37. Patricia K. Hunt, "Clothing as an Expression of History: The Dress of African-American Women in Georgia, 1880–1915," *Georgia Historical Quarterly* 76, no. 2 (1992): 459–71.

38. "Nannie Helen Burroughs," *Voice of the Negro*, June 1904, 227; Tera W. Hunter, *To 'Joy My Freedom: Southern Black Women's Lives and Labors after the Civil War* (Cambridge, MA: Harvard University Press, 1997), 182–83.

39. Quoted in Deborah Gray White, *Too Heavy a Load: Black Women in Defense of Themselves, 1894–1994* (New York: W. W. Norton, 1999), 21–23.

40. The separate skirt that went along with the shirtwaist was also mass-produced, yet it was the shirtwaist that became the symbol of the ready-made industry. Claudia Brush Kidwell and Margaret C. S. Christman, *Suiting Everyone: The Democratization of Clothing in America* (Washington, DC: Smithsonian Institution Press, 1974), 145.

41. G.S.H., "Shirt-Waists, Bodices, Skirts and Sleeves," *Ladies' World*, June 1897, 19.

42. Jean L. Parsons, "The Shirtwaist: Changing the Commerce of Fashion," *Fash-

ion, Style, and Popular Culture 5, no. 1 (2018): 18; *Sears Roebuck & Co. Catalog*, no. 109 (Spring 1900): 605, 730; Mme. Rumford, "The Prevailing Styles for Early Summer," *Colored American Magazine*, June 1901, 130.

43. Quote appears in Kidwell and Christman, *Suiting Everyone*, 143, 145.

44. Kidwell and Christman, *Suiting Everyone*, 143; Parsons, "Shirtwaist," 8–9, 13.

45. Ella J. Cannady, "Shirt-Waists," *Ladies' World*, April 1903, 20; "The Season's Sensation in Waists," *Half-Century Magazine*, April 1917, 15.

46. Margaret Walsh, "The Democratization of Fashion: The Emergence of the Women's Dress Pattern Industry," *Journal of American History* 66, no. 2 (1979): 304, 311.

47. *Sears Roebuck & Co. Catalog*, no. 102 (Spring 1896): 168.

48. G.S.H., "Fashion Notes," *Ladies' World*, September 1901, 41.

49. Wendy Gamber, *The Female Economy: The Millinery and Dressmaking Trades, 1860–1930* (Urbana: University of Illinois Press, 1997), 131–33, 151, 153, 216; Nancy L. Green, *Ready-to-Wear and Ready-to-Work: A Century of Industry and Immigrants in Paris and New York* (Durham, NC: Duke University Press, 1997), 32.

50. Green, *Ready-to-Wear and Ready-to-Work*, 46–47.

51. Cannady, "Shirt-Waists," 20.

52. Parsons, "Shirtwaist," 8. For more on professional dressmakers, see Gamber, *Female Economy*.

53. "Waist," *John Wanamaker Catalogue*, Fall Winter 1902–3, 19; "Ladies' Waists," *H. O'neill & Co. Fashion Catalogue*, Spring and Summer 1898, 24.

54. Parsons, "Shirtwaist," 18–20; Nan Enstad, *Ladies of Labor, Girls of Adventure: Working Women, Popular Culture, and Labor Politics at the Turn of the Twentieth Century* (New York: Columbia University Press, 1999), 28–29. Cheap shirtwaists and patterns costing about 20 cents for a pattern and 45–75 cents for a waist could also be bought through trade catalogs. See, for example, *Standard Fashion Company Trade Pattern Catalog*, May 1900, 5; *Sears Roebuck & Co. Catalog*, no. 102 (Spring 1896): 168.

55. Enstad, *Ladies of Labor*, 30.

56. Quoted in Barbara Schreier, *Becoming American Women: Clothing and the Jewish Immigration Experience 1880–1920* (Chicago: Chicago Historical Society, 1994), 69.

57. Rose Schneiderman, *All for One* (New York: P. S. Eriksson, 1967), 44, 175.

58. Quoted in Schreier, *Becoming American Women*, 56.

59. Enstad, *Ladies of Labor*, 64–67.

60. Ibid., 30, 64–67; Schreier, *Becoming American Women*, 68–69. Working-class saleswomen had different tactics for using workplace resources, turning to stealing if they could not afford what they wanted. Susan Porter Benson, *Counter Cultures: Saleswomen, Managers, and Consumers in American Department Stores, 1890–1940* (Urbana: University of Illinois Press, 1986), 238–39.

61. Paul Nystrom, *Economics of Fashion* (New York: Roland Press Co., 1928), 375.

62. Benson, *Counter Cultures*, 139–40.

63. "Marshall Field's Book of Rules," 1902, folder 5, box 03024, MFR.

Notes to Chapter 1

64. "Marshall Field's Book of Rules," n.d. (ca. 1910), box 18001, RG18, MFR. Employee resistance to the regulations might have prompted management's stricter enforcement. Benson, *Counter Cultures*, 236–238.

65. "Notices," September 25, 1912, box 03082, MFR, emphasis in original.

66. Schreier, *Becoming American Woman*, 69; Deirdre Clemente, "Striking Ensembles: The Importance of Clothing on the Picket Line," *Labor Studies Journal* 30, no. 4 (2006): 4.

67. Clara Lemlich, "The Inside of a Shirtwaist Factory," *Good Housekeeping*, March 1912, 368.

68. "Leader Tells Why 40,000 Girls Struck," *New York Evening Journal*, November 26, 1909, 3.

69. Enstad, *Ladies of Labor*, 50, 82–83.

70. For more information on Lemlich and the 1909 strike, see Enstad, *Ladies of Labor*; Annelise Orleck, *Common Sense and Little Fire: Women and Working-Class Politics in the United States 1900–1965* (Chapel Hill: University of North Carolina Press, 1995).

71. Sarah Comstock, "The Uprising of the Girls," *Collier's*, December 25, 1909, 14–15; Clemente, "Striking Ensembles," 6; Enstad, *Ladies of Labor*, 117, 131–33, 148–50.

72. Enstad, *Ladies of Labor*, 128; Maxine Schwartz Seller, "The Uprising of the Twenty Thousand: Sex, Class and Ethnicity in the Shirtwaist Markers' Strike of 1909," in *Struggle and a Hard Battle: Essays on Working-Class Immigrants*, ed. Dirk Hoerder (DeKalb: Northern Illinois University Press, 1986), 261.

73. "College Girls as Pickets in a Strike," *New York Times*, December 19, 1909, SM5.

74. Elizabeth Walling, "The Girl of the Period," *Ladies' World*, October 1896, 10.

75. Patricia Campbell Warner, *When the Girls Came Out to Play: The Birth of American Sportswear* (Amherst: University of Massachusetts Press, 2006), 118–19.

76. Ibid., 117–18.

77. Mary Wheeler, "The Fortunate Woman of To-Day," *Ladies' World*, June 1901, 11. Mary Wheeler was Mary Sargent Hopkins's pseudonym.

78. Warner, *When the Girls*, 114–15.

79. Indiana Bicycle Co. advertisement, *Harper's Bazaar*, May 23, 1896, 450; Columbia Bicycle advertisement, *Vogue*, April 2, 1896, vii; "Bicycle Department," *Sears Roebuck & Co. Catalog*, Fall 1900, 417.

80. Evan Friss, *The Cycling City: Bicycles and Urban America in the 1890s* (Chicago: University of Chicago Press, 2015), 160–61; Sarah A. Gordon, "Clothing for Sport: Home Sewing as a Laboratory for New Standards," chapter 5 of *Make It Yourself: Home Sewing, Gender, and Culture, 1890–1930* (New York: Columbia University Press, 2007), http://www.gutenberg-e.org/gordon/chap5.html#pgtop.

81. Nellie Bly, "Champion of Her Sex," *New York World*, February 2, 1896, 10.

82. Mary Sargent Hopkins, "Random Notes and Reminiscences," *Ladies' World*, February 1898, 10.

83. Lisa S. Strange and Robert S. Brown, "The Bicycle, Women's Rights, and Eliza-

beth Cady Stanton," *Women's Studies: An Interdisciplinary Journal* 31, no. 5 (2002): 615–16; Friss, *Cycling City*, 161–63, 171–76.

84. Hopkins, "Random Notes and Reminiscences," 10.

85. "Will They Wear 'Em?," *Washington Evening Star*, November 16, 1895, 16.

86. Warner, *When the Girls*, 104–5, 114, 117; Diana Crane, *Fashion and Its Social Agendas: Class, Gender, and Identity in Clothing* (Chicago: University of Chicago Press, 2000), 117.

87. Elizabeth Cady Stanton, Susan Brownell Anthony, and Matilda Joslyn Gage, *History of Women Suffrage*, vol. 1, *1848–1861* (New York, 1881), 844; Patricia A. Cunningham, *Reforming Women's Fashion, 1850–1920: Politics, Health, and Art* (Kent, OH: Kent State University Press, 2003), 33, 57. The scandal that followed Bloomer's and other activists' adoption of the outfit caused the press to identify every reform dress that included trousers with the name Bloomer.

88. Elizabeth Cady Stanton, "Shall Women Ride the Bicycle?," reel 35, 1066–73, *Papers of Elizabeth Cady Stanton and Susan B. Anthony: Microfilm Edition*, ed. Patricia G. Holland and Ann D. Gordon.

89. Frances Willard, *A Wheel within a Wheel: How I Learned to Ride a Bicycle* (New York: F. H. Revell Co., 1895), 39; Elizabeth Cady Stanton, "The Era of the Bicycle," *Woman's Tribune*, July 20, 1895, 112.

90. Warner, *When the Girls*, 122, 127; Friss, *Cycling City*, 171–76.

91. "Will They Wear 'Em?," 16.

92. G.S.H., "Bicycle Costumes," *Ladies' World*, January 1896, 17.

93. Constance Astor Choate, "Paris and New York Fashions," *American Woman*, August 1897, 11.

94. G.S.H., "Bicycle Outing Fashions," *Ladies' World*, July 1896, 12.

95. Adelia K. Brainerd, "The Outdoor Woman," *Harper's Bazaar*, May 2, 1896, 383.

96. Friss, *Cycling City*, 165–68, 171.

97. See, for example, C. J. Taylor, "Independence Day of the Future," Library of Congress, https://www.loc.gov/pictures/item/2012648736/, accessed January 13, 2021; "The New Woman—Wash Day," Library of Congress, https://www.loc.gov/pictures/item/90706169/, accessed January 13, 2021.

98. Warner, *When the Girls*, 123; "Suit, Bicycling," 48.611, Permanent Collection, Western Reserve Historical Society, Cleveland.

99. Onlex Cycling Costume advertisement, *Harper's Bazaar*, April 25, 1896, 371.

100. Choate, "Paris and New York Fashions," 11; Brainerd, "Outdoor Woman."

101. Mary Sargent Hopkins, "Suitable Costumes for Rainy Days," *Ladies' World*, April 1897, 10.

102. Ibid.

103. Ibid.

104. "Rainy Day Euchre Party," *New-York Tribune*, November 22, 1899, 7; Emma Churchman Hewitt, "The Business Woman and Her Uniform," *Ladies' World*, March

1902, 11; "Approve Short Skirts," *New-York Tribune*, March 3, 1904, 7; "Baltimore's Rainy Day Club," *New-York Tribune*, March 4, 1897, 5.

105. "Rainy Day Club Meets," *New York Times*, February 4, 1897, 7; "New York Women Imitated," *New York Times*, January 1, 1898, 9.

106. Hopkins, "Suitable Costumes for Rainy Days."

107. "Rainy Day Club Meets," 7.

108. "Rainy Day Club Queries," *New York Times*, March 21, 1897, 11.

109. "'Rainy Day' Discussion," *New-York Tribune*, April 7, 1898, 5.

110. Hopkins, "Suitable Costumes for Rainy Days."

111. "'Rainy Day' Discussion."

112. "The Rainy Day Club," *New-York Tribune*, January 7, 1897, 5.

113. Martha Clark Rankin, "Woman's Greatest Lack," *Ladies' World*, March 1899, 27. Club members were not the only ones to frame pockets as a feminist issue; Elizabeth Cady Stanton also mentioned the lack of pockets in her feminist struggle for suffrage. Elizabeth Cady Stanton, "Fashions Against Suffrage," *New-York Tribune*, June 14, 1899, 7.

114. Hopkins, "Suitable Costumes for Rainy Days"; "The Rainy Day Club," *New-York Tribune*, November 6, 1896, 5.

115. "Harper's Miscellaneous Patterns," *Harper's Bazaar*, September 1, 1900, B15; "Cut Paper Patterns and Hints for Home Dressmaking," *Harper's Bazaar*, February 24, 1900, 166; "Outing Costumes," *Harper's Bazaar*, February 1902, 151; "Dress and Gossip of Paris," *Delineator*, 1903, 583.

116. Emily Wight, "The Dress of the Business Girl," *Ladies' Home Journal*, January 1900, 29.

117. "Beauty and Dress Reform," *New York Times*, December 2, 1897, 5.

118. "No Needle or Hourglass Style for Universal Gown," *New-York Tribune*, April 12, 1915, 5.

119. "Rainy Daisies' Triumph," *New York Times*, October 31, 1921, 35.

Chapter 2. Styling Women's Rights

1. Florence Flynn, "'Attract and Allure,' Cries the Suffragette," *New-York Tribune*, April 30, 1911, V7.

2. For further discussion on the suffrage campaign and the change in strategy, see Robert Booth Fowler and Spenser Jones, "Carrie Chapman Catt and the Last Years of the Struggle for Woman Suffrage: 'The Winning Plan,'" 130–42, and Linda Ford, "Alice Paul and the Politics of Nonviolent Protest," 174–88, both in *Votes For Women: The Struggle for Suffrage Revisited*, ed. Jean Baker (New York: Oxford University Press, 2002); Ellen Dubois, "Working Women, Class Relations, and Suffrage Militance: Harriot Stanton Blatch and the New York Woman Suffrage Movement 1894–1909," *Journal of American History*, 74, no. 1 (June 1987): 34–58; Michael McGerr, "Political

Style and Women's Power 1830–1930," *Journal of American History* 77, no. 3 (December 1990): 864–85.

3. On the spectacular aspects of the suffrage campaign, see Susan Glenn, *Female Spectacle: The Theatrical Roots of Modern Feminism* (Cambridge, MA: Harvard University Press, 2000); Lisa Tickner, *The Spectacle of Women: Imagery of the Suffrage Campaign, 1907–1914* (Chicago: University of Chicago Press, 1988); McGerr, "Political Style and Women's Power"; Margaret Finnegan, *Selling Suffrage: Consumer Culture and Votes for Women* (New York: Columbia University Press, 1999); Mary Chapman, *Making Noise, Making News: Suffrage Print Culture and U.S. Modernism* (New York: Oxford University Press, 2014).

4. Sandra Adickes, *To Be Young Was Very Heaven: Women in New York Before the First World War* (New York: St. Martin's Press, 1997), 89–90; Nancy F. Cott, *The Grounding of Modern Feminism* (New Haven, CT: Yale University Press, 1987), 13–15, 35. According to Cott, feminism was born ideologically on the left of the political spectrum and was influenced by socialism.

5. Marie Jenny Howe, "Feminism," *New Review* 2, no. 8 (August 1914): 441–42.

6. Elizabeth Francis, *The Secret Treachery of Words: Feminism and Modernism in America* (Minneapolis: University of Minnesota Press, 2002), xx, xxii.

7. Nina Wilcox Putnam, "Fashion and Feminism," *Forum*, October 1914, 580.

8. Melyssa Wrisley, "'Fashion I Despised': Charlotte Perkins Gilman and American Dress Reform, 1880–1920," *Dress* 33, no. 1 (2006): 97.

9. Elizabeth Cady Stanton, "Letter to the National Dress Reform Association Convention," *Sibyl*, February 1, 1857, 119–20, reel 8:833–34, *Papers of Elizabeth Cady Stanton and Susan B. Anthony: Microfilm Edition*, ed. Patricia G. Holland and Ann D. Gordon. The notion that in order for women to achieve freedom they need to discard their slavish adherence to fashion dictates was a common argument among woman's rights advocates. See, for example, Elisabeth Stuart Phelps, *What to Wear?* (Boston: J. R. Osgood and Co., 1873), 34.

10. Putnam, "Fashion and Feminism," 584.

11. There was never a single suffrage movement, and suffragists, like feminists, presented diverse approaches to the best way to secure the vote. The National American Woman's Suffrage Association (NAWSA), which was the largest suffrage organization, supported a more conservative tactic of convincing state legislators to grant women the vote. Frustrated by what they saw as a timid approach, some of the younger members in the movement formed in 1913 the Congressional Union, an affiliate body within NAWSA, to fight for a constitutional amendment, and later left NAWSA to form the National Woman's Party (NWP), which was a more radical and militant organization.

12. For White middle-class suffragists, this approach and use of fashion helped them in stressing their class and race privilege when they campaigned for suffrage. On the racist and classist attitudes in the suffrage movement, see Louise Newman, *White Woman's Rights: The Racial Origins of Feminism in the United States* (New York: Oxford University Press, 1999), 56–85.

13. Maud C. Hessler, "Better Dress Standards," *Journal of Home Economics*, November 1912, 469.

14. Finnegan, *Selling Suffrage*, 2, 79–81; Marlis Schweitzer, *When Broadway Was the Runway: Theater, Fashion, and American Culture* (Philadelphia: University of Pennsylvania Press, 2009), 156–57, 159.

15. Helena Hill Weed, "A Feminist Rises in Defense of Bobbed Hair," *New-York Tribune*, September 18, 1921, D6; "Loveable Nature to Win Men in Vote War," *San Francisco Examiner*, April 6, 1913, 70.

16. Quoted in Flynn, "Attract and Allure," V7.

17. Finnegan, *Selling Suffrage*, 93; Marth Banta, *Imaging American Women: Idea and Ideals in Cultural History* (New York: Columbia University Press, 1987), 82. For depictions of suffragists as masculine women, see "Why Shouldn't We Vote?," Library of Congress Prints and Photographs Division, http://www.loc.gov/pictures/resource/var.0899/, accessed January 13, 2021; Rodney Thompson, "Militants," *Life*, March 27, 1913, 616.

18. Inez Milholland quoted in "Mrs. Belmont Home for Suffrage War," *New York Times*, September 16, 1910. For more on Milholland's use of her fashionable image in the service of suffrage, see Ann Marie Nicolosi, "'The Most Beautiful Suffragette': Inez Milholland and the Political Currency of Beauty," *Journal of Gilded Age and Progressive Era* 6, no. 3 (2007): 287–309; Linda J. Lumsden, *Inez: The Life and Times of Inez Milholland* (Bloomington: Indiana University Press, 2004).

19. "'Throw-Away-Your-Corset' Crusade opens here Today," *Washington Post*, March 1, 1912, 2.

20. Inez Milholland quoted in "Vote an Aid to Beauty," *Washington Post*, March 3, 1913, 10.

21. Maud Wood Park quoted in "Ballot First Aid to Beauty, Says Crusader," n.d., reel D47, Maud Wood Park Papers (Woman's Rights Collection), SL.

22. Charlotte Perkins Gilman, *The Dress of Women: A Critical Introduction to the Symbolism and Sociology of Clothing*, ed. by Michael R. Hill and Mary Jo Deegan (Westport, CT: Greenwood Press, 2002), 134. Gilman differentiated between beauty and femininity, which she perceived as human and desirable qualities, and sex distinction, which she understood as the use of appearance to distort the "true" meaning of femininity so that women will be kept in their subservient position.

23. Laura L. Behling, *The Masculine Woman in America, 1890–1935* (Urbana: University of Illinois Press, 2001), 35–39.

24. Cott, *Grounding of Modern Feminism*, 19–20; Alieen S. Kraditor also identified two arguments for suffrage yet she divides them to arguments based on justice (equality to men) and arguments based on expediency (difference from men). Kraditor, *The Ideas of the Woman Suffrage Movement, 1890–1920* (New York: Columbia University Press, 1965), 44–47.

25. Lydia Commander quoted in Dubois, "Working Women," 56.

26. Cott, *Grounding of Modern Feminism*, 29–30.

27. Glenn, *Female Spectacle*, 133.

28. Mary Holland Kinkaid, "The Feminine Charms of the Woman Militant," *Good Housekeeping*, February 1912, 146–55; Banta, *Imaging American Women*, 64–67.

29. Cornelia is remembered as an archetype of a virtuous Roman woman who played a vital role in her two sons' political careers and who has been frequently depicted in art as the "mother of the Gracchi," an image that Milholland and other suffragists adroitly utilized.

30. Kinkaid, "Feminine Charms of the Woman Militant," 152.

31. Behling, *Masculine Woman in America*, 43.

32. Treva B. Lindsey, *Colored No More: Reinventing Black Womanhood in Washington, D.C.* (Urbana: University of Illinois Press, 2017), 100, 106.

33. Mary Church Terrell, "Woman's Case in Equity," *Colored American*, February 17, 1900, 1. Other Black suffragists also harnessed motherhood and domesticity as arguments for suffrage. See, for example, Adella Hunt Logan, "Colored Women as Voters," *Crisis*, September 1912, 242–43; Mrs. Coralie Franklin Cook, "Votes for Mothers," *Crisis*, August 1915, 184–85.

34. Elizabeth Newport Hepburn, "Suffragists' Clothes," *New York Times*, May 15, 1913, 10.

35. For further discussion on the importance of looking feminine and respectable to working women strikers' success, see Nan Enstad, *Ladies of Labor, Girls of Adventure: Working Women, Popular Culture, and Labor Politics at the Turn of the Twentieth Century* (New York: Columbia University Press, 1999).

36. More on the 1913 parade, see James Glen Stovall, *Seeing Suffrage: The Washington Suffrage Parade of 1913, Its Pictures, and Its Effect on the American Political Landscape* (Knoxville: University of Tennessee Press, 2013).

37. Lumsden, *Inez*, 84, 87.

38. After Milholland's premature death in 1916 while she was on the campaign—probably from undiagnosed pernicious anemia—the NWP used her image (see fig. 2.1) as the movement's logo to harness support for suffrage by emphasizing Milholland's martyrdom and sacrifice. Milholland collapsed on the podium while giving a speech in Los Angeles on October 23, 1916. She was hospitalized and died a month later. Nicolosi, "Most Beautiful Suffragette," 305–7.

39. Chapman, *Making Noise*, 5–6.

40. Lindsey, *Colored No More*, 106, 108.

41. Elizabeth Ewing, *History of Twentieth Century Fashion* (New York: Costume and Fashion Press, 2001), 66.

42. "Paris (From Our Own Correspondent)," *Vogue*, May 21, 1908, 706.

43. Ewing, *History of Twentieth Century Fashion*, 62; Caroline Rennolds Milbank, *New York Fashions: The Evolution of American Style* (New York: Harry N. Abrams, 1996), 52–54.

44. Patricia A. Cunningham, *Reforming Women's Fashion, 1850–1920: Politics, Health, and Art* (Kent, OH: Kent State University Press, 2003), 206–10.

45. "For Outdoor Wear," *Harper's Bazaar*, September 1911, 416.

46. "Farmer's Wife Fashions," *Farmer's Wife*, April 1914, 375; "Fashions of To-day," *New Idea Woman's Magazine*, May 1911, 12; "Fashion Engravings," *Young Ladies Journal*, November 1912, 205; "[?] to Minute One-Piece Frocks for the Jaunty Summer Girl," *Sears Catalog*, no. 124 (1912): 155.

47. Richard Martin and Harold Koda, *Orientalism: Visions of the East in Western Dress* (New York: Metropolitan Museum of Art, 1994), 12–13. Any number of geographical cultures, even those not in Asia, could fall under the definition of the "Orient," as they symbolized a primitive, romantic, non-modern past. These included Western cultures such as Native Americans, or ancient European cultures such as ancient Greece or medieval Europe, or even contemporary Eastern European peasantry.

48. Milbank, *New York Fashions*, 56; Ewing, *History of Twentieth Century Fashion*, 68.

49. Paul Poiret, *King of Fashion: The Autobiography of Paul Poiret*, trans. Stephen Haden Guest (Philadelphia: J. B. Lippincott, 1931), 77.

50. Valerie S. Steele, *Fashion and Eroticism: Ideals of Feminine Beauty from the Victorian Era to the Jazz Age* (New York: Oxford University Press, 1985), 230–32; "The Triumph of French Traditions," *Dress and Vanity Fair*, October 1913, 29; "The Charm of Certain Lines," *Delineator*, July 1913, 35.

51. Irene Castle and Vernon Castle, *Modern Dancing* (New York: Da Capo Press, 1914), 139–40.

52. Ewing, *History of Twentieth Century Fashion*, 66; Daniel James Cole and Nancy Deihl, *The History of Modern Fashion* (London: Laurence King, 2015), 110–11.

53. "Timely Facts from the World of Fashion," *New York Times*, January 2, 1910, X3.

54. Cole and Deihl, *History of Modern Fashion*, 108–11.

55. "American Manufacturers Provide Models for Sale in Department Stores," *New York Times*, March 9, 1913, 99.

56. "Plenty of Pockets in Suffragette Suit," *New York Times*, October 10, 1910, 5.

57. Ibid.

58. Alice Duer Miller, "Why We Oppose Pockets for Women?," *New-York Tribune*, May 3, 1914, sec. 3, 12.

59. For more on the feminist meanings of pockets, see chapter 1.

60. "The 'Suffragette Gown,'" *Women's Wear*, March 21, 1913, 11; "Fifth Avenue Modiste Arrives Wearing Self-Designed 'Suffragette' Skirt," *Women's Wear*, July 7, 1913, 4; "Costumes," *Women's Wear*, July 5, 1913, 1, 12.

61. "Woman Modelling Marching Costume for Chicago's Suffrage Parade, June 6, 1916," Library of Congress Prints and Photographs Division, https://www.loc.gov/resource/cph.3a21391/, accessed January 20, 2020.

62. "Suffragette Does Not Want Trouserette," *Women's Wear*, February 21, 1911, 3.

63. "The Suffrage Blouse," *Woman Citizen*, June 2, 1917, 10; "Blouses," *Women's Wear*, May 29, 1917, 10; Finnegan, *Selling Suffrage*, 126.

64. MC546-PD2, Doris Stevens Papers, SL.

65. Mary Ware Dennett quoted in "Suffragette Does Not Want Trouserette," 3.

66. Harriot Stanton Bltach, "Final Word to the Women Marchers," *New-York Tribune*, May 4, 1912, 1.

67. Suffragists were jailed along with African American and poor women, a fact that Stevens, who was White and college educated, found abhorrent, especially when she was required to wear the same prison uniforms. From her account, it seems that the idea that she was dressed like a Black woman bothered Stevens more than the quality of the clothes. Doris Stevens, *Jailed for Freedom* (New York: Boni & Liveright, 1920), 108–9.

68. "Prison Special," *Suffragist*, February 15, 1919, 5.

69. Katherine Feo Kelly, "Performing Prison: Dress, Modernity, and the Radical Suffrage Body," *Fashion Theory* 15, no. 3 (2011): 316; Malcolm Barnard, *Fashion as Communication*, 2d ed. (New York: Routledge, 2002), 140.

70. The U.S. suffrage colors were inspired by the British suffragettes, whose movement's colors stood for loyalty (purple), purity (white), and hope (green). The NWP replaced the green with golden yellow as a tribute to Susan B. Anthony and Elizabeth Cady Stanton, who used the sunflower—Kansas' state flower—when they campaigned in the state in 1867.

71. Glenna Smith Tinnin, "Why the Pageant?," *Woman's Journal*, February 15, 1913, 50.

72. "March 3, 1913: Parade Plan-List of Floats," folder 239, box 16, Papers of Alice Paul, 1785–1985 (inclusive), 1805–1985 (bulk), SL.

73. "10,000 March in Suffrage Line," *New York Times*, March 4, 1913, 1.

74. Finnegan, *Selling Suffrage*, 93.

75. "White Gown Wanted for Suffragists," *Women's Wear*, September 29, 1911, 8; "Why Parade," folder 6, box 2, Suffrage Collection, SSC.

76. NAWSA members embraced yellow as a suffrage color and combined it with white in their parades, while purple and gold were more popular among the NWP. White, although never adopted as an official suffrage color, was used by all the organizations. Finnegan, *Selling Suffrage*, 93. Yellow was also popular among western suffragists and was used heavily in the campaign in California during 1911. Jessica Ellen Sewell, *Women and the Everyday City: Public Space in San Francisco 1890–1915* (Minneapolis: University of Minnesota Press, 2011), 146–48.

77. Mary Beard quoted in Mary K. Trigg, *Feminism as Life's Work: Modern American Women through Two World Wars* (New Brunswick, NJ: Rutgers University Press, 2014), 48; Mary Church Terrell, *A Colored Woman in a White World* (Salem, NH: Ayer Co. Publishers, 1992 [a reprint of the edition published by Ransdell, Washington, 1940]), 212; "Suffrage Parades," *Crisis*, April 1913, 296.

78. "Illinois Women Feature Parade," *Chicago Daily Tribune*, March 4, 1913, 3. A photograph of Wells marching alongside her fellow white suffragists was published a day later on page 5.

Notes to Chapter 2

79. Lindsey, *Colored No More*, 100–101, 105–6, 109–10.
80. "The Silent Parade," *New York Age*, July 26, 1917, 4.
81. "Negroes in Protest March in Fifth Av.," *New York Times*, July 29, 1917, 12.
82. Chapman, *Making Noise*, 71; Sewell, *Women and the Everyday City*, 143–44, 148.
83. "Women's Political Union leaflet," folder 9, box 6, Suffrage Collection; "Daily Notes for New York Show Windows," *Women's Wear*, November 6, 1912, 1; "Daily Notes for New York Show Windows," *Women's Wear*, November 8, 1912, 6.
84. Finnegan, *Selling Suffrage*, 66–69.
85. Hepburn, "Suffragists' Clothes," 10.
86. Unfortunately, media coverage of fashionably dressed suffragists also solidify the image of the suffragist as a White woman. Alice Duer Miller, "Who Is Sylvia? An Aspect of Feminism," *Scribner's Magazine*, July 1914, 55.
87. "Massachusetts Woman Suffrage Association memo," December 15, 1913, reel D39, Maud Wood Park Papers.
88. "Bifurcation," *Independent*, March 16, 1911, 581.
89. "The Type Has Changed," *New-York Tribune*, February 24, 1911, 7.
90. "Beauty's Vote," *Century Magazine*, July 1915, 480.
91. "10,000 Marchers in Suffrage Line," 1; "Race Women Make Good Showing in Suffrage Parade," *Chicago Defender*, May 9, 1914, 1.
92. "Feminists Ask for Equal Chance," *New York Times*, February 21, 1914, 18; Curiously enough, the topic of suffrage was not discussed as a key element of modern feminism.
93. "Feminists Ask for Equal Chance"; Nina Wilcox Putnam, "Fashion and Feminism," *Forum*, October 1914, 584.
94. Wrisley, "Fashion I Despised," 103.
95. Gilman, *Dress of Women*, 139.
96. Ibid., 140, 133, 57, 136.
97. Putnam, "Fashion and Feminism," 584.
98. Lucy Delap, *The Feminist Avant-Garde: Transatlantic Encounters of the Early Twentieth Century* (Cambridge: Cambridge University Press, 2007), 5–10, 103–12, 117.
99. Cott, *Grounding of Modern Feminism*, 5.
100. Gilman, *Dress of Women*, 133.
101. For more on Greenwich Village Bohemia, see Christine Stansell, *American Moderns: Bohemian New York and the Creation of a New Century* (New York: Owl Books, 2001).
102. Henrietta Rodman to Rebecca Hourwich Reyher, December 19, 1914, folder 23, box 124, Rebecca Hourwich Reyher Papers 1877–1988, SL.
103. Untitled, undated speech, reel 3, Papers of Inez Milholland, 1906–1916, SL.
104. Gilman, *Dress of Women*, 54.
105. Midori Takagi, "Consuming the 'Orient': Images of Asians in White Women's Beauty Magazines, 1900–1930," in *Sexual Borderlands: Constructing an American Sexual Past*, ed. Kathleen Kennedy and Sharon Ullman (Columbus: Ohio State University

Press, 2003), 310; Mary Yoshihara, *Embracing the East: White Women and American Orientalism* (New York: Oxford University Press, 2003), 78–79; Martin and Koda, *Orientalism*, 74.

106. Reina Lewis, *Rethinking Orientalism: Women, Travel, and the Ottoman Harem* (London: I. B. Tauris, 2004), 217, 245, 247–48. For further discussion of how white women used the Orient to claim their equal position in American society, see Yoshihara, *Embracing the East*; Newman, *White Women's Rights*.

107. "Costumes from Drecoll and Premet," *Harper's Bazaar*, October 1913, 51; "Draperies in Waists and Skirts," *Delineator*, April 1914, 29; Alice Long, "What I see On Fifth Avenue," *Ladies' Home Journal*, January 1914, 24.

108. "The Kimono Coats," *New York Times*, June 5, 1910; "The Paris Fall Openings," *Harper's Bazaar*, October 1913, 26; "Three Summer Frocks," *Vogue*, May 15, 1914, 29; Marie Beauchamp, "Fashion Hints from Paris," *Pictorial Review*, March 1911, 55; "Mrs. Ralston's Chat About the New Things in Women's Dress for Spring," *Ladies' Home Journal*, April 1913, 38.

109. Barnard, *Fashion as Communication*, 152.

110. Nina Wilcox Putnam quoted in "Nina Wilcox Putnam," *American Magazine*, May 1913, 34.

111. Nina Wilcox Putnam, *Laughing Through, Being the Autobiographical Story of a Girl Who Made Her Way* (New York: Sears Publishing Company, 1930), 236.

112. Putnam, "Fashion and Feminism," 584; Sarah A. Gordon, "Boundless Possibilities," chapter 2 of *"Make It Yourself": Home Sewing, Gender and Culture, 1890–1930* (New York: Columbia University Press, 2007), http://www.gutenberg-e.org/gordon/chap2.html.

113. Moreover, for professional dressmakers, almost all of whom were women, easy-to-follow patterns threatened their business and devalued their profession. Wendy Gamber, *The Female Economy: The Millinery and Dressmaking Trades, 1860–1930* (Urbana: University of Illinois Press, 1997), 128–29, 134.

114. "The Woman's Forum," *New York Tribune*, March 22, 1914, B10; "Henrietta Rodman," Library of Congress Prints and Photographs Division, http://www.loc.gov/pictures/resource/ggbain.17763/, accessed January 13, 2021.

115. "Woman's Forum."

116. Deborah Saville, "Dress and Culture in Greenwich Village," in *Twentieth-Century American Fashion*, ed. Linda Walters and Patricia A. Cunningham (Oxford: Berg, 2005), 48.

117. Putnam, *Laughing Through*, 237.

118. "Nina Wilcox Putnam," 34.

119. Takagi, "Consuming the 'Orient,'" 313.

120. "Woman's Forum."

121. "Feminists Ask for Equal Chance"; "Feminist Inhabitants of a Feminist Village," *New-York Tribune*, December 27, 1914, B11; "Radicals," *Quill*, April 1923, 15. The photojournalist Jessie Tarbox Beals spent a couple of years in Greenwich Village and

also adopted the kimono style. She took pictures of Village inhabitants, in which the women are dressed in the kimono style and the "Village Smock." Folders 7 and 60f–66, Jessie Tarbox Beals Photographs, SL.

122. Harry Kemp, *More Miles: An Autobiographical Novel* (New York: Boni and Liveright, 1926), 85–86; "Feminists Ask for Equal Chance"; "Radicals," 15.

123. Rebecca Hourwich Reyher, "Search and Struggle for Equality and Independence: An Interview Conducted by Amelia R. Fry and Fern Ingersoll," 1977, Suffragists Oral History Project, accessed at CaliSphere, http://content.cdlib.org/view?docId=kt6xonb1ts&query=&brand=calisphere, accessed November 28, 2020.

124. Stansell, *American Moderns*, 273–76; Saville, "Dress and Culture," 38.

125. Folder 6, 60, Jessie Tarbox Beals Photographs; Kemp, *More Miles*, 199; Deborah Saville, "Freud, Flappers, and Bohemians: The Influence of Modern Psychological Thought and Social Ideology on Dress 1910–1923," *Dress* 30 (2003): 70–72; Irvin S. Cobb, "'Twixt the Bluff and the Sound," *Saturday Evening Post*, July 28, 1917, 14.

126. Allen Churchill, *The Improper Bohemians: A Re-Creation of Greenwich Village in Its Heyday* (New York: Dutton, 1959), 66; "Greenwich Village Art in Bonwit Teller Costumes," *Women's Wear*, April 11, 1917, 15; Saville, "Freud, Flappers, and Bohemians," 67; Saville, "Dress and Culture," 44.

127. "Women Fighting for Modest Clothes," *New York Times*, June 17, 1917, X3.

128. Schweitzer, *When Broadway Was the Runway*, 177.

129. Putnam, "Fashion and Feminism," 580.

130. Crystal Eastman, "Short Hair and Short Skirts," in *Crystal Eastman on Women and Revolution*, ed. Blanche Wiesen Cook (New York: Oxford University Press, 1978), 75.

Chapter 3. Dressing the Modern Girl

1. Mary Alden Hopkins, "Do Women Dress for Men?," *Delineator*, July 1921, 3.

2. Valerie Steele, *Fashion and Eroticism: Ideals of Feminine Beauty from the Victorian Era to the Jazz Age* (New York: Oxford University Press, 1985), 225, 237; Joshua Zeitz, *Flapper: A Madcap Story of Sex, Style, Celebrity, and the Women Who Made America Modern* (New York: Crown Publishers, 2006), 5–6, 8.

3. John D'Emilio and Estelle B. Freedman, *Intimate Matters*, 3d ed. (Chicago: Chicago University Press, 2012), 233–34, 241; Paula Fass, *The Damned and the Beautiful: American Youth in the 1920s* (New York: Oxford University Press, 1977), 262–70; Zeitz, *Flapper*, 23.

4. Carolyn Kitch, *The Girl on the Magazine Cover* (Chapel Hill: University of North Carolina Press, 2001), 121–22; G. Stanley Hall, "Flapper Americana Novissima," *Atlantic Monthly*, June 1922, 771–80; Fass, *Damned and the Beautiful*, 308–9.

5. Penny Tinkler and Cheryl Krasnik Warsh, "Feminine Modernity in Interwar Britain and North America," *Journal of Women's History* 20, no. 3 (Fall 2008): 113–15; Alys Eve Weinbaum, "Racial Masquerade: Consumption and Contestation of Ameri-

can Modernity," in *The Modern Girl around the World: Consumption, Modernity, and Globalization*, ed. Alys Eve Weinbaum, Lynn M. Thomas, Priti Ramamurthy, Uta G. Poiger, and Madeleine Yue Dong (Durham, NC: Duke University Press, 2008), 121.

6. The Modern Girl Around the World Research Group, "The Modern Girl as Heuristic Device," in Weinbaum et al., *Modern Girl*, 7–8; Ilya Parkins and Elizabeth Sheehan, "Introduction," in *Cultures of Femininity in Modern Fashion*, ed. Ilya Parkins and Elizabeth Sheehan (Durham: University of New Hampshire Press, 2012), 1–3.

7. Mary Louise Roberts, "Samson and Delilah Revisited: The Politics of Women's Fashion in 1920s France," *American Historical Review* 98, no. 3 (1993): 665.

8. Kitch, *Girl on the Magazine Cover*, 122–23; Martin Pumphrey, "The Flapper, the Housewife and the Making of Modernity," *Cultural Studies* 1, no. 2 (1987): 186; Zeitz, *Flapper*, 39–49, 63; Maria Elena Buszek, *Pin-Up Grrrls: Feminism, Sexuality, Popular Culture* (Durham, NC: Duke University Press, 2006), 174–76.

9. Davarian L. Baldwin, *Chicago's New Negroes: Modernity, the Great Migration, and Black Urban Life* (Chapel Hill: University of North Carolina Press, 2007), 5–9, 247–48; Laila Haidarali, *Brown Beauty: Color, Sex, and Race from the Harlem Renaissance to World War II* (New York: New York University Press, 2018), 7–11, 17; Einav Rabinovitch-Fox, "Fabricating Black Modernity: Fashion and African American Womanhood during the First Great Migration," *International Journal of Fashion Studies* 6, no. 2 (2019): 253–56.

10. On the global dissemination of the flapper image, see Weinbaum et al., *Modern Girl*; Mary Louise Roberts, *Civilization without Sexes: Reconstructing Gender in Postwar France, 1917–1927* (Chicago: University of Chicago Press, 1994); Brigitte Soland, *Becoming Modern: Young Women and the Reconstruction of Womanhood in the 1920s* (Princeton, NJ: Princeton University Press, 2000); Liz Conor, *The Spectacular Modern Woman: Feminine Visibility in the 1920s* (Bloomington: Indiana University Press, 2004); Jane Nicholas, *The Modern Girl: Feminine Modernities, the Body, and Commodities in the 1920s* (Toronto: University of Toronto Press, 2015).

11. Scholars Martin Pumphrey and Estelle Freedman argue that emancipation in the 1920s was often a matter of appearance rather than substance. According to them, although fashion provided women with new freedoms that presented an image of equality, discrimination was still abundant. Pumphrey, "Flapper," 183; Estelle B. Freedman, "The New Woman: Changing Views of Women in the 1920s," *Journal of American History* 61 (September 1974): 373.

12. Between 1916 and 1930 over one million African Americans, many of them young women, left the rural South to settle in urban centers, mainly in the Northeast and the Midwest. These migrants sought better lives and to improve their economic status, as well as to escape the violence of Jim Crow. On Black experience during the first Great Migration, see Baldwin, *Chicago's New Negroes*; Carol Marks, *Farewell—We're Good and Gone: The Great Black Migration* (Bloomington: Indiana University Press, 1989); Daniel Johnson, *Black Migration in America: A Social Demographic History*

(Durham, NC: Duke University Press, 1981); Ann Douglas, *Terrible Honesty: Mongrel Manhattan in the 1920s* (New York: Noonday Press, 1995).

13. Nancy F. Cott, "The Modern Woman of the 1920s, American Style," in *Toward a Cultural Identity in the Twentieth Century*, vol. 5 of *A History of Women in the West* (Cambridge, MA: Harvard University Press, 1994), 67–91; Rayna Rapp and Ellen Ross, "Feminism, Consumerism, and Political Backlash in the United States," in *Women in Culture and Politics: A Century of Change*, ed. Judith Friedlander (Bloomington: Indiana University Press, 1986), 52–61; Freedman, "New Woman," 373–93. Although Freedman questions the paradigm that sees the 1920s as the demise of feminism, arguing that historical accounts of the flapper are too often based on stereotypes than evidence, she does not attend to the political aspects of the image.

14. Nancy F. Cott, *The Grounding of Modern Feminism* (New Haven, CT: Yale University Press, 1987), 172.

15. Hopkins, "Do Women Dress for Men?," 3.

16. Elizabeth Francis, *The Secret Treachery of Words: Feminism and Modernism in America* (Minneapolis: University of Minnesota Press, 2002), xxi–xxii; Michele R. Finn, "Modern Necessity: Feminism, Popular Culture, and American Womanhood 1920–1960," PhD diss. (University of Rochester, 2012), 15–16.

17. Cheryl Buckley and Hilary Fawcett, *Fashioning the Feminine: Representation and Women's Fashion from the Fin de Siècle to the Present* (London: I. B. Tauris, 2002), 109.

18. Elizabeth Ewing, *History of Twentieth Century Fashion* (New York: Costume and Fashion Press, 2001), 92–93; Daniel James Cole and Nancy Deihl, *The History of Modern Fashion* (London: Laurence King, 2015), 136–37.

19. Caroline Rennolds Milbank, *New York Fashions: The Evolution of American Style* (New York: Harry N. Abrams, 1996), 79. Evening wear of the 1920s is usually associated with the flapper culture of dancing and flirting and has a distinct class component. Yet styles, mainly the short hemline, penetrated to everyday wear as well and disseminated across all sectors of society. See, for comparison, Orange and Gold Brocade Dress, 1926–1927, 1983.001.0347 ab, and Lanvin Evening Dress, 1925–1928, 1983.001.0395, Digital Collections, Kent State University Museum, https://www.kent.edu/museum/online-collection, accessed January 15, 2021.

20. Dean L. Merceron, *Lanvin* (New York: Rizzoli, 2007), 83, 88–89, 97; Cole and Deihl, *History of Modern Fashion*, 137.

21. Marjorie Howard, "Paris Offers Her Midseason Models," *Harper's Bazaar*, July 1927), 87; Marjorie Howard, "Why Clothes Are Not Changing," *Harper's Bazaar*, March 1926), 80–87, 158.

22. Cole and Deihl, *History of Modern Fashion*, 146–48. Although Chanel became associated with flapper fashions, she did not invent the flapper.

23. Coco Chanel quoted in Ewing, *History of Twentieth Century Fashion*, 100, see also 99–101.

24. Ewing, *History of Twentieth Century Fashion*, 86, 119–20, 122–14; Nancy Green,

Ready-to-Wear and Ready-to-Work: A Century of Industry and Immigrants in Paris and New York (Durham, NC: Duke University Press, 1997), 119–21.

25. Green, *Ready-to-Wear*, 48, 56–58. For more on labor struggles in the women's garment industry, see Richard Greenwald, *The Triangle Fire, the Protocols of Peace, and Industrial Democracy in Progressive Era New York* (Philadelphia: Temple University Press, 2005); Michelle Haberland, *Striking Beauties: Women Apparel Workers in the U.S. South, 1930–2000* (Athens: University of Georgia Press, 2015).

26. Carmen Nicole Keist, "Rayon and Its Impact on the Fashion Industry at its Introduction 1910–1924," MSc thesis (Iowa State University, 2009), 8–14, 16–17, 21; Cole and Deihl, *History of Modern Fashion*, 142–43; Ewing, *History of Twentieth Century Fashion*, 88–91.

27. Paul H. Nystrom, *The Economics of Fashion* (New York: Roland Press Company, 1928), 423–29; Alice Kessler-Harris, *Out to Work: A History of Wage-Earning Women in the United States* (New York: Oxford University Press, 1983), 224.

28. Ewing, *History of Twentieth Century Fashion*, 119, 122–23.

29. Nystrom, *Economics of Fashion*, 405.

30. "To-Day's Morals and Manners—The Side of 'The Girls,'" *Literary Digest*, July 9, 1921, 34–36.

31. "Slenderness Achieved!," *Lane Bryant Spring and Summer 1926*, catalog, 4.

32. "Designed Especially for Short Stout Women," *Lane Bryant Spring and Summer 1928*, catalog, 21.

33. Claudia Brush Kidwell and Margaret C. S. Christman, *Suiting Everyone: The Democratization of Clothing in America* (Washington, DC: Smithsonian Institution Press, 1974), 165; "Styles to Please Those Accustomed to the Finest," *Montgomery Ward Spring and Summer 1927 Catalogue*, 6; "Superb New Paris Models," *Bellas Hess Fall Winter Catalogue 1920–21* (1920), 40.

34. Grace Elizabeth Hale, "'For Colored' and 'For Whites': Segregating Consumption in the South," in *Jumpin' Jim Crow: Southern Politics from Civil War to Civil Rights*, ed. Jane Daily, Glenda Gilmore, and Bryant Simon (Princeton, NJ: Princeton University Press, 2000), 170–71, 176–77; Ted Ownby, *American Dreams in Mississippi: Consumers, Poverty, and Culture, 1830–1998* (Chapel Hill: University of North Carolina Press, 1999), 75–77.

35. Susannah Walker, *Style and Status: Selling Beauty to African American Women, 1920–1975* (Lexington: University Press of Kentucky, 2007), 7, 15; Bernard-Hewitt & Co. advertisement, *Crisis*, May 1924, 45; "The Macy's Fur Shop," *Inter-State Tattler*, October 19, 1928, 6; Goodyear Raincoat Co. advertisement, *Baltimore Afro-American*, November 23, 1929, 17; World Mail Order Co. advertisement, *Baltimore Afro-American*, December 6, 1924, 10.

36. Ann Devon, "Will Women Wear Them?," *Outlook*, November 6, 1929, 372.

37. Robert Lynd and Hellen Lynd, *Middletown: A Study in Modern American Culture* (New York: Harcourt, Brace, & World, 1956), 161.

38. Mary Alden Hopkins, "Women's Rebellion Against Fashions," *New Republic*, August 16, 1922, 332.
39. P. K Crocker, "Mass Representation of Style Seen as Artistic Expression of the Age," *Women's Wear Daily*, January 7, 1928, 3.
40. "Fashion's Effect on Business," *Literary Digest*, 25 February 1928, 18.
41. Franklin S. Clark, "Who Sets Fashions—and How?," *Review of Reviews*, January 1930, 56; Frances Anne Allen, "Fig Leaves," *American Mercury*, January 1928, 66; Devon, "Will Women Wear Them?," 373.
42. Muriel Draper, "The Trail of America Abroad," folder 420, box 12, Muriel Draper Papers, Beinecke Rare Book and Manuscript Library, Yale University; Milbank, *New York Fashions*, 72.
43. Caroline Evans, "Jean Patou's American Mannequins: Early Fashion Shows and Modernism," *Modernism/Modernity* 15, no. 2 (April 2008): 243–63.
44. "Attractive Frocks In and After Office Hours," *Ladies' Home Journal*, January 1924, 57.
45. "Paris Design for Summer," *Ladies' Home Journal*, September 1929, 42.
46. Hopkins, "Women's Rebellion Against Fashions," 331.
47. "Dark orange silk crepe dress, American ca. 1925–1929," 1990.042.0091, Digital Collections, Kent State University Museum. Accessed January 15, 2021.
48. Delator Pattern Service ad, *Delineator*, February 1922, 56–57; "A Revolutionary Idea," McCall's Printed Patterns advertisement, *Ladies' Home Journal*, October 1922, 163; "Reproductions of Paris Ensembles," *Vogue*, March 1, 1925, 76–77. Sarah A. Gordon, "New Business Strategies," in *"Make It Yourself": Home Sewing, Gender, and Culture, 1890–1930* (New York, 2007), http://www.gutenberg-e.org/gordon/chap4.html#newbus.
49. Ruth Sykes, "Paris Gowns That Are Easily Made at Home," *Woman's World*, October 1926, 22.
50. Mary Brooks Picken, "The One Hour Dress—And How to Make It" (Scranton, PA: Institute of Domestic Arts & Sciences, 1923), Winterthur Museum and Library; Linda Przybyszewski, *The Lost Art of Dress: The Women Who Once Made America Stylish* (New York: Basic Books, 2014), 230.
51. "'It's the Prettiest Dress I Ever Had—'," *Ladies' Home Journal*, January 1920, 91; Anna Steese Richardson, "The New Way to Happiness," *Ladies' Home Journal*, September 1921, 99; Mary Brooks Picken, "It's Fun to Make a Dress," *Pictorial Review*, October 1925, 96.
52. Florence Maylin, "Fashion Flashes," *Inter-State Tattler*, January 20, 1928, 8; "Fashion News," *Baltimore Afro-American*, September 22, 1928, 18; "Smart Fashion for Limited Incomes," *Half-Century Magazine*, September 1917, 7; "What Clothes Shall I Wear?," *Half-Century Magazine*, May–June 1924, 19–20, 22.
53. "Dame Fashions," *Negro World*, May 16, 1925, 7. Amy Jacques Garvey was Marcus Garvey's second wife, becoming an influential journalist and activist after she took

over the editing of the *Negro World*, the UNIA paper, and the movement after her husband was arrested, playing an important leading role in Garveyism.

54. "Half-Century Pattern Service," *Half-Century Magazine*, October 1920, 15; Noliwe M. Rooks, *Ladies' Pages: African American Women's Magazines and the Culture That Made Them* (New Brunswick, NJ: Rutgers University Press, 2004), 75–76; Aunt Dilsey, "Afro Fashions," *Baltimore Afro-American*, May 19, 1928, 15; *Baltimore Afro-American*, July 17, 1926, 15; *Baltimore Afro-American*, June 6, 1924, A11.

55. Reader letter, "The People's Forum," *Half-Century Magazine*, November 1920, 17.

56. Bruce Bliven, "Flapper Jane," *New Republic*, September 1925, 65–67.

57. Ibid.

58. While my analysis focuses on garments, short hair was also central to the construction of the "boyish" look, and it was as controversial as short skirts. For more on the hair controversies, see Roberts, "Samson and Delila Revisited," 657–84; Fass, *Damned and the Beautiful*, 280–81; Helena Hill Weed, "A Feminist Rises in Defense of Bobbed Hair," *New-York Tribune*, September 18, 1921, D6.

59. Kathleen Eddy, "The Source of Beauty," *Pictorial Review*, February 1924, 40.

60. Alfredo Panzini, "The Flapper—A New Type," *Vanity Fair*, September 1921, 63.

61. Ewing, *History of Twentieth Century Fashion*, 92–93; Roberts, *Civilization without Sexes*, 69–71. Historian Jill Fields, on the contrary, suggests that the look, which required the modeling of the body through flattening undergarments, symbolized the further feminization of women as it included discomfort and the molding of women's bodies, two elements that were associated with women's fashion. Jill Fields, *An Intimate Affair: Women, Lingerie, Sexuality* (Berkeley: University of California Press, 2007), 90.

62. Zeitz, *Flapper*, 156–58; Kitch, *Girl on the Magazine Cover*, 130–31.

63. Richard Le Gallienne, "The Modern Girl and Why She's Painted," *Vanity Fair*, January 1924, 27–28.

64. Anne Hollander, *Sex and Suits: The Evolution of Modern Fashion* (New York: Kodansha, 1995), 145–47.

65. Christina Simmons, *Making Marriage Modern: Women's Sexuality from the Progressive Era to World War II* (New York: Oxford University Press, 2009), 121–27, 145–47.

66. Laura Doan, "Passing Fashions: Reading Female Masculinities in the 1920s," *Feminist Studies*, 24, no. 3 (Fall 1998): 663–700.

67. D'Emilio and Freedman, *Intimate Matters*, 200–201, 256–57, 263–65; Zeitz, *Flapper*, 33–35; Fass, *Damned and the Beautiful*, 218, 268–70; Beth Baily, *From Front Porch to Back Seat: Courtship in Twentieth-Century America* (Baltimore: Johns Hopkins Press, 1988), 19, 86–87.

68. "Rouge and Progress," *Half-Century Magazine*, May–June 1921, 6; "African Girl Like Flapper of America," *Chicago Defender*, May 30, 1925, A1; Deirdre Clemente, *Dress Casual: How College Students Redefined American Style* (Chapel Hill: University of North Carolina Press, 2014), 61–63.

69. "Judging by Your Clothes," *Half-Century*, September–October 1922, 19.

70. I have addressed in length elsewhere the fashionable practices of Black flappers: Rabinovitch-Fox, "Fabricating Black Modernity," 239–60.

71. "Display Many Styles at Fashion Show," *Chicago Defender*, October 13, 1928, 11; "Two Types of Beauty from Two States," *Baltimore Afro-American*, May 14, 1927, 12; "New York Daily Uses Pretty Picture of Some Harlem Bobbed Hair Beauties," *Pittsburgh Courier*, December 18, 1926, 4.

72. Of course, trousers for women also provided visible proof that women had two legs, and in many ways they were even more comfortable than the short skirt in regard to ease of movement. Yet, whereas trousers were worn by women well before the 1920s, they never managed to infiltrate the mainstream to become fashionable. For more on women's wearing of pants before the 1920s, see Gayle V. Fischer, *Pantaloons and Power: Nineteenth-Century Dress Reform in America* (Kent, OH: Kent University Press, 2001); Cynthia Craig and Catherine Smith, *Women in Pants: Manly Maiden, Cowgirls, and Other Renegades* (New York: H. N. Abrams, 2003).

73. "To-Day's Morals and Manners," 34, 36, 39. Interestingly, Brown considered the Gibson Girl fashions—which as a young girl allowed her to engage in sports, ride bicycles, and live an active life—as very uncomfortable compared to the 1922 fashions. For more on the Gibson Girl and her fashions, see chapter 1.

74. "Editorial Paragraphs," *Nation*, 9 October 1929, 373, emphasis in original.

75. "Dress Reform for Men," *Review of Reviews*, August 1929, 128.

76. Bliven, "Flapper Jane," 65.

77. Eleanor Chalmers, "'Let Go' Is the Law of the New Corset and the Corsetless Figure," *Delineator*, April 1922, 41.

78. "Corset," 1983.003.0061; and "Brassiere," 1999.072.0003, both in Digital Collections, Kent State University Museum.

79. Chalmers, "'Let Go' Is the Law," 41.

80. Fields, *Intimate Affair*, 56–61, 90–92; Jenna Weissman Joselit, *A Perfect Fit: Clothes, Character, and the Promise of America* (New York: Owl Books, 2001), 60.

81. Kathy Peiss, *Hope in a Jar: The Making of America's Beauty Culture* (New York: Owl Books, 1998), 213; "When Is a Contest Not a Contest?," *Crisis*, June 1924, 80; "Popularity Contest of N.Y. Paper Abandoned," *Chicago Defender*, April 12, 1924, 1. Also see Tiffany Melissa Gill, *Beauty Shop Politics: African American Women's Activism in the Beauty Industry* (Urbana: University of Illinois Press, 2010), for further discussion on how beauty served as a useful avenue for political action.

82. Gemma James, "Shall We Lengthen Our Skirts?," *Half-Century Magazine*, September–October 1922, 17; "Pope Wars on Fashion," *Baltimore Afro-American*, October 26, 1923, 16.

83. Dorothy Ilone Embry, "Leader of Harlem Sub-Debs Defends 'Virtue' of Modern Girl," *Pittsburgh Courier*, July 2, 1927, 12.

84. "Cotton Stocking, Long Sleeves Are Too Much for Fisk," *Baltimore Afro-American*, February 28, 1925, 1; "Fisk College Students Quit by Hundreds," *Baltimore Afro-American*, February 14, 1925, 1.

85. "A Nifty Bunch of Damsels . . .," *Inter-State Tattler*, June 29, 1928, 15.

86. Graham White and Shane White, *Stylin': African American Expressive Culture from Its Beginnings to the Zoot Suit* (Ithaca, NY: Cornell University Press, 1998), 245–46; Hazel Carby, "Policing the Black Woman's Body in an Urban Context," *Critical Inquiry* 18, no. 4 (Summer 1992): 741; Tera W. Hunter, *To 'Joy My Freedom: Southern Black Women's Lives and Labors after the Civil War* (Cambridge, MA: Harvard University Press, 1997), 182–83.

87. Kathy Peiss, *Cheap Amusements: Working Women and Leisure in Turn-of-the-Century New York* (Philadelphia: Temple University Press, 1986), 67–72; Vicki L. Ruiz, "The Flapper and the Chaperon," in *From Out of the Shadows: Mexican Women in Twentieth-Century America* (New York: Oxford University Press, 1998), 54–56; Valerie J. Matsumoto, *City Girls: The Nisei Social World in Los Angeles, 1920–1950* (New York: Oxford University Press, 2014), 60–62; Judy Yung, *Unbound Feet: A Social History of Chinese Women in San Francisco* (Berkeley: University of California Press, 1995), 115–16, 122–25.

88. Roberts, *Civilization without Sexes*, 85.

89. Cott, *Grounding of Modern Feminism*, 172–74; Fields, *Intimate Affair*, 90–92; Einav Rabinovitch-Fox, "Baby, You Can Drive My Car: Advertising Women's Freedom in 1920s America," *American Journalism: A Journal of Media History* 33, no. 4 (2016): 372–400; Peiss, *Hope in a Jar*, 146–51.

90. Cole and Deihl, *History of Modern Fashion*, 142.

91. Fields, *Intimate Affair*, 90; Valerie Steele, *The Corset: A Cultural History* (New Haven, CT: Yale University Press, 2001), 152–54.

92. Scott Peirce, "What It Costs to Be a Well-Dressed Flapper," *Motion Picture Classic*, March 1927, 44.

93. On treating see Peiss, *Cheap Amusements*, 51–55.

94. "Courting Danger in the Automobile," *Literary Digest*, July 5, 1924, 35; "Is the Young Generation in Peril?," *Literary Digest*, May 14, 1921, 9–12, 58–73; "The Case against the Younger Generation," *Literary Digest*, June 17, 1922, 38–42, 51–63; Barton W. Currie, "Eliminate Flapperism, Male and Female," *Ladies' Home Journal*, October 1922, 30; Hall, "Flapper Americana Novissima," 771–80; Stephan Ewing, "Blue Laws for School Teachers," *Harper's Magazine*, February 1928, 329–38.

95. Richard Le Gallienne, "The Return of the Artificial," *Harper's Bazaar*, July 1927, 63.

96. Angela Latham, *Posing a Threat: Flappers, Chorus Girls, and Other Brazen Performers in the American 1920s* (Hanover, NH: Wesleyan University Press, 2000), 69.

97. "Case against the Younger Generation," 42.

98. Currie, "Eliminate Flapperism," 30.

99. "Short Skirts and Business," Winifred Harper Cooley Scrapbook, 1920s, SSC.

100. "Conduct of Modern Flapper Deplored," *Chicago Defender*, July 18, 1925, A1; "Fear Collapse of Home Life in Extreme Styles," *Chicago Defender*, February 12, 1927, A1.

101. "The 'Flapper's Age,'" *Chicago Defender*, July 29, 1922, 12.
102. "'Flapper Styles' Attacked by Rev. J. Milton Walrond," *Pittsburgh Courier*, February 5, 1927, 5.
103. "Is the Young Generation in Peril?," 10.
104. There was a great difficulty in enforcing these rules, though. For more, see Latham, *Posing a Threat*, 65–97.
105. Myrtle Heileman, "The Modern Riddle," *Flapper*, October 1922, 10.
106. "Our Monthly Chat," *Flapper*, July 1922, 2.
107. James, "Shall We Lengthen Our Skirts?," 17.
108. Devon, "Will Women Wear Them?," 372.
109. Alexander Black, "Legs," *Century*, July 1921, 339, 341.
110. Emily Newell Blair, "New Styles in Feminine Beauty," *Outlook*, June 26, 1929, 331, 360.
111. Cott, *Grounding of Modern Feminism*, 172–73; Francis, *Secret Treachery of Words*, xiv–xv.
112. Adams, "Did They Know What They Wanted?," *Outlook*, December 8, 1927, 528–29.
113. Ida Clyde Clarke, "Feminism and the New Technique," *Century Magazine*, April 1929, 760.
114. Dorothy Dunbar Bromley, "Feminist—New Style," *Harper's Magazine*, October 1927, 557.
115. Elise Jerard, "High Heels and Blue Stockings," *Pictorial Review*, May 1929, 98.
116. Roberts, *Civilization without Sexes*, 66.
117. "Urges Long Skirts for Cotton Relief," *New York Times*, May 14, 1927, 19; "Textile Mills See Aid in Long Easter Frocks," *New York Times*, April 1, 1929, 3; "Retailers Urge Radical Style Change to Combat Home Dressmaking Growth," *Women's Wear*, June 24, 1925, 26.
118. "Editorial Paragraphs."
119. Marjorie Howard, "Paris Sounds a New Note," *Harper's Bazaar*, April 1928, 96–97.
120. Marjorie Howard, "Highlights on the Paris Collections," *Harper's Bazaar*, April 1929, 88.
121. Devon, "Will Women Wear Them?," 373, 396.
122. "Must Women Go Back to Tripping Over Their Trains?," *Literary Digest*, November 16, 1929, 39.
123. Ethel Traphagen, "Fighting the New Fashions," *New York Times*, November 3, 1929, E5.
124. Mildred Adams, "Revolt Rumbles in the Fashion World," *New York Times*, October 27, 1929, SM3.
125. "Will Women Wear Them?," *Woman's Journal*, December 1929, 27.
126. Lucie R. Sayler, "Long Skirts?," *Nation*, October 9, 1929, 384.
127. Latham, *Posing a Threat*, 48–49, 52–53; Joeslit, *Perfect Fit*, 64–70; "The Pope's

Notes to Chapter 3

Appeal to Men to Reform Women's Dress," *Literary Digest,* January 29, 1927, 27–28, 57–59.

128. Emily Newell Blair, "Discourage Feminists," *Outlook,* July 8, 1931, 302–3, 318–19.

129. Adams, "Did They Know What They Wanted?," 530.

130. Fannie Hurst, "Let's Not Wear Them," *New Republic,* October 30, 1929, 294.

131. Carrie Chapman Catt, "Short Skirts and French Dictators," *Forum,* April 1927, 584.

132. "Jersey City Y.W.C.A. Girls Opposing New Style Dictates," *Women's Wear Daily,* October 21, 1929, sec. 3, 1.

133. "70% of Hunter Girls Rebel at Long Skirts," *New York Times,* November 25, 1929, 23; "Radcliffe, Smith Girls Cling to Short Skirts," *Chicago Tribune,* November 27, 1929, 30.

134. "New Mode Seen Resisted in Far West Town," *Women's Wear Daily,* October 30, 1929, sec. 3, 9; "Midwestern Women Declared Opposed to the New Silhouette," *Women's Wear Daily,* October 14, 1929, sec. 3, 3.

135. "Call Long Skirts 'Cruel,'" *New York Times,* December 25, 1928, 38.

136. S.I.K., "Another Woman Revolts," *New York Times,* October 21, 1929, 24.

137. Sayler, "Long Skirts?," 384. Mildred Harrington, "Clothes Don't Make the Woman But They Help a Lot," *American Magazine,* May 1927, 18–19, 72–80; Elsievans, "The Trend of Fashion: Business Women," *Chicago Defender,* November 19, 1927, 5.

138. "Are Long Dresses Silly?—Well, Read This," *Baltimore Afro-American,* August 30, 1930.

139. "'To Be or Not To Be'—Long," *Pittsburgh Courier,* January 18, 1930, 1.

140. "Women Balk at Long Skirts That are Decreed by Fashion," *Baltimore Afro-American,* November 23, 1929, 3; "Leaders Name People They would Like to Hang," *Baltimore Afro-American,* November 30, 1929, 5; "No Skirt At All Plea Of Women," *Chicago Defender,* May 5, 1928, 9.

141. Devon, "Will Women Wear Them?," 396.

142. "The Battle of Styles," *New Republic,* December 11, 1929, 58; "Must Women Go Back to Tripping Over Their Trains?," 39–51.

143. "Skirts Are Shorter at Spring Display," *New York Times,* December 8, 1929, 13.

144. "Finds Long Skirt Curtailing Sales," *New York Times,* December 14, 1929, 40.

145. "Longer Dress Seen Big Selling Problem," *Women's Wear Daily,* October 8, 1929), sec. 3, 5.

146. "Gives Short Skirts Five Years More," *New York Times,* November 2, 1929, 32.

147. "New Styles Seen Problem for Women of Large Sizes," *Women's Wear Daily,* October 1, 1929, sec. 3, 23; "Lays Higher Returns to New Styles," *Women's Wear Daily,* October 23, 1929, sec. 3, 1.

148. "Midwestern Women Declared Opposed," 3.

149. "Columbus Stores Note Interest in Daytime Dresses," *Women's Wear Daily,* October 22, 1929, sec. 3, 10; "Consumers Readily Accept New Silhouette, Survey

Shows," *Women's Wear Daily*, October 22, 1929, sec. 1, 13; "Phila. Retail Trade Favors Newer Modes," *Women's Wear Daily*, October 1, 1929, sec. 3, 17.

150. "Wellesley Adopts Long Skirt Mode," *New York Times*, November 27, 1929, 32; "Long vs. Short Skirt Controversy Given Publicity in Chicago," *Women's Wear Daily*, February 4, 1930, sec. 3, 6.

151. "New York Women's Acceptance of Longer Silhouette Generally Expressed in 4–5 Inch-Below-Knee Length," *Women's Wear Daily*, October 25, 1929, sec. 1, 3.

152. "Spring Fashions Are Out," *Nation*, January 1, 1930, 3.

153. "The Battle of the Skirt," *Woman's Journal*, January 1930, 27.

154. "Fashion Settles Down," *Outlook*, January 29, 1930, 177.

155. "Society's Verdict Favors New Silhouette At Opening of Los Angeles Opera," *Women's Wear Daily*, October 8, 1929, sec. 1, 3; "Omaha Ball Reveals Society Women Unanimous in Approval of New Mode," *Women's Wear Daily*, October 10, 1929, sec 3, 1; "New York Dressmaker Cater to the Opera Opening In Gown With Trailing Silhouette and Short Wrap," *Women's Wear Daily*, October 29, 1929, sec. 1, 3; "New Silhouettes Endorsed at Capitol State Dinner," *Women's Wear Daily*, October 8, 1929, sec. 1, 1; "Fashion Settles Down," 177.

156. "Wearability Gains Importance," *Women's Wear Daily*, May 6, 1932, sec. 1, 15.

157. Versatility advertisement, *Women's Wear Daily*, August 12, 1931, sec. 1, 8.

158. Marjorie Howard, "Paris Signs a Triple Entente in Skirts," *Harper's Bazaar*, January 1930, 60.

159. "Fashion Significances," *Women's Wear Daily*, February 5, 1932, sec. 1, 5; *Bellas Hess & Co. Autumn Winter 1931–1932 Catalog* (1931), 49.

Chapter 4. Designing Power

1. "Address by Miss Dorothy Shaver, President of Lord & Taylor before the Fashion Group, November 13, 1951," folder 14, box 75, FGI.

2. Annemarie Strassel, "Designing Women: Feminist Methodologies in American Fashion," *Women's Studies Quarterly* 41, no. 1 (2013): 41.

3. "Address by Miss Dorothy Shaver."

4. Edna Woolman Chase, *Fashion Group Bulletin* 1 (February 1942): 1, folder 14, box 144, FGI.

5. Annelise Orleck, *Common Sense and a Little Fire: Women and Working-Class Politics in the United States* (Chapel Hill: University of North Carolina Press, 1995); Dorothy Sue Cobble, *The Other Woman's Movement: Workplace Justice and Social Rights in Modern America* (Princeton, NJ: Princeton University Press, 2003); Nancy F. Cott, *The Grounding of Modern Feminism* (New Haven, CT: Yale University Press, 1987). A notable exception to the dearth of attention to women in the fashion industry is Annemarie Strassel, "Redressing Women: Feminism in Fashion and the Creation of American Style 1930–1960," PhD diss. (Yale University, 2008).

6. Landon R. Y. Storrs argues that historians should pay more attention to the creation of women's professional networks outside the women's movement as important places where feminism continued to reverberate in the interwar period. See Storrs, *Civilizing Capitalism: The National Consumers' League, Women's Activism, and Labor Standards during the New Deal Era* (Chapel Hill: University of North Carolina Press, 2000), 7, and *The Second Red Scare and the Unmaking of the New Deal Left* (Princeton, NJ: Princeton University Press, 2012), 45–50. Other historians also made a similar argument, emphasizing the importance of female networks to keeping feminism alive "between the waves." See, for example, Emily Westkaemper, *Selling Women's History: Packaging Feminism in Twentieth-Century American Popular Culture* (New Brunswick, NJ: Rutgers University Press, 2017).

7. Claire McCardell, *What Shall I Wear? The What, Where, When, and How Much of Fashion* (New York: Simon and Schuster, 1956), 21.

8. Estelle Hamburger, "The First Fifty Years," in *The Fashion Group 1930/80* (New York: Fashion Group, 1980), folder 5, box 151, FGI; Rebecca Arnold, *The American Look: Fashion, Sportswear, and the Image of Women in 1930s and 1940s New York* (New York: I. B. Tauris, 2008), 93; Marie Clifford, "Working with Fashion: The Role of Art, Taste, and Consumerism in Women's Professional Culture 1920–1940," *American Studies* 44, no. 1/2 (Spring/Summer 2003): 74.

9. "Fashion Group International History," Fashion Group International, https://www.fgi.org/system/about-fgi/#history, accessed January 8, 2021.

10. "List of Members 1931," folder 3, box 182, FGI.

11. "Aids Fashion Show Plan," *New York Times*, December 18, 1940, 34.

12. Eleanor Roosevelt, "The Times, the Job, and the Girl," *Vogue*, April 26, 1930, 45, 102.

13. Kenneth Collins quoted in "Fashion Group Luncheon Meeting, February 10, 1941," minutes, folder 10, box 73, FGI.

14. Strassel, "Designing Women," 46.

15. Sheryl Leipzig, Jean Parsons, and Jane Farrell-Beck, "It Is a Profession that Is New Unlimited and Rich: Promotion of the American Designer in the 1930s," *Dress* 35, no. 1 (2008): 38–39; Clifford, "Working with Fashion," 80.

16. Hamburger, "First Fifty Years."

17. Sara B. Marketti and Jean L. Parsons, "American Fashions for American Women: Early Twentieth Century Efforts to Develop an American Fashion Industry," *Dress* 34, no. 1 (2007): 82, 89. See also chapter 3.

18. Nettie Rosenstein quoted in Margaret Case Harriman, "Profiles: Nettie Rosenstein," *New Yorker*, October 19, 1940, 28.

19. Elizabeth Hawes, *Fashion Is Spinach* (New York: Grosset & Dunlap, 1938), 286–87.

20. Arnold, *American Look*, 95; Edna Woolman Chase, "The Business of Fashion," *Vogue*, May 1, 1932, 41, 89, 107.

21. "The Fashion Group Inc. Constitution and By-laws," folder 1, box 183, FGI.

Notes to Chapter 4

22. Ibid.

23. In 1988 the Fashion Group changed its name to Fashion Group International to reflect the global reach of the organization. In 1997 it opened its membership to men. Today, FGI has twenty-six branches around the world.

24. "Fashion Group Monthly Meeting, June 19, 1933," minutes, folder 9, box 72, FGI. See also "New Fashions in Unionism Discussed at April and May Luncheons," *Fashion Group Bulletin*, May 1941 folder 13, box 144, FGI.

25. Clifford, "Working with Fashion," 69. Westkaemper, *Selling Women's History*, makes a similar argument about professional societies of women in advertising.

26. "The Fashion Group Inc. Constitution and By-laws."

27. "Annual Report 1955–1956," folder 2, box 6, series 5, NAFAD.

28. Nancy Deihl, "Zelda Wynn Valdes: Uptown Modiste," in *The Hidden History of American Fashion: Rediscovering Twentieth-Century Women Designers*, ed. Nancy Deihl (London: Bloomsbury, 2018), 226–27.

29. Rosemary E. Reed Miller, *Threads of Time, the Fabric of History: Profiles of African American Dressmakers and Designers, 1850 to the Present* (Washington, DC: Toast and Strawberries Press, 2002), 34–37.

30. Deihl, "Zelda Wynn Valdes," 224–25.

31. "Jubilee Fashion Show Accepts Negro Girl," *New York Amsterdam News*, August 21, 1948, 1, 23.

32. "Constitution of National Association of Fashion and Accessory Designers, Inc.," folder 15, box 7, series 5, NAFAD; "3rd Annual Fashion Show Convention Program," folder 4, box 2, series 2, NAFAD; "Do You Design Clothes? Here's a New Outlet," *Baltimore Afro-American*, April 2, 1949, B11; "Designers Set to Study Plans for New York Office," *Baltimore Afro-American*, April 28, 1951, 11.

33. Mary McLeod Bethune to Mrs. Kay Linden, December 15, 1948, folder 1, box 1, series 1, NAFAD; Jeannetta W. Brown to Mrs. Ethel Kreemer, May 20, 1950, folder 4, box 1, series 1, NAFAD.

34. Leipzig, Parsons, and Farrell-Beck, "It Is a Profession," 32–33; Arnold, *American Look*, 77.

35. "See American Women Standardizing Garb," *New York Times*, March 3, 1931, 9; "New York Couture" *Vogue*, April 15, 1933, 33; Arnold, *American Look*, 75–76; Caroline Rennolds Milbank, *New York Fashions: The Evolution of American Style* (New York: Harry N. Abrams, 1996), 98.

36. Lonsdale Sport Clothes advertisement, *Women's Wear Daily*, December 20, 1932, 9.

37. Sandra Stansbery Buckland, "Promoting American Designers, 1940–1944: Building Our Own House," in *Twentieth-Century American Fashion*, ed. Linda Welters and Patricia A. Cunningham (Oxford, UK: Berg, 2005), 112–13; Virginia Pope, "New York: Twofold Fashion Center," *New York Times*, January 5, 1941; Mary Lewis, "Fashion Group Luncheon, July 11, 1940," minutes, box 73, folder 8, FGI.

38. *New York's Fashion Futures 1940*, program book, folder 8, box 151, FGI.

Notes to Chapter 4

39. "20,000 Retailers to See American Style Show," *New York Times*, January 2, 1941, 58; Virginia Pope, "Fashion Futures Opens in Splendor," *New York Times*, January 9, 1941, 25.

40. The success of Fashion Futures inspired other similar events that showcased American design, such as the Fashions of the Times, organized by Virginia Pope in 1942, and New York Fashion Week, organized by the publicist Eleanor Lambert in 1943, both members of the Fashion Group.

41. Adrian, "Do American Women Want American Clothes?," *Harper's Bazaar*, February 1934, 37; Arnold, *American Look*, 100–101; Leipzig, Parsons, and Farrell-Beck, "It Is a Profession," 36.

42. Lewis, "Fashion Group Luncheon."

43. Dorothy Shaver quoted in "Finds Style Centre Here," *New York Times*, April 14, 1932, 18.

44. Tiffany Webber-Hanchett, "Dorothy Shaver: Promoter of 'The American Look,'" *Dress* 30, no. 1 (2003): 83; Marketti and Parsons, "American Fashions for American Women," 93.

45. Lord & Taylor advertisement, *New York Times*, April 17, 1932, 16, emphasis in original.

46. Buckland, "Promoting American Designers," 112.

47. "Fashions America Does Best," *Vogue*, February 1, 1938, 114–15.

48. "7th Avenue Designers," *Harper's Bazaar*, September 1, 1940, 43.

49. "American Designers: U.S. Public Is Getting to Know Their Names and Styles," *Life*, May 8, 1944, 63–69; Selma Robinson, "They Have Your Number," *Collier's Weekly*, March 24, 1934, 24, 33; "New York Couture," 33–34, 96.

50. Virginia Pope quoted in "Virginia Pope Oral History, 1971," 13–16, New York Times Company records, folder 9, box 9, Oral History files, Manuscripts and Archives Division, New York Public Library, Astor, Lenox and Tilden Foundations.

51. Virginia Pope, "Styles by Potter Are Personalized," *New York Times*, February 6, 1944, 39; "Designer Studies Small-Town Needs," January 30, 1944, 36.

52. Robinson, "They Have Your Number," 24.

53. "The Dressmakers of the U.S.," *Fortune*, December 1933, 36–40; "American Designers," *Good Housekeeping*, September 1938, 56–57; Arnold, *American Look*, 180.

54. "Coif-Style Revue Ultra in Chic, Unique in Entertainment Value," *Chicago Defender*, December 30, 1950, 9; "Fashions by L'Tanya," *Ebony*, August 1947, 24–27.

55. "600 View '57 Clothes of Cleveland Designers," *Cleveland Call and Post*, March 23, 1957; "Cleveland's NAFADs to Show Spring Summer Collections," *Cleveland Call and Post*, March 1, 1958; "Designers Talk Shop," *Colored Magazine*, July 1951, all in NAFAD Scrapbook, box 10, NAFAD.

56. Robinson, "They Have Your Number," 24.

57. "Beauty and Four Women," *Vogue*, September 15, 1934, 78–79; Arnold, *American Look*, 83–85.

58. "Best-Dressed Women—and Why," *Vogue*, February 1, 1938, 87; Nora Caroé, "Coming Back to Town," *Good Housekeeping*, September 1938, 60–61; Sarah Comstock, "The Girls Are Marching," *Good Housekeeping*, September 1938, 52–54, 104; Roosevelt, "The Times," 45, 102.

59. "The Busy Woman's Wardrobe Does 24 Hours Duty," *Pictorial Review*, August 1936, 32–33.

60. Arnold, *American Look*, 86; Clifford, "Working with Fashion," 79.

61. "Glamour—For the Girl with a Job," *Glamour*, August 1943, front cover.

62. Marjorie Stewart Joyner, "Irresistible Charm," *Chicago Defender*, January 21, 1933, 15; Helen Woodward, "The Woman Who Makes Good," *Chicago Defender*, August 15, 1931, 15; "Career Clothes," *Ebony*, October 1954, 53–57.

63. Woodward, "Woman Who Makes Good," 15. The column ran from 1931 to 1935.

64. J. E. Smyth, *Nobody's Girl Friday: The Women Who Ran Hollywood* (New York: Oxford University Press, 2018), 200; William Dieterle, dir., *Fashions of 1934*, Warner Brothers, 1934, 78 min.

65. Sarah Berry, *Screen Style: Fashion and Femininity in 1930s Hollywood* (Minneapolis: University of Minnesota Press, 2000), 143.

66. "Katharine Hepburn in a Linen Duster," *Vogue*, May 15, 1933, 60; Smyth, *Nobody's Girl Friday*, 183–84.

67. Pattullo advertisement featuring Joan Crawford, *Harper's Bazaar*, September 1, 1940, 31.

68. Stephen Gundle, *Glamour: A History* (New York: Oxford University Press, 2008), 174–75, 194–95; "Does Hollywood Creates?," *Vogue*, February 1, 1933, 59–61, 76–77.

69. Edith Head quoted in Smyth, *Nobody's Girl Friday*, 189.

70. "Business Girl Modes Created in Hollywood," *Milwaukee Journal*, September 27, 1942, 7.

71. Smyth, *Nobody's Girl Friday*, 190, 196–97; Patricia Campbell Warner, "The Americanization of Fashion: Sportswear, the Movies, and the 1930s," in Welters and Cunningham, *Twentieth-Century American Fashion*, 86; Berry, *Screen Style*, 28–29, 179, 182.

72. Buckland, "Promoting American Designers," 108; William P. Gaines, "Hollywood Snubs Paris," *Photoplay*, April 1934, 78–79, 107.

73. Stephanie Lake, *Bonnie Cashin: Chic is Where You Find It* (New York: Rizzoli Press, 2016), 43.

74. *Sears Roebuck and Co. Catalog Spring 1933*, 14, 33; Warner, "Americanization of Fashion," 84–85.

75. Berry, *Screen Style*, 17, 21–22; Joy Spanabel Emery, "Dress Like a Star: Hollywood and the Pattern Industry," *Dress* 28, no. 1 (2001): 92–99.

76. "Styled in Hollywood," *Women's Wear Daily*, October 6, 1937, sec. 1, 7.

77. Smyth, *Nobody's Girl Friday*, 186–87.

78. Berry, *Screen Style*, 56; Tracy E. Robey, "Depression-Era Movies and Their Bizarre Fashion Show Montages," *Racked*, December 28, 2017, https://www.racked.com/2017/12/28/16790280/mid-movie-fashion-show-great-depression.
79. Smyth, *Nobody's Girl Friday*, 198.
80. Robey, "Depression-Era Movies."
81. McCardell, *What Shall I Wear?*, 156.
82. Strassel, "Designing Women," 41.
83. McCardell, *What Shall I Wear?*, 91.
84. Arnold, *American Look*, 105–7, 113; Milbank, *New York Fashion*, 106.
85. McCardell, *What Shall I Wear?*, 1.
86. Arnold, *American Look*, 180.
87. Warner, "Americanization of Fashion," 81; Daniel James Cole and Nancy Deihl, *The History of Modern Fashion* (London: Laurence King, 2015), 166; Strassel, "Designing Women," 36.
88. Bonnie Cashin quoted in Lake, *Bonnie Cashin*, 59; Bonnie Cashin, "The Contribution of the Designer," *American Fabrics* 23 (Fall 1952): 66–67.
89. McCardell, *What Shall I Wear?*, 18.
90. "Fashions America Does Best," 114–15.
91. "Style Leadership for America Seen," *New York Times*, January 12, 1945, 18; Dorothy Shaver quoted in "What Is the American Look?," *Life*, May 21, 1945, 87–88.
92. Arnold, *American Look*, 112–13.
93. Claire McCardell quoted in Kohle Yohannan and Nancy Nolf, *Claire McCardell: Redefining Modernism* (New York: Harry N. Abrams, 1998), 98.
94. Arnold, *American Look*, 179.
95. Deihl, "Zelda Wynn Valdes," 224, 227–28.
96. "Town Still Talking about Fashion Show," *New York Amsterdam Star-News*, May 2, 1942, 1, 24.
97. Milbank, *New York Fashion*, 100–102; Cole and Deihl, *History of Modern Fashion*, 164, 166–67.
98. Hawes, *Fashion Is Spinach*, 254–55.
99. "Diagram Specifications and Limitations, Authorized Measurement for Daytime Dresses," *Women's Wear Daily*, April 8, 1942, SII10.
100. Cole and Deihl, *History of Modern Fashion*, 202–3; Sally Kirkland, "McCardell," in *American Fashion: The Life and Lines of Adrian, Mainbucher, McCardell, Norell, and Trigere*, ed. Sarah Tomerlin Lee (New York: Quadrangle, 1975), 253.
101. Jessica Daves quoted in "November 19 Luncheon," *Fashion Group Bulletin*, December 1943, folder 15, box 144, FGI.
102. Strassel, "Redressing Women," 92; Arnold, *American Look*, 170.
103. Elizabeth Hawes, *Why Is a Dress?* (New York: Viking Press, 1942), 64–65.
104. Ibid., 104; Michael Denning, *The Cultural Front: The Laboring of American Culture in the Twentieth Century* (London: Verso, 1996), 456–57.
105. Cashin, "Contribution of the Designer," 66–67.

106. Claire McCardell quoted in Yohannan and Nolf, *Claire McCardell*, 7, 73; Kirkland, "McCardell," 235.

107. Strassel, "Designing Women," 42, 44; Yohannan and Nolf, *Claire McCardell*, 41.

108. Beryl Williams, *Fashion Is Our Business* (New York: J. B. Lippincott Co., 1945), 85, 90.

109. For more on the Gibson Girl, see chapter 1.

110. "Be Nifty—Be New—Be Interchangeable," *Harper's Bazaar*, September 1944, 82–83.

111. Bonnie Cashin quoted in Lake, *Bonnie Cashin*, 55.

112. Lake, *Bonnie Cashin*, 60, 96–98.

113. "Fashions America Does Best," 114–15; "Best-Dressed Women—and Why," 87; "For Summer Evenings," *Life*, May 9, 1938, 19; "Shirtwaist and Skirt: Town Meeting," *Vogue*, April 1, 1947, 176–77.

114. Best & Co. advertisement, *Harper's Bazaar*, March 1, 1939, 1.

115. "Promotable Ties for a Gibson Girl Look," *Women's Wear Daily*, August 22, 1947, 8; "Gibson Girl Gives Her Good Name to Many Types," *Women's Wear Daily*, October 29, 1947, 29.

116. "A New Era of Masculine Fashions," *Women's Wear Daily*, January 13, 1933, sec. 1, 3–4; "1933 Inspiration—The Mannish Fashions of the 90's," *Women's Wear Daily*, January 24, 1933, 3.

117. Sara B. Marcketti and Emily Thomsen Angstman, "The Trend for Mannish Suits in the 1930s," *Dress* 39, no. 2 (2013): 138, 142–43; Virginia Pope, "The Tailor-Made Look," *New York Times*, February 12, 1933, 146; Berry, *Screen Style*, 144. The mannish suit of the 1930s was a precursor to the pantsuit of the 1980s and 1990s, which was a symbol for women's empowerment in the workplace.

118. "Trousered Ladies Frequent Street of Stars in Hollywood," *Women's Wear Daily*, January 10, 1933, 41; Marcketti and Angstman, "Trend for Mannish Suits," 139–42.

119. Berry, *Screen Style*, 144–45, 150–51; Marcketti and Angstman, "Trend for Mannish Suits," 142; Lois Banner, "'The Mystery Woman of Hollywood': Greta Garbo, Feminism, and Stardom," *Feminist Media Histories* 2, no. 4 (2016): 84–115.

120. Carol Dyhous, *Glamour: Women, History, Feminism* (London: Zed Books, 2010), 3, 46–47; Gundle, *Glamour*, 188–89.

121. "Marlene Dietrich," *Vogue*, July 1, 1942, 35.

122. Rosalind Shaffer, "Marlene Dietrich Tells Why She Wears Men's Clothes!," *Motion Picture*, April 1933, 45, 70.

123. "This Is the Life!," Kotex advertisement, *Good Housekeeping*, September 1938, 15; Berry, *Screen Style*, 165.

124. Deirdre Clemente, *Dress Casual: How College Students Redefined American Style* (Chapel Hill: University of North Carolina Press, 2014), 35–37.

125. Elizabeth Hawes, *Men Can Take It* (New York: Random House, 1939), 2.

126. Clemente, *Dress Casual*, 58–59.

127. Strassel, "Redressing Women," 175–76.

128. Sylva Weaver, "New Series of Fashions Designed for War Workers," *Los Angeles Times*, May 6, 1943, A10; "Give Civilian Women Workers Streamlined Clothes," *Fashion Group Bulletin*, July 1943, 1, folder 15, box 144, FGI.

129. "At Home in Pants," *Harper's Bazaar*, September 1944, 110.

130. Elizabeth Hawes joined the war effort as a machine operator at Wright Aeronautics and later abandoned her career as a fashion designer and became a union organizer for the UAW. Hawes's *Why Women Cry* (1943) was a memoir of her wartime experience in which she discussed the changing status of women in the workforce. Denning, *Cultural Front*, 456–58; Strassel, "Designing Women," 35.

131. Kirkland, "McCardell," 254; Yohannan and Nolf, *Claire McCardell*, 67–68.

132. "The Pop-Over," *Harper's Bazaar*, November 1942, 54.

133. Helen Valentine quoted in "Fashion from 3 Vantage Points," December 1950, Monthly Luncheon Meeting, folder 5, box 145, FGI.

134. "Address by Miss Dorothy Shaver."

135. Mildred Smolze quoted in "Fashion Personalities Agree We Will Share Post-War Leadership With Paris," *Fashion Group Bulletin*, November 1944, folder 16, box 144, FGI.

136. "Fashion Group Luncheon Meeting, November 17, 1941," minutes, folder 12, box 73, FGI.

137. On the backlash against women and the return to domesticity, see Elaine Taylor May, *Homeward Bound: American Families in the Cold War Era* (New York: Basic Books, 1988); Karal Ann Marling, *As Seen on TV: The Visual Culture of Everyday Life in the 1950s* (Cambridge, MA: Harvard University Press, 1994). A growing body of literature complicates this narrative, most notably Joanne Meyerowitz, "Beyond the Feminine Mystique: A Reassessment of Postwar Mass Culture, 1946–1958," *Journal of American History* 79, no. 4 (1993): 1455–82; Susan J. Douglas, *Where the Girls Are: Growing Up Female with Mass Media* (New York: Three Rivers Press, 1994); Stephanie Coontz, *The Way We Never Were: American Families and the Nostalgia Trap* (New York: Basic Books, 1992). Anna Lebovic demonstrates how *Vogue* served as a site where feminist ideas of individuality and independence were encouraged and propagated throughout the 1950s. See her "'How to Be in Fashion and Stay an Individual': American *Vogue*, The Origins of Second Wave Feminism, and Mass Culture Criticism in 1950s America," *Gender and History* 31, no. 1 (March 2019): 178–94.

138. Cole and Deihl, *History of Modern Fashion*, 209–10.

139. "First Notes from the Paris Collections," *Harper's Bazaar*, April 1947, 186.

140. Cole and Deihl, *History of Modern Fashion*, 210–11.

141. "Resistance," *Time*, September 1947, 14.

142. "WOWS War on New Styles and the Wow Public," *Oakland (CA) Tribune*, 23 August 1947; "Resistance," 14.

143. "Protest Launched on Skirt Lengths on Coast," *Women's Wear Daily*, August 11, 1947, 4; "Southwest Women Protest Skirts Are Too Far South," *Women's Wear Daily*,

August 18, 1947, 4; "Women in Dallas Deride Long Skirts," *New York Times*, August 24, 1947, 24.

144. Lake, *Bonnie Cashin*, 45.
145. "Counter Revolution," *Time*, September 15, 1947, 87–88.
146. Strassel, "Redressing Women," 268–71.
147. "Paris Tendencies," *Vogue*, March 1, 1950, 124–25.
148. "Gibson Girl Is Retailers' Heroine," *Women's Wear Daily*, October 6, 1947, 34.
149. "Gibson Girl Clothes: They Accent Hips and Sweetness," *Life*, August 25, 1947, 113–14, 116; "American Resort Idea—The Gibson Girl Dress," *Vogue*, November 15, 1951, 128–29.
150. On the influence of college students in popularizing casual wear, see Clemente, *Dress Casual*, esp. 54–69.
151. "Real Gone Garb for Fall, Beat but Neat," *Life*, August 8, 1959, 48–49; Linda Welters, "The Beat Generation: Subcultural Style," in Welters and Cunningham, *Twentieth-Century American Fashion*, 158–64.
152. Cole and Deihl, *History of Modern Fashion*, 235–36; Milbank, *New York Fashion*, 179.
153. Lake, *Bonnie Cashin*, 68; Arnold, *American Look*, 195; Milbank, *New York Fashion*, 175.
154. Virginia Pope, "Fashions of Today . . . and Fashions of Tomorrow," *New York Times*, October 11, 1942, SM28.
155. "The American Look," *Time*, May 2, 1955, front cover, 85–90.
156. Betty Friedan, "The Gal Who Defied Dior," *Town Journal*, October 1955, 98.
157. Betty Friedan, *The Feminine Mystique*, with a new introduction by Anne Quindlen (New York: W. W. Norton, 2001), originally published 1963.

Chapter 5. This Is What a Feminist Looks Like

1. "No More Miss America," in *Dear Sisters: Dispatches from the Women's Liberation Movement*, ed. Rosalyn Baxandall and Linda Gordon (New York: Basic Books, 2000), 184–85.
2. Patricia Bradley, *Mass Media and the Shaping of American Feminism, 1963–1975* (Oxford: University Press of Mississippi, 2003), 62; For further discussion on the No More Miss America Protest, see Alice Echols, *Daring to Be Bad: Radical Feminism in America, 1967–1975* (Minneapolis: University of Minnesota Press, 1989), 92–101.
3. Art Buchwald, "The Bra Burners," *New York Post*, September 12, 1968, 42; Helen Lawrenson, "The Feminine Mistake," illustration by Asian, *Esquire*, January 1971, 82.
4. Judy Duffett, "WLM vs. Miss America," *Voice of the Woman's Liberation Movement* 1, no. 4 (October 1968): 4, emphasis in original.
5. Ellen Willis, "'Consumerism' and Women," in *Notes from the Second Year: Women's Liberation; Major Writings of the Radical Feminists* (New York: Radical Feminism, 1969), 72–73.

6. "Miss America Beauty Pageant Protest," Bev Grant Photography, https://www.bevgrantphotography.com/miss-america, accessed January 15, 2021.

7. For more on the politics of fashion in 1960s social movements, see Betty Luther Hillman, *Dressing for the Culture Wars: Styles and the Politics of Self-Presentation in the 1960s and 1970s* (Lincoln: University of Nebraska Press, 2015); Tanisha C. Ford, *Liberated Threads: Black Women, Style, and the Global Politics of Soul* (Chapel Hill: University of North Carolina Press, 2015); Maxine Leeds Craig, *Ain't I a Beauty Queen? Black Women, Beauty, and the Politics of Race* (New York: Oxford University Press, 2002).

8. Hillman, *Dressing for the Culture Wars*, xvi, 62.

9. Ruth Rosen, *The World Split Open: How the Modern Women's Movement Changed America* (New York: Penguin Books, 2006); Echols, *Daring to Be Bad*.

10. Of course, these are not clear definitions, and women did not necessarily define themselves under one label. Many women were members of both NOW and other women's liberation groups, and not all lesbian feminists belonged to separatist organizations. In general, I use the term "liberal feminist" to describe women who were members of mainstream organizations like NOW, and "radical" or "women's liberationist" for younger women who belonged to leftist and radical groups. I define "lesbian feminist" as women who identify as such or wrote specifically on these issues in periodicals.

11. Bradley, *Mass Media*, 81, 84–85.

12. Betty Friedan quoted in Trucia Kushner, "Finding a Personal Style," *Ms.*, February 1974, 85.

13. Hillman, *Dressing for the Culture Wars*, 81–82.

14. Kaye Northcott, "At War with the Pink Ladies," *Mother Jones*, November 1977, 21–28.

15. Bella Abzug quoted in Kushner, "Finding a Personal Style," 47.

16. Gloria Steinem quoted in Kushner, "Finding a Personal Style," 83.

17. Hillman, *Dressing for the Culture Wars*, 65–66; Rosen, *World Split Open*, 196–201; Bradley, *Mass Media*, 48–49; Joshua Clark Davis, *From Head Shops to Whole Foods: The Rise and Fall of Activist Entrepreneurs* (New York: Columbia University Press, 2017), 136–37; Sara Evans, *Personal Politics: The Roots of Women's Liberation in the Civil Rights Movement and the New Left* (New York: Vintage Books, 1980), 214–16.

18. Evans, *Personal Politics*, 214–16; Rosen, *World Split Open*, 196–201.

19. "No More Miss America," 184–85; Willis, "Consumerism and Women," 72–75.

20. "Rita Right on Radical Fashion," *Lesbian Tide*, February 1973, 11.

21. Toby Silvey, "Letters," *Voice of the Women's Liberation Movement* 1, no. 4 (October 1968): 11.

22. Ellen Maslow, "I Dreamed . . . I Took Myself Seriously in My Maidenform Bra," *Up from Under* 1, no. 1 (May–June 1970): 23.

23. Sara Davidson, "An 'Oppressed Majority' Demands Its Rights," *Life*, December 12, 1969, 69.

24. Barbara Falconer, "Are Blue Jeans Mandatory?," *San Francisco Chronicle*, May 3, 1970, 18.

25. Kushner, "Finding a Personal Style," 83–84.

26. Craig, *Ain't I a Beauty Queen?*, 14; Linda M. Scott, *Fresh Lipstick: Redressing Fashion and Feminism* (New York: Palgrave Macmillan, 2005), 270; Georgia Paige Welch, "'Up against the Wall Miss America': Women's Liberation and Miss Black America in Atlantic City, 1968," *Feminist Formations* 27, no. 2 (2015): 72, 78.

27. Bradley, *Mass Media*, 94, 154.

28. Jordan Bonfante, "Germaine Greer," *Life*, May 7, 1971, 30.

29. Judy Klemesrud, "And a Word from Our Leader: Gloria, Our Leader," *New York Times*, March 4, 1973, 84, 87, 114.

30. Richard Boeth, "Gloria Steinem: A Liberated Women Despite Beauty, Chic, and Success," *Newsweek*, August 16, 1971, 51.

31. Scott, *Fresh Lipstick*, 268–69, 297; Bradley, *Mass Media*, 150–54. *Newsweek*, August 16, 1971, front cover; *McCall's*, January 1972, front cover.

32. Liz Smith, "Coming of Age in America: Gloria Steinem," *Vogue*, June 1, 1971, 90–92, 150, 158; Klemesrud, "And a Word," 84, 87, 114.

33. "Gloria in Excelsis: It's the Steinem Look," *Life*, August 11, 1972, 66–67.

34. *Life*, May 7, 1971, front cover.

35. Helen Gurley Brown, *Sex and the Single Girl* (New York: Pocketbooks, 1962), 171–86; Jennifer Scanlon, *Bad Girls Go Everywhere: The Life of Helen Gurley Brown* (New York: Penguin Books, 2010), 103–4, 113–15, 177.

36. Scanlon, *Bad Girls Go Everywhere*, 182–85, quote on 185.

37. Stephanie Harrington, "Two Faces of the Same Eve: Ms. versus Cosmo," *New York Times Magazine*, August 11, 1974, 10–11. Jennifer Scanlon argues that despite Gurley Brown's erasure from histories of second-wave feminism, her views on sexuality and beauty practices, as well as her pro-capitalist approach made her an important voice of the women's movement. Scanlon, *Bad Girls Go Everywhere*, xi–xiv, 98–117.

38. Bradley, *Mass Media*, 144.

39. "What Do You Women Want?," *No More Fun and Games* 2 (February 1969): 11.

40. Dana Densmore, "On the Temptation to Be a Beautiful Object," *No More Fun and Games* 2 (February 1969): 43–48.

41. Andrea Dworkin, *Women Hating* (New York: Dutton, 1974), 113–16.

42. "Rita Right on Radical Fashion," 11.

43. Anne Thompson, "Dress," *Women: A Journal of Liberation* 4, no. 1 (Winter 1974): 24.

44. Kushner, "Finding a Personal Style," 88.

45. Liza Cowan, "What the Well-Dressed Dyke Will Wear," *Cowrie* 1, no. 2 (June 1973): 6.

46. Lawrenson, "Feminine Mistake," 153.

47. "Virginia Slims American Women's Poll 1970," August 1970, Louis Harris & Associates (Cornell University, Ithaca, NY: Roper Center for Public Opinion Research,

1970), dataset, https://doi.roper.center/?doi=10.25940/ROPER-31107583, accessed January 8, 2021.

48. The photograph by Dan Wynn (fig. 5.3) was reenacted many times over the years, and again by Steinem and Pitman-Hughes in 2014.

49. Leonard Levitt, "She: The Awesome Power of Gloria Steinem," *Esquire*, October 1971, photo by Dan Wynn, 88.

50. Lawrenson, "Feminine Mistake," illustration by Aslan, 82.

51. Liza Cowan, "What the Well-Dressed Dyke Will Wear," *Dyke: A Quarterly* 1 (Winter 1975–76), 23.

52. Liza Cowan, "What the Well-Dressed Dyke Will Wear," *Cowrie* 1, no. 3 (October 1973), 12.

53. Linda Buzzell, "The Haircut," *NOW News LA*, 1972, Periodical Collection, SSC.

54. Kirsten Grimstad and Susan Rennie, eds., *The New Woman's Survival Catalog* (New York: Coward, McCann and Geoghegan, 1973), 182; Davis, *From Head Shops to Whole Foods*, 140–42.

55. Ford, *Liberated Threads*, 112–15.

56. "Pacemakers in the World of Fashion," *Ebony*, September 1966, 131–35; "Fashion's Flower Child" and "It was 'Goodbye Paris, Hello Seventh Avenue,'" *Ebony*, March 1968, 56–63; Eunice W. Johnson, "Some Together Black Designers," *Ebony*, December 1972, 184–89.

57. Thompson, "Dress."

58. Vivian Rothstein, "Women vs. Madison Avenue," *Voice of the Women's Liberation Movement* 1, no. 3 (August 1968): 7.

59. Ibid. For a visual interpretation of how "feminist uniforms" would function in a feminist's daily routine, see Cherie Westmoreland (photographer), "New Looks for Spring!," *Branching Out* 4, no. 1 (March/April 1977): 35–40.

60. "Letters," *Voice of the Women's Liberation Movement* 1, no. 4 (October 1968): 11.

61. Hillman, *Dressing for the Culture Wars*, 72; Scott, *Fresh Lipstick*, 289; Astrid Henry, "Fashioning a Feminist Style, Or, How I Learned to Dress from Reading Feminist Theory," in *Fashion Talks: Undressing the Power of Style*, ed. Shira Tarrant and Marjorie Jolles (Albany: State University of New York Press, 2012), 18.

62. "The Woman-Identified Woman," Radicalesbians, 1970, https://dukelibraries.contentdm.oclc.org/digital/collection/p15957coll6/id/771, Women's Liberation Movement Print Culture Collection, https://repository.duke.edu/dc/wlmpc, Sally Bingham Center for Women's History & Culture, David M. Rubenstein Rare Book and Manuscript Library, Duke University.

63. Hillman, *Dressing for the Culture Wars*, 70–71.

64. Susan Walsh quoted in Mary Jean Haley, "What Gay Women Wear," *Rags* 10 (March 1971): 20.

65. Cowan, "What the Well-Dressed Dyke Will Wear," *Dyke*, 21.

66. Rosen, *World Split Open*, 86; Echols, *Daring to Be Bad*, 162.

67. "Notes on Cutting My Hair," *Ain't I a Woman?* 1, no. 11 (January 29, 1971): 2.

68. Ford, *Liberated Threads*, 75.
69. Craig, *Ain't I a Beauty Queen?*, 92.
70. Phyl Garland, "The Natural Look," *Ebony*, June 1966, 144.
71. Susannah Walker, "Black Is Profitable: The Commodification of the Afro, 1960–1975," in *Beauty and Business: Commerce, Gender, and Culture in Modern America*, ed. Philip Scranton (New York: Routledge, 2001), 256, 263.
72. Charlotte Anne Heavirapp, "On the Yin Side: Fall Fashions for Feminists," *Second Wave* 2, no. 2 (1972): 45.
73. "Our Own Feelings about Androgyny by the Journal *Women*," *Women: A Journal of Liberation* 4, no. 1 (Winter 1974): 32.
74. "How Do I Feel about Androgyny?" *Women: A Journal of Liberation* 4, no. 1 (Winter 1974): 33.
75. "Our Own Feelings about Androgyny," 33.
76. Betty Friedan, *It Changed My Life: Writings on the Women's Movement* (New York: Random House, 1976), 138.
77. Rosen, *World Split Open*, 85–88.
78. On political conservative use of fashion, see Hillman, *Dressing for the Culture Wars*, 86–87; Northcott, "At War," 21–28.
79. Daniel James Cole and Nancy Deihl, *The History of Modern Fashion* (London: Laurence King, 2015), 310–11.
80. Nancy Willamson, "The Case for Studied Ugliness," *Second Wave* 1, no. 1 (Spring 1971): 11; Sheilah Drummond, "Hairy Legs Freak Fishy Liberal," in Baxandall and Gordon, *Dear Sisters*, 187.
81. Falconer, "Are Blue Jeans Mandatory?," 18.
82. Hillman, *Dressing for the Culture Wars*, 78.
83. Florynce Kennedy quoted in Kushner, "Finding a Personal Style," 83–84.
84. Mrs. D. E. Wilson, "Back to the Hot Comb," *Ebony*, letter, November 1969, 19.
85. "Letters," *Cowrie* 1, no. 5 (February 1974): 11, emphasis in original.
86. Cowan, "What the Well-Dressed Dyke Will Wear," *Dyke*, 23.
87. Dixie McMills quoted in Haley, "What Gay Women Wear," 21.
88. Maureen Turner quoted in Mopsy Strange Kennedy, "What Does a Feminist Wear?," *Boston Globe Magazine*, December 30, 1979, 25.
89. Bernadine Morris, "Summer's Miniskirt Brigade Leads the Rush to Pants for Fall," *New York Times*, September 6, 1968, 46; Isadore Barmash, "Pants Emphasized as Women's Sportswear," *New York Times*, July 15, 1968, 43.
90. Ed Baynard quoted in Hope B. Simon, "Girls Invade Boys' Shops for Fashion Rebel Look," *Women's Wear Daily*, August 16, 1966, 21.
91. "Wide Ranging Retail Fallout in Unisex Explosion," *Women's Wear Daily*, November 25, 1968, 16.
92. "The New Genderation," *Women's Wear Daily*, August 23, 1968, 1, 4–5.
93. Jo B. Paoletti, *Sex and Unisex: Fashion, Feminism, and the Sexual Revolution* (Bloomington: Indiana University Press, 2015), 51.

94. On commodity feminism, see Robert Goldman, Deborah Heath, and Sharon L. Smith, "Commodity Feminism," *Critical Studies in Mass Communication* 8 (1991): 333–51. Also see Thomas Frank, *The Conquest of Cool: Business Culture, Counterculture, and the Rise of Hip Consumerism* (Chicago: University of Chicago Press, 1997), on the market co-option of the counter culture.

95. Deirdre Clemente, *Dress Casual: How College Students Redefined American Style* (Chapel Hill: University of North Carolina Press, 2014), 58–60; Elizabeth Ewing, *History of Twentieth Century Fashion* (New York: Costume and Fashion Press, 2001), 239.

96. Scott, *Fresh Lipstick*, 293.

97. Caterine Milinaire and Carol Troy, *Cheap Chic: Hundreds of Money-Saving Hints to Create Your Own Great Look* (New York: Random House, 1975, 2015), 9.

98. John T. Molloy, *The Woman's Dress for Success Book* (Chicago: Follet, 1977), 33–40, 49–50, 108–25.

99. Paoletti, *Sex and Unisex*, 38, 56.

100. "The Bosom," *Ladies' Home Journal*, October 1969, 79; "Braless Mannequins Make Fashion Scene," *Daily Hampshire Gazette*, December 30, 1971, 5.

101. Phyllis Battelle, "The Bra . . . Then and Now," *Ladies' Home Journal*, October 1969, 80–81, 154, 156.

102. "FBI Wanted" poster for Angela Davis (1970), 2012.60.8, Collection of the Smithsonian National Museum of African American History and Culture, https://collections.si.edu/search/record/ark:/65665/fd55e759e7383354bf68d11a753a2e96b2a.

103. Marcia Gillespie, "Angela Davis: Black Woman on the Run," *Essence* 1, no. 7 (November 1970): 50–51; Robert DeLeon, "A Revealing Report on Angela Davis' Fight for Freedom," *Jet*, November 1971, 12–17; "The Paths of Angela Davis," *Life*, September 11, 1970, 20D-27.

104. Craig, *Ain't I a Beauty Queen?*, 101–4; Ford, *Liberated Threads*, 1–2.

105. Angela Y. Davis, "Afro Images: Politics, Fashion, and Nostalgia," *Critical Inquiry* 21, no. 1 (1994): 37–45.

106. Afro Sheen advertisement, *Ebony*, March 1970, 39; Raveen advertisement, *Ebony*, February 1971, 22; Royal Shied advertisement, *Ebony*, February 1973, 133.

107. Walker, "Black Is Profitable," 266–69, 274; Ultra Sheen advertisement, *Ebony*, April 1970, 2.

108. Davis, "Afro Images," 37–38.

109. oedipussy tuddé, "Fashion Politics and the Fashion in Politics," *Off Our Backs*, July 1974, 17–18, emphasis in original.

110. Ewing, *History of Twentieth Century Fashion*, 180–81.

111. Diana Vreeland quoted in "Up, Up & Away," *Time*, December 1, 1967, 70.

112. Diana Vreeland, "The New York Collection," *Vogue*, September 1, 1966, 234.

113. Isadore Barmash, "Miniskirts Are Raising Some Retailing Eyebrows," *New York Times*, December 4, 1966, F9.

114. Ibid.; "Up, Up & Away," 78.

115. Barmash, "Miniskirts," F9.

116. Bernadine Morris, "After the Decision to Raise the Hem: How to Live with It," *New York Times*, April 9, 1966, 28; "Seventeen's Fashion Independents," *Women's Wear Daily*, June 7, 1966, 76.
117. "To the Editor . . .," *Women's Wear Daily*, March 25, 1970, 27.
118. Morris, "After the Decision," 28.
119. "Women Got the Vote, Now What?," *Hartford Courant*, May 5, 1968, 37A.
120. Hillman, *Dressing for the Culture Wars*, 16.
121. "Health Aide Casts Vote for Miniskirts," *Women's Wear Daily*, December 29, 1966, 8; "Protests in High Schools," *New York Times*, March 3, 1969, 18.
122. For more on the flapper and the reaction to her styles, see chapter 3.
123. "Legislators Ban the Mini Skirt," *Washington Post*, January 12, 1969, 30; "Students in Cleveland Reject Miniskirts Etc.," *New York Times*, February 4, 1967, 22; "A Miniskirt and Maxihair Story: Schools Reinstate Girl and Boy," *New York Times*, November 4, 1966, 23; "The Mini's Moment of Truth," *Women's Wear Daily*, September 20, 1966, 19.
124. "Fashion Show in the Office," *Time*, August 2, 1968, 58; "Up, Up & Away," 70.
125. "Out on a Limb with the Midi," *Time*, September 14, 1970, 76–81; "The Battle of the Hemlines," *Newsweek*, March 16, 1970, 72–73.
126. Bernadine Morris, ". . . Unless, Like Everyone Else, You're Insecure . . .," *New York Times*, September 25, 1970, 49; "Independent Thinkers Oppose the Midi Lengths," *Chicago Defender*, June 24, 1970, 12.
127. "Out on a Limb with the Midi," 76; Enid Nemy, "Leggy Parade on 5th Ave. Rallies to the Mini," *New York Times*, March 22, 1970, 74.
128. "Battle of the Hemlines," 71D; "Virginia Slims American Women's Poll 1970"; Sara Slack, "The Mini—the Midi—the Maxi—Which Do You Prefer? Harlem Women Pick Their Favorite Style," *New York Amsterdam News*, March 21, 1970, 5.
129. "An Open Letter to All Concerned with Fashion," *Pittsburgh Courier*, March 21, 1970, 21.
130. Enid Nemy, ". . . But Outside, Battle for Mini Continued," *New York Times*, 5 May 1970), 74; Judi Klemesrud, ". . . Or You Belong to One of the Protest Groups," *New York Times*, September 25, 1970, 49.
131. Enid Nemy, "Petitions and Parades: War of Descending Hemline Escalates," *New York Times*, April 28, 1970, 46.
132. Ibid.
133. Nemy, "Leggy Parade."
134. Ibid.
135. Marylou Luther, "Dissenters Say 'POOFF' to Style World," *Los Angeles Times*, March 2, 1970, F1.
136. Marylou Luther, "No Shortage of Long Skirt Foes," *Los Angeles Times*, March 9, 1970, E1.
137. "Dead of Acute Rejection," *NOW Acts*, December 1970, 16, Periodical Collection, SSC.

138. Norma Lesser, "Hemlines," *Off Our Backs* 1, no. 2 (March 19, 1970): 4.

139. Patricia Kent, "Some Hemlines to Fall, But Mini Will Stay On," *Women's Wear Daily*, January 30, 1970, 17; "Store-by-Store Lowdown on the Great Hemdown," *Los Angeles Times*, June 14, 1970, I1; Marylou Luther, "Pantsuits Voted Tops for Fall," *Los Angeles Times*, September 13, 1970, H1, 14.

140. Hillman, *Dressing for the Culture Wars*, 140.

141. Paoletti, *Sex and Unisex*, 41.

142. Luther, "Pantsuits Voted Tops for Fall," 14.

143. Barmash, "Pants Emphasized as Women's Sportswear," 43.

144. Margie Albert, "Something New in the Women's Movement," *New York Times*, December 12, 1973, 47.

145. Susan Brownmiller, *Femininity* (New York: Fawcett Columbine, 1984), 80.

146. Hillman, *Dressing for the Culture Wars*, 19.

147. "The New Femininity," *Vogue*, January 15, 1967, 88; Barmash, "Pants Emphasized as Women's Sportswear," 43.

148. Grace Glueck, "Now His *Is* Hers," *New York Times*, September 20, 1964, SM48.

149. As Jennifer Baumgardner and Amy Richards argue, this approach fell short of instilling radical structural social change, partly because Girlie feminists refrained from traditional avenues of politics and preferred to limit themselves to cultural expressions. Nevertheless, while these young feminists distanced themselves from the older generation of the movement, their emphasis on beauty and fashion, Baumgardner and Richards claimed, was an important addition to it, mostly because it made feminism relevant and appealing to larger audiences. Jennifer Baumgardner and Amy Richards, *Manifesta: Young Women, Feminism, and the Future* (New York: Farrar, Straus and Giroux, 2000), 136–38, 161–66.

Epilogue

1. Debbie Stoller, "Editor's Letter: The Devil Wears Nada," *BUST*, August/September 2006, 6.

2. Jennifer Baumgardner and Amy Richards, *Manifesta: Young Women, Feminism, and the Future* (New York: Farrar, Straus and Giroux, 2000), 80, 136–38, 161.

3. Scholars identify the 1990s and early 2000s as the third wave of feminism, arguing that what distinguishes it from previous waves is its inclusivity, emphasis on intersectionality, and greater focus on the cultural realm. See, for example, Baumgardner and Richards, *Manifesta*; Leslie Heywood and Jennifer Drake, eds., *Third Wave Agenda: Being Feminist, Doing Feminism* (Minneapolis: University of Minnesota Press, 1997); Jo Reger, ed., *Different Wavelengths: Studies of the Contemporary Women's Movement* (New York: Routledge, 2005). Yet, as I discuss in the introduction, and as some of these studies argue, the clear division into waves is problematic and refers not only to generational differences. For more on that, see Leandra Zarnow, "Bringing the Third Wave into History," *Feminist Formations* 22, no. 1 (2010): 110–20.

4. Kristen Stocks, "Skirting the Issue," *BUST*, August/September 2006, 62–66.

5. "Our Outfits, Ourselves," *BUST*, August/September 2006, 55–61.

6. *BUST*, August/September 2006, front cover.

7. According to media scholar Elizabeth Groeneveld, while *BUST* positioned itself as pro-fashion, its approach actually validated rather than challenged the perceived myth of feminism's hostility to fashion. *Making Feminist Media: Third-Wave Magazines on the Cusp of the Digital Age* (Waterloo, ON: Wilfrid Laurier University Press, 2016), 93–94. While I don't disagree with Groeneveld, I see the root of this problem in the failure to recognize the continuity of feminism's pro-fashionable approaches from the early twentieth century, not in portraying all second-wavers as antifashionable, a position many antifeminists embraced.

8. Joyann King, "Chanel Taps Gisele and Kendall for Feminist Protest on the Runway," *Harper's Bazaar*, September 30, 2014, https://www.harpersbazaar.com/fashion/fashion-week/a3773/chanel-spring-2015/; Steff Yotka, "Maria Grazia Chiuri Makes a Feminist Statement at Her Dior Debut," *Vogue*, September 30, 2016, https://www.vogue.com/article/dior-we-should-all-be-feminists-t-shirt-maria-grazia-chiuri.

9. Maura Brannigan, "Proceeds from Dior's 'We Should All Be Feminists' T-Shirt Will Benefit Rihanna's Charity," *Fashionista*, February 28, 2017, https://fashionista.com/2017/02/dior-feminists-shirts-to-rihanna-charity; Emma McClendon, *Power Mode: The Power of Fashion* (Milano: Skira, 2019), 78.

10. *Time*, February 6, 2017, front cover; Robin Givhan, "For Nancy Pelosi and the New Women in Congress, Fashion Was a Defiant Statement of Purpose—and Resistance," *Washington Post*, January 3, 2019, https://www.washingtonpost.com/lifestyle/style/for-nancy-pelosi-and-the-new-women-in-congress-fashion-was-a-defiant-statement-of-purpose—and-resistance/2019/01/03/0f8c2836-0f7a-11e9-831f-3aa2c2be4cbd_story.html.

11. "FAQ," Pussyhat Project, https://www.pussyhatproject.com/faq/, accessed January 17, 2020.

12. Alexandria Ocasio-Cortez (@AOC), "I wore all-white today to honor the women . . .," Twitter, January 3, 2019, 7:39pm, https://twitter.com/AOC/status/1081032307262345216.

13. For examples of women politicians embracing suffrage imagery to promote their agendas, see Cara Kelly, "Hillary Clinton Was a Modern Suffragette in Ralph Lauren White for Historic DNC Speech," *USA Today*, July 29, 2016, https://www.usatoday.com/story/life/entertainthis/2016/07/29/hillary-clinton-modern-suffragette-white-historic-dnc-speech/87694618/; Emily Crockett, "House Democratic Women Are Wearing White—A Symbol of Women's Suffrage—To Trump's Speech" *Vox*, February 28, 2017, https://www.vox.com/identities/2017/2/28/14748562/trump-congress-women-house-wear-white-suffragists; Marisa Iati, "Why Did Women in Congress Wear White for Trump's State of the Union Address?," *Washington Post*, February 6, 2019, https://www.washingtonpost.com/history/2019/02/05/why-are-women-lawmakers-wearing-white-state-union/?utm_term=.b2fd51d2fcc4; Emilia

Petrarca, "Wearing White, Kamala Harris Recalls the Past—And Looks Forward," *Cut,* November 8, 2020, https://www.thecut.com/2020/11/kamala-harris-white-suit-acceptance-speech.html.

14. Givhan, "For Nancy Pelosi."

15. Robin Givhan, "Gabriela Hearst Is Dressing Women for a New Era of Political Power," *Washington Post,* January 17, 2019, https://www.washingtonpost.com/lifestyle/style/gabriela-hearst-is-dressing-women-for-a-new-era-of-political-power/2019/01/16/e8f71b0c-f8d8-11e8-8d64-4e79db33382f_story.html.

16. BUST, August/September 2006, front cover.

Index

Abzug, Bella, 159, 190
Academy Award, 135
Adams, John H., 23
Adams, Mildred, 106, 109
Adrian, 135, 145
African Americans: African-inspired clothing, 155, 169, 171, 175, 179; and the Black Press, 23, 82–83, 88, 92, 96, 130, 133, 169; community, 23–24, 55, 57, 95–96, 98–101, 104, 124, 130, 161, 169, 172; as consumers, 87–88, 98–99, 111, 138, 169, 180; design, 124, 130, 138, 169 (*see also* fashion designers); fashion styles, 24, 67–68, 95–96, 98–101, 111, 138, 157, 169, 175 (*see also* African-inspired clothing; Afro hairstyles); and notions of Black womanhood, 22–24, 55, 82–83, 99–100, 104, 133, 159, 161–62 (*see also under* Black beauty); and politics of appearance, 4, 22–25, 51, 55, 56–57, 96, 99–101, 105–6, 159, 161–62, 166–67, 171–72, 179–80; and respectability politics, 15, 23–25, 46, 55–57, 67–68, 82–83, 95–97, 99–100, 104–5, 159, 162, 171. *See also* Black Power
Afro hairstyles, 171–72, 175, 179–80, 181

American design, 117–22, 125, 126–28, 139, 142, 226n40
American Look, 11, 118, 135, 136, 138, 149, 152, 153, 191
androgynous: look, 94–95, 157, 163, 170, 176, 177, 181; styles, 172–75. *See also* unisex clothing
androgyny, 170, 172
Anthony, Susan B., 35, 36, 210n70
Arden, Elizabeth, 119

ballet flats, 139
Ballets Russes, 59
Baltimore Afro-American, 92, 111
Barthes, Roland, 6
bathing suits. *See* swimwear
Beat fashions, 151
beauty: beauty culture, 22, 154, 160, 162, 164, 171, 180, 189; beauty culturists, 40, 119, 180; belts, 87, 139, 140, 164; Black beauty, 22–25, 55, 99, 104, 106, 133, 161–62, 171–72, 175, 179, 180; emphasis on, 44–45, 49, 50–51, 53–54, 56, 71–72, 118, 186, 238n149; ideal, 13, 15, 18, 26, 59, 69–70, 75, 82, 87, 93–94, 103, 104, 130, 133, 145, 149, 162, 164;

as identity, 52, 54, 56, 128, 134, 163; notions of, 38, 44, 52, 75, 104, 106, 115, 130, 155, 160–62, 164, 171, 174–75, 180, 181, 186, 191, 207n22; as political tool, 4, 21, 22–24, 52–53, 55, 56, 66, 68, 72, 154–55, 157, 162, 171–72, 188; practices of, 102, 154, 155, 157, 163, 164, 166, 168, 188, 189
Best & Co., 127, 142, 143
Bethune, Mary McLeod, 124
bicycle costume, 34, 36–37, 39. *See also* rainy-day costume
bicycles, 10, 15, 35–36, 37, 38, 39, 40, 45
bicycle skirt, 9, 10, 16, 17, 34, 39. *See also* rainy-day costume
Black Power, 155, 157, 180. *See also* civil rights
Blair, Emily Newell, 106
Blatch, Harriot Stanton, 64
Bliven, Bruce, 93
Bloomer, Amelia, 1–3
bloomer costume, 1–3, 36, 38, 39, 43, 64, 77, 196n5, 196n7, 204n87
bloomers, 18, 20, 34, 36–38, 39, 69
blue jeans, 145, 151, 155, 158, 159, 162, 172, 175–78, 187. *See also* denim
bra burner, 155, 161, 166–67, 179, 196n8
bras, 98, 154, 161, 179
brassiere, 98, 99, 102. *See also* bras
Bromley, Dorothy Dunbar, 107
Brown, Helen Gurley, 163, 233n37
Brown, Jeanette Welch, 124
Brownmiller, Susan, 187
Bryant, Anita, 159
Bryant, Lane, 87
Burroughs, Nannie Helen, 24
BUST magazine, 189, 190, 192, 193, 239n7

Cashin, Bonnie, 118, 127, 135, 137, 140, 142, 143, 150, 152
Castle, Irene, 59–60
Catt, Carrie Chapman, 54, 110
Cell 16 (group), 164, 171
Century magazine, 17, 71
Chase, Edna Woolman, 119
Chanel, Coco, 85, 191, 215n22
Charm magazine, 131, 132, 148
Cheap Chic, 178–79
Chicago Defender, 96, 104, 133
Chisholm, Shirley, 159, 192

Chiuri, Maria Grazia, 191
Choate, Constance Astor, 37, 39
civil rights, 24, 99, 155, 157, 171, 181. *See also* Black Power
Clarke, Ida Clyde, 107
clothing: and class, 21–22, 24–34, 44–45, 65, 75, 87–90, 111, 174; and esthetics, 49, 51, 66, 72, 74–75, 136–37; and functionality, 16, 26, 37, 40–45, 60–64, 77, 85, 90, 110–11, 113–14, 129, 130–31, 137, 139–43, 145–46, 170; and physical mobility, 6, 16–17, 19, 34–36, 39–41, 62–63, 85, 96, 98, 100, 110–11, 137, 149; as rhetorical tool, 1–3, 65. *See also* fashion
Coburn, Julia, 119
college students, 10, 34, 110, 111, 137, 143, 145, 149–50, 151, 177, 181, 183; Black students, 23–24, 66–67, 100, 169; White students, 15, 17, 19–21, 46, 82, 112–13, 163
collegiate culture, 18–19, 21–22, 32, 35, 145, 151. *See also* youth culture
Collier's Weekly, 13
Collins, Kenneth, 120
Columbia Pictures, 134
consciousness-raising, 159–60, 169, 171
consumerism: consumer culture, 3, 4, 7–10, 12, 29, 32, 51, 82–84, 88, 154, 160, 168, 193; consumerist ideology, 96, 119, 132–33, 170, 178–79; consumer market, 7, 17, 22–23, 25, 29, 35, 45, 51, 68–69, 78, 86–89, 100, 125–26, 135, 151, 155, 157, 160, 169, 171–72, 183 (*see also under* feminism, commercialization of; ready-made industry); women as consumers, 4, 11, 15, 28–29, 31, 68, 84, 86–89, 92, 107, 112, 114, 115, 119, 121, 126–28, 130, 138, 140, 150, 168–69, 184, 186
Copeland, Jo, 134, 150
corsets, 5, 6, 13, 16, 18, 36, 52, 59, 75, 77, 81, 93, 98, 102–4, 108–10, 114, 115, 145, 150, 179
Cosmo Girl, 163–64
Coty Awards, 142
Cowan, Liza, 166, 168, 171
Crawford, Joan, 133, 134, 135
Cuyjet, Helen Cornele, 124

Davis, Angela, 9, 179–80, 190
Davis, Bette, 133
denim, 145, 146, 174. *See also* blue jeans

Index

Dennett, Mary Ware, 64
Devon, Ann, 106, 108, 111, 112
Dietrich, Marlene, 9, 11, 118, 133, 134, 144–45
Dior, Christian, 149, 150, 151, 153, 167, 191
Draper, Muriel, 89
dress. *See* fashion
dressmakers, 26, 28, 87, 89, 90, 212n113
dress reform, 2, 3, 10, 36, 37, 39, 41, 43, 45, 58, 62, 72, 74, 98, 145, 198n24
Duffett, Judith, 155
Dunbar, Roxanne, 164
Duskin, Nan, 119
Dworkin, Andrea, 164
dyke fashions. *See* lesbian fashions

Eastman, Crystal, 80
Ebony, 175
E. Butterick & Co., 26, 90, 135
Embry, Dorothy Ilone, 99–100
Empire-style, 59, 60
ensemble, 15–16, 19, 21, 24, 29, 44–47, 58, 60, 69, 142, 143, 151, 152

fashion: and conveying political messages, 5–6, 12, 158, 167, 191; and demands for gender equality, 1, 49, 53, 62, 100, 158; democratization of, 16, 28–29, 86–89, 90–92, 140; as empowering force, 4, 12, 16, 75, 115, 119, 122, 140, 157, 160–61, 166, 168, 179, 187, 189, 192; as expression of feminist ideas, 3, 4, 7, 41, 49, 50, 62, 77–78, 105, 114–15, 117–19, 137, 142, 148, 150–51, 161, 185–86, 190–91, 193; as expression of feminist identity, 7, 10, 19–20, 49, 50, 72, 75–79, 155, 157, 160–61, 163, 169–70, 171, 188, 190; as expression of identity, 5–6, 8, 15, 31, 74, 82, 107, 114, 115, 159, 163, 170–71, 181, 193; as expression of national identity, 29, 101–2, 118, 126–27, 137–38; as expression of professional identity, 40, 41–42, 89–90, 130–32, 134, 136–37, 179, 187; and feminist politics, 4, 7–8, 11, 79–80, 83–84, 106–7, 155, 157–58, 173–74, 192; as feminist practice, 5, 7–8, 12, 50, 73, 75, 153, 168, 169–70, 188, 189; as a form of gender critique, 71, 77, 170; and freedom, 16, 34, 46–47, 51, 72, 80, 81, 83, 93, 102–3, 106, 108–9, 112–16, 149–51, 181, 182, 185, 188; and mainstreaming of feminism, 5, 8–9, 71, 79–80, 84, 106–7, 115, 119, 179, 186, 191; meaning of, 5–6, 9, 197n16; and modernity, 13, 16, 22–24, 50, 58–60, 74, 83–85, 105, 115; and political expression, 5–7, 25, 31–32, 34, 81, 83–84, 106, 109, 157, 182, 191–92, 196n12; as political statement, 3, 7, 62, 65–66, 68, 154–55, 160, 166–67, 169, 171–72, 175–76, 187, 191–92, 196n12; as political strategy, 1, 4, 8, 12, 50, 159, 192; as political tool, 8, 34, 48, 51, 56–57, 62–63, 65–68, 79–80, 155, 158–59; as a professional field, 121, 122–25, 135; and promoting feminist agendas, 4, 8, 12, 52, 68, 71, 77–78, 155–56, 176, 187, 191, 193; as a realm of freedom, 12, 93, 115, 189, 192; and a redefinition of gender notions, 4, 5–6, 77, 82, 94–95, 170, 172, 177, 187; and sexuality, 59, 84, 94–95, 103–5, 177–78, 181–83; and shaping attitudes towards feminism, 106–7, 119, 157; and struggles for race equality, 22–25, 57–58, 66–68, 83, 98–99, 100–101, 111, 124, 161–62, 169, 171–72. *See also* clothing
fashionability, 16, 43, 46, 62, 88, 94, 146, 152; as a concept, 4–5, 10, 138, 161, 162, 180, 190, 193; as political tool, 21, 22, 25, 34, 49, 50–51, 52, 55, 57, 66, 95, 155, 174; as a right, 31, 44, 92, 134, 140; and race, 4–5, 22–25, 55, 57, 69, 82, 100, 102, 162
fashion designers, 8, 9, 11, 60, 79–80, 108, 114, 126, 168, 176, 186, 190; Black designers, 123, 124–25, 130, 138, 169, 172; as role model, 117, 127–30, 133, 135; White designers, 58–59, 85, 89, 109, 117–22, 127–28, 134–40, 142, 145, 146, 148, 149, 150, 152, 153, 177, 181, 182, 191
Fashion Futures, 120, 126–27, 226n40
Fashion Group, 117–28, 148, 149, 168, 225n23
fashion industry, 8, 11, 25, 107–8, 119, 126–27, 134–36, 144, 149, 158, 176–77, 179, 183; criticism of, 72, 155, 160, 169, 176, 184; developments in, 60, 79, 86–87, 121, 126; women in, 117–18, 121–22, 123, 124–25; women's relationship with, 89, 113, 114, 148, 158, 162, 168, 184, 185–86
Fashions of 1934 (film), 133, 136
feminism: commercialization of, 176–81, 186; concept of choice 73, 158, 161, 181,

185–86, 188; cultural aspects of, 4, 7, 8, 83–84, 106, 115–16, 119, 120, 157, 160, 162, 185, 189, 190–93, 238n3, 238n149; as cultural style, 6, 78, 84, 107, 115, 176, 190, 191, 193; and dress reform, 5, 72; feminist aesthetics, 77, 118, 152; feminist critique of fashion, 12, 160, 164, 168–71, 176, 196n10; as an identity, 10, 49, 72, 76, 77, 161, 162–63, 185, 190; as ideology, 7, 49, 50, 53–54, 71, 73, 83–84, 115, 119, 155, 158, 160, 176, 188, 195n3; the mainstreaming of, 5, 9, 11, 71, 79, 80, 84, 107, 115–16, 119, 153, 176, 179, 186, 191; movement, 3, 5, 7, 11, 12, 83, 106, 109, 118, 120, 153–59, 161, 163, 166, 168–71, 173–74, 176, 182, 186, 187, 190, 193, 215n13, 224n6, 232n10; and its relationship with fashion, 1–3, 4, 7–10, 12, 46, 49, 51, 71, 79, 157, 166, 188–90, 193; "waves" metaphor, 7, 190, 197n21, 197–98n22, 238n3. *See also* feminists; woman's suffrage; women's liberation
Feminist Alliance, 74, 78
feminists, 7–8, 9, 12, 21, 45–46, 106–10, 113–14, 162–63, 169, 179, 183, 187, 188, 190; as anti-fashion, 2–3, 12, 20, 38, 50, 52, 54–55, 64, 69–70, 77, 155, 157, 162, 164, 166, 174, 191, 239n7; Black, 156, 157, 159, 161, 162, 171, 175, 176 (*see also* African Americans); bohemian, 10, 49, 50, 51, 71, 72–74, 75, 77–80, 190 (*see also* Greenwich Village feminists); "The Feminist" image, 3–4, 10, 14–15, 51, 54, 69–70, 79, 154–55, 158, 164, 166, 168, 180, 181; Girlie, 188, 189, 192, 238n149; lesbian, 156, 166, 168, 170, 173, 175, 176, 232n10; liberal, 156–59, 168, 232n10; radical, 18, 20, 155–57, 159–61, 163, 164, 171–74, 177, 180–81, 184–86, 196n8, 232n10 (*see also* women's liberationists). *See also* feminism; suffragists
the Feminists, 161
feminist style, 5, 107, 157, 168–70, 172, 175, 176, 180–81, 188, 199n26
Fight Against Dictating Designers (FADD), 184
Fisk University, 100
Fitzgerald, Scott F., 82
flapper, 3, 8, 10, 81–82, 105, 107, 109, 113, 115–16, 183, 190; Black flappers, 11, 82–83, 95–96, 98–101, 104, 105–6; image, 10, 80, 83, 85, 88, 90, 92, 95, 102–3, 104, 115, 137, 215n13; and modernity, 81–82, 90, 93, 102, 103; and morality, 100, 103–5; and sexuality, 82, 83, 94–95, 96, 218n61; styles, 6, 11, 82–85, 87, 93–96, 98–107, 110, 114, 115, 137, 183, 215n19; wage-earning, 88–90, 111; and youth, 82, 93–94, 98, 104
flapperism, 84, 102, 103, 104
Friedan, Betty, 153, 158–59, 160, 173–74
Funny Face (film), 151

Garbo, Greta, 118, 133, 134, 144
garment workers, 10, 29, 31–32, 33, 40, 111, 123, 135. *See also* strikers
Garvey, Amy Jacques, 92, 217n53
gender: and Black femininity, 22, 24, 55, 57, 96, 99–100, 159, 161, 162, 169, 172, 175; blurring lines, 74, 94–95, 157, 170, 172–73, 176–78, 187; challenge to notions, 1–2, 15, 16, 18, 52–54, 56, 62, 74, 77, 82, 94, 99–100, 144–45, 154–55, 157, 170, 187–88; critique, 5, 49, 50, 71, 77, 157, 170; demands for equality, 1, 4, 7, 38, 46, 49, 51, 55, 100, 120, 122, 125, 159–60, 188, 192; and feminine appearance, 18, 38, 52–54, 66, 68, 82, 94, 115, 140, 157, 159, 162, 164, 170, 172–73, 183; redefinition of notions, 4–5, 17, 31, 34, 47, 83, 92, 94, 102, 115, 121, 122, 125, 144; and White femininity, 17–18, 31, 52, 54, 56, 163
Gibson, Charles Dana, 13, 17, 18, 20, 21, 35
Gibson Girl, 3, 10, 13–21, 25, 30, 32, 35, 46, 54, 82, 142, 151, 190, 219n73; African American adoption of, 21–25; fashions of, 15–16, 18–21, 24, 25, 45–47, 142, 143, 151, 191, 219n73
Gilman, Charlotte Perkins, 9, 13, 21, 53, 72–74, 207n22
Gimbel, Sophie, 150
Girls/Guys Against More Skirts (GAMS), 184
Glamour, 131, 132, 161
Good Housekeeping, 31, 54
Great Migration, 83, 214n12
Greenwich Village feminists, 10, 49–51, 71, 73–79, 212n121. *See also* feminists, bohemian
Greer, Germaine, 162–63

Index

hair: bobbed, 81, 84, 93, 94, 96, 101–5, 115, 218n58; cutting of, 171; products, 82, 92, 154, 180; short, 52, 55, 69–70, 170, 172, 176; styles, 24, 32, 56, 92, 104, 110, 155, 157, 159, 162, 163, 170–72, 175. *See also* Afro hairstyles
Half-Century magazine, 92, 95, 106
Hamburger, Estelle, 120
Harper's Bazaar, 37, 39, 45, 59, 85, 108, 119, 128, 134, 142, 145, 146, 149
Hawes, Elizabeth, 118, 122, 127, 130, 137, 139, 140, 145, 152, 230n130
Head, Edith, 119, 134, 135, 136
Heileman, Myrtle, 105
hemlines, 6, 46, 59, 60, 62, 84–86, 94, 96, 101, 106, 140, 149, 150, 179, 181–84, 215n19; debates over, 11, 107–14, 186–87. *See also* skirts
Hepburn, Audrey, 151
Hepburn, Elizabeth Newport, 56, 69
Hepburn, Katherine, 9, 11, 118, 133, 134, 144
hobble skirt, 59–60
Hollywood, 3, 11, 118, 133, 134–36, 144, 145, 151, 177, 190
Hopkins, Mary Holden, 81, 84, 88, 89, 90
Hopkins, Mary Sargent, 35, 36, 39
hosiery industry, 86, 107
Howard, Marjorie, 85, 108, 114
Howe, Marie Jenny, 49
Hughes, Frances, 119
Hunter, Juli, 184, 185
Hurst, Fannie, 110

immigrant women, 10, 15, 22, 25, 29–30, 46, 95, 101–2
Irwin, Inez Haynes (Gilmore), 19, 21

Japanese style, 59, 74, 75, 80. *See also* kimonos; Oriental style

Kearon, Pam, 161
Kennedy, Florynce "Flo," 161, 175
Kenton, Edna, 75, 77
kimonos, 59, 74, 75, 77, 78, 80, 212n121. *See also* Japanese style
King, Muriel, 127, 130, 134, 145
Kinkaid, Mary Holland, 54
Kirkland, Sally, 128

L-85 regulation, 139
Ladies' Home Journal, 13, 45, 89, 90, 104, 119, 179
Ladies' World, 26, 28, 34, 37
La Follette, Fola, 52
Lanvin, Jeanne, 85
Lastex, 139
layering, 142–43
League of Women Voters (LWV), 109, 110
LeMaire, Eleanor, 119
Lemlich, Clara, 9, 31–33
lesbian fashions, 95, 168, 170, 173, 175, 176. *See also* feminist styles; unisex styles
Letty Lynton (film), 135
Liberation Enterprises, 168–69
Life magazine, 13, 128, 163
Lily, 1
Literary Digest, 87, 89, 105
Lord & Taylor, 114, 117, 119, 127, 128, 129, 134
Lowe, Ann, 124

Macy's department store, 69, 120, 135
Mademoiselle, 119
mail-order catalogs, 26, 59, 87–88, 168
makeup, 81, 94–96, 101, 102, 104, 155, 159, 163, 164, 170, 172, 174
marching costume, 62–63
Marshall Field's department store, 30–31
Maxwell, Vera, 118, 137
McCall's (magazine), 162
McCall's (pattern company), 90
McCardell, Claire, 9, 118, 119, 127, 136–40, 142, 145–47, 153
MGM Studios, 135
middle class: and fashions, 10, 28, 44–45, 49, 123, 138, 129; notions of femininity, 14–15, 17, 21, 22, 24, 30, 34, 82, 83, 95, 119, 120, 138, 163; and respectability, 22–24, 32, 40, 55–56, 68, 96, 101, 104–5, 130, 133; status, 24, 29, 32, 35, 56, 65, 68, 69, 75–76, 206n12; tensions with working class, 30–31, 32, 44, 65, 163, 174–75
midi skirt, 181, 183–84, 186, 187, 188
Milholland, Inez, 9, 52, 53–54, 55, 56–57, 74, 208n38
Miller, Alice Duer, 62
mini skirt, 155, 158, 162, 163, 174, 178, 181–88
modern woman: Black women as, 23, 24–25,

82–83, 96, 100–101, 159; identity, 8, 31, 50, 72–75, 80, 82, 94, 107, 114, 128, 148, 190; image, 10–13, 22, 50, 52, 56, 78, 81–82, 87, 108, 117, 121, 127–29, 134–38, 142, 148, 162; meanings of, 16, 21, 82, 89, 103, 104, 109, 115, 117, 118, 122, 133, 134, 136, 148
Molloy, John T., 179
Monastic dress, 140–42
Montgomery Ward, 26
Ms. magazine, 166

Nation, 96, 108, 113
National American Woman's Suffrage Association (NAWSA), 52, 64, 69, 206n11, 210n70
National Association for the Advancement of Colored People (NAACP), 68
National Association of Fashion and Accessory Designers (NAFAD), 124–25, 130, 138
National Council of Negro Women (MCNW), 124, 125
National Organization for Women (NOW), 158–61, 168, 173, 185, 186, 232n10
National Woman's Party (NWP), 52, 56, 65, 206n11, 208n38, 210n70, 210n76
Neiman Marcus Fashion Award, 142
Negro World magazine, 92, 217n53
New Left, 155, 160, 181, 182
New Look, 149–50, 151
New Negro Woman, 22–24, 82
New Republic, 90, 93, 112
Newsweek, 162
New Woman: and African Americans, 22, 24–25; and collegiate culture, 18–20, 35; global aspects, 199n3; image, 9, 13–21, 26, 32, 34–35, 38, 40, 42, 45, 46, 56, 82; meanings of, 10, 13–18, 22, 25, 32, 34, 36, 46–47, 80, 143, 199n3; and modernity, 15, 16, 22, 29, 34, 45, 73, 80; and politics, 15, 16, 19, 25, 32, 34, 36, 49, 50, 56, 80. *See also* modern woman
New York Amsterdam News, 138, 184
New York Radical Women (NYRW), 154, 155
New York Times, 33, 41, 42, 60, 62, 68, 79, 111, 113, 119, 128, 152, 162–64, 182, 187
New-York Tribune, 48, 70

No More Miss America, 154–55, 162
nylon, 139

Ocasio-Cortez, Alexandria, 192
Off Our Backs, 186
"one-hour dress," 90
one-piece dress, 58, 59, 62, 64, 71, 75, 77, 143
Oriental style, 50, 59, 60, 64, 74, 75–78, 155, 209n47. *See also* Japanese style; kimonos
Our Bodies, Ourselves, 190

pantaloon skirt, 64. *See also* bloomers
pants, 1, 6, 56, 64, 74, 142, 144–46, 151, 152, 158, 161, 162, 170–79, 186–87, 219n72. *See also* trousers
pantsuits, 138, 158, 179, 187, 229n117. *See also* mannish suit; trouser-suit
Paquin, Jeanne, 58
Paramount Pictures, 134, 135, 136
Park, Maud Wood, 19, 21, 53
Patou, Jean, 85, 89
pattern companies, 17, 26, 44, 90, 92, 135, 149
patterns, 9, 26, 28, 30, 37, 59, 60, 65, 75, 90, 92, 136, 202n54, 212n113
Picken, Mary Brooks, 90
Pictorial Review, 107, 130
Pitman-Hughes, Dorothy, 166–67
Pittsburgh Courier, 111, 184
pockets, 44, 62, 140, 145, 146, 150, 170, 205n113
Poiret, Paul, 58, 59
Pope, Virginia, 119, 128, 143
pop-over dress, 146–47
Potter, Clare, 119, 127, 128, 130, 134, 137, 145–46
Preservation of Our Femininity and Finances (POOFF), 184, 185, 186
pussyhat, 191–92
Putnam, Nina Wilcox, 49, 71–73, 75–77, 80

Quant, Mary, 181

racial uplift, 22, 24–25, 46, 51, 55, 96, 115, 133
Radicalesbians, 170
Rainy Day Club, 8, 10, 38, 40–45, 46, 190
rainy-day costume, 6, 41, 43–45, 46, 60. *See also* bicycle costume; bicycle skirt
rayon, 86

Index

ready-made clothes, 5, 10, 21, 25–29, 60, 64, 75, 86–88, 92, 98, 102, 115, 124, 136, 139
ready-made industry, 3, 10, 28, 44, 60, 82, 84, 86–88, 92, 121–22, 125–27, 135, 136, 138, 139, 145, 151, 152, 176, 182, 201n40. *See also* fashion industry
respectability: and appearance, 15, 16, 23, 42, 50, 56, 60, 66–67, 95–96, 99–100, 115, 158–59, 161–62, 168, 174–76, 181, 183; through fashion, 15, 24–25, 29, 31–32, 34, 46, 55–56, 60, 66–68; and middle-class propriety, 22, 24, 32, 40, 42, 67, 68, 82, 95, 96, 100, 130, 133; politics of, 21, 23, 31, 55, 66, 95–96, 99, 100, 103, 171, 181, 208n35. *See also* African Americans
Rihanna, 191
robe de style, 85, 102
Rodman, Henrietta, 73–74, 75, 76, 78
Roosevelt, Eleanor, 120, 123
Rose, Helen, 135
Rosenstein, Nettie, 121–22
Rubinstein, Helena, 119

Saks Fifth Avenue, 150, 185
Schlafly, Phyllis, 159, 174
Schneiderman, Rose, 29
Sears, Roebuck & Co., 26, 135. *See also* mail-order catalogs
separates, 137, 142. *See also* ensemble
sewing, 6, 9, 23, 26, 28, 29, 42, 54, 75, 86, 88–90, 92, 135, 168, 169
sexual revolution, 82, 163, 178, 183
Shaver, Dorothy, 117, 118, 119, 127, 129, 138, 145, 148
Shaw, Anna Howard, 52, 54
shirtwaist, 8, 9, 13, 15–19, 21, 24, 45, 46, 47, 58, 60, 191; and Americanism, 29–30; and class conflict, 28, 30–31; and mass production, 10, 25–28, 29, 46, 201n40, 202n54; political aspects, 24–25, 31–34, 46; revivals and adaptations, 59, 143, 151; strike, 32–34; working class adoption of, 15, 26, 28–29, 31–32
shirtwaist dress, 143
silhouette, 5, 10, 58, 59, 65, 66, 74, 77, 80, 84, 87, 93–96, 102, 106, 137, 140, 149–51, 174
Simpson, Adele, 119, 128
skirt length, 5, 6, 39, 43, 58, 85, 103, 105, 106, 109, 112, 114, 115, 150, 182, 184–87. *See also* hemlines
skirts: bell-shaped, 13, 15 (*see also* Gibson Girl fashions); circumference of, 6, 58, 62, 139; debates over skirt length, 11, 103, 107–14, 149–51, 183–87 (*see also* hemlines); divided skirt, 38–39, 60, 62–64 (*see also* bicycle costume; bloomers); full, 3, 15, 39, 85, 149, 150–52; knee-length, 6, 39, 84, 93, 101, 112, 140, 174, 179, 182, 183, 186; long skirt, 3, 6, 36, 40, 41, 63, 96, 108, 110–13, 142, 149, 150; as part of ensemble, 15–16, 18, 21, 24, 29, 32, 46, 58, 201n40; as part of a suit, 60–61, 62–63, 143, 179; short skirt, 1, 8, 20, 34, 36, 38–42, 44–47, 55, 84, 94–115, 150, 182, 183, 193, 219n72; skirts for men, 177; wrap, 151; walking skirt, 19, 39. *See also* bicycle skirt; hobble-skirt; midi skirt; mini skirt
slacks, 8, 134, 138, 144, 145. *See also* pants; trousers
Snow, Carmel, 119, 146
sportswear, 6, 134, 136–40, 142–43, 145, 149, 150, 152–53, 177; as design language, 11, 118, 136, 140, 142, 149, 151; and feminist ideas, 11, 119, 136–37, 146–48, 150–51, 152, 153. *See also* monastic dress; pop-over dress; shirtwaist dress
Stanton, Elizabeth Cady, 1–2, 36–37, 54, 190, 205n113, 210n70
Steinem, Gloria, 9, 159, 162–63, 164, 166–67, 190
Stevens, Doris, 19–21, 65, 210n67
Stoller, Debbie, 189
STOP-ERA, 174
strikers, 32–34
Student Nonviolent Coordinating Committee (SNCC), 171
suffragists, 8, 10, 32, 49, 79, 109, 190; Black suffragists, 51, 55, 56–58, 66–68, 69, 208n33; image, 3, 15, 52, 57, 69–71; legacies, 158, 174, 192; use of fashion, 10, 21, 48, 50, 51, 52–57, 60, 62–66, 68, 69; White suffragists, 19, 20, 55, 56, 58, 65, 81, 106, 107, 110, 206n12. *See also* Women's suffrage
suits, 77, 114, 137, 142, 152; dress suits, 131, 134, 159; mannish, 143–44, 175 (*see also* trouser-suit); "suffragette" suit, 60–64,

247

80; tailored, 26, 58, 60, 62, 80, 133, 143–45, 159, 179; trouser (*see* mannish suit). *See also* pantsuits; rainy-day costume
swimwear, 104, 105, 138

Terrell, Mary Church, 9, 23, 24, 55, 57, 66, 67
Time magazine, 153
Tobé, 119, 148
Traphagen, Ethel, 109
trousers, 1, 2, 36, 39, 62–64, 95, 140, 143–46, 170, 187, 196n5, 219n72. *See also* pants; slacks
True Woman, 15
Twiggy, 181

Unique Fashion Club, 96, 97
unisex clothing, 158, 173, 174, 176–78, 181, 191

Vanity Fair, 93
Vogue, 58, 90, 119, 120, 128, 130, 134–39, 144, 161, 162, 181, 230n137
Voice of the New Negro, 23
Vreeland, Diana, 146, 181–82

waistline, 59, 60, 74, 84, 85, 137, 150
Wells-Barnett, Ida B., 24, 67, 210n78
Willard, Frances, 37
Woman's Dress for Success Book, 178–79
Woman's Journal, 109, 113
woman's rights advocates, 1, 16, 21, 36, 38, 45, 50, 144, 195–6n3, 206n9. *See also* feminists; suffragists
women's liberation, 12, 154, 157, 160–66, 179, 185, 188, 198n24. *See also* feminism

women's liberationists, 8, 11, 155–56, 160–63, 168, 172, 174, 176, 190, 232n10. *See also* feminists
women's suffrage: as a beautifying force, 53–54; campaign, 10, 15, 21, 48, 50, 52, 54–57, 60, 62, 65–71, 81, 106, 109, 110; colors, 65–69, 210n70, 210n76; movement, 7, 10, 19, 21, 49, 206n11, 207n24 (*see also* NAWSA; NWP); Nineteenth Amendment, 7, 71, 115, 118; and race, 55, 56–58, 66–68, 206n12, 208n33, 210n67; suffrage parades, 6, 56, 58, 62–69; suffrage styles, 54, 58–65, 67, 69–71. *See also* suffragists
Women's Trade Union League (WTUL), 33
Women's Wear Daily (news journal), 62, 89, 110, 113, 143, 144, 177, 182, 183, 186
working class: and fashions, 25, 28–29, 34, 44, 46, 59, 88–89, 100–101, 111, 130, 138, 143, 145–46, 163, 174, 175, 202n60; and identity, 15, 25, 46, 163; notions of femininity, 17, 22, 32, 82–83, 89–90, 95, 132, 146, 163; respectability, 31, 34, 56, 69, 100, 103; tensions with middle class, 24, 30, 32–33, 65, 174. *See also* garment workers
Wynn Valdes, Zelda, 123, 124, 138

youth, 15, 80, 82, 87, 93–94, 104, 106–8, 112, 134, 151, 162, 174, 177, 182, 183
youth culture, 82, 93, 95, 98, 102, 104, 106, 151, 155, 177, 181
YWCA (Young Women's Christian Association), 110

zipper, 139

EINAV RABINOVITCH-FOX teaches history at Case Western Reserve University.

WOMEN, GENDER, AND SEXUALITY IN AMERICAN HISTORY

Women Doctors in Gilded-Age Washington: Race, Gender, and Professionalization   *Gloria Moldow*
Friends and Sisters: Letters between Lucy Stone and Antoinette Brown Blackwell, 1846–93   *Edited by Carol Lasser and Marlene Deahl Merrill*
Reform, Labor, and Feminism: Margaret Dreier Robins and the Women's Trade Union League   *Elizabeth Anne Payne*
Private Matters: American Attitudes toward Childbearing and Infant Nurture in the Urban North, 1800–1860   *Sylvia D. Hoffert*
Civil Wars: Women and the Crisis of Southern Nationalism   *George C. Rable*
I Came a Stranger: The Story of a Hull-House Girl   *Hilda Satt Polacheck; edited by Dena J. Polacheck Epstein*
Labor's Flaming Youth: Telephone Operators and Worker Militancy, 1878–1923   *Stephen H. Norwood*
Winter Friends: Women Growing Old in the New Republic, 1785–1835   *Terri L. Premo*
Better Than Second Best: Love and Work in the Life of Helen Magill   *Glenn C. Altschuler*
Dishing It Out: Waitresses and Their Unions in the Twentieth Century   *Dorothy Sue Cobble*
Natural Allies: Women's Associations in American History   *Anne Firor Scott*
Beyond the Typewriter: Gender, Class, and the Origins of Modern American Office Work, 1900–1930   *Sharon Hartman Strom*
The Challenge of Feminist Biography: Writing the Lives of Modern American Women   *Edited by Sara Alpern, Joyce Antler, Elisabeth Israels Perry, and Ingrid Winther Scobie*
Working Women of Collar City: Gender, Class, and Community in Troy, New York, 1864–86   *Carole Turbin*
Radicals of the Worst Sort: Laboring Women in Lawrence, Massachusetts, 1860–1912   *Ardis Cameron*
Visible Women: New Essays on American Activism   *Edited by Nancy A. Hewitt and Suzanne Lebsock*
Mother-Work: Women, Child Welfare, and the State, 1890–1930   *Molly Ladd-Taylor*
Babe: The Life and Legend of Babe Didrikson Zaharias   *Susan E. Cayleff*
Writing Out My Heart: Selections from the Journal of Frances E. Willard, 1855–96   *Edited by Carolyn De Swarte Gifford*
U.S. Women in Struggle: A *Feminist Studies* Anthology   *Edited by Claire Goldberg Moses and Heidi Hartmann*
In a Generous Spirit: A First-Person Biography of Myra Page   *Christina Looper Baker*

Mining Cultures: Men, Women, and Leisure in Butte, 1914–41
   Mary Murphy
Gendered Strife and Confusion: The Political Culture of Reconstruction
   Laura F. Edwards
The Female Economy: The Millinery and Dressmaking Trades, 1860–1930
   Wendy Gamber
Mistresses and Slaves: Plantation Women in South Carolina, 1830–80
   Marli F. Weiner
A Hard Fight for We: Women's Transition from Slavery to Freedom in
   South Carolina   *Leslie A. Schwalm*
The Common Ground of Womanhood: Class, Gender, and Working Girls'
   Clubs, 1884–1928   *Priscilla Murolo*
Purifying America: Women, Cultural Reform, and Pro-Censorship Activism,
   1873–1933   *Alison M. Parker*
Marching Together: Women of the Brotherhood of Sleeping Car Porters
   Melinda Chateauvert
Creating the New Woman: The Rise of Southern Women's Progressive Culture
   in Texas, 1893–1918   *Judith N. McArthur*
The Business of Charity: The Woman's Exchange Movement, 1832–1900
   Kathleen Waters Sander
The Power and Passion of M. Carey Thomas   *Helen Lefkowitz Horowitz*
For Freedom's Sake: The Life of Fannie Lou Hamer   *Chana Kai Lee*
Becoming Citizens: The Emergence and Development of the California
   Women's Movement, 1880–1911   *Gayle Gullett*
Selected Letters of Lucretia Coffin Mott   *Edited by Beverly Wilson Palmer
   with the assistance of Holly Byers Ochoa and Carol Faulkner*
Women and the Republican Party, 1854–1924   *Melanie Susan Gustafson*
Southern Discomfort: Women's Activism in Tampa, Florida, 1880s–1920s
   Nancy A. Hewitt
The Making of "Mammy Pleasant": A Black Entrepreneur in Nineteenth-Century
   San Francisco   *Lynn M. Hudson*
Sex Radicals and the Quest for Women's Equality   *Joanne E. Passet*
"We, Too, Are Americans": African American Women in Detroit and Richmond,
   1940–54   *Megan Taylor Shockley*
The Road to Seneca Falls: Elizabeth Cady Stanton and the First Woman's
   Rights Convention   *Judith Wellman*
Reinventing Marriage: The Love and Work of Alice Freeman Palmer and
   George Herbert Palmer   *Lori Kenschaft*
Southern Single Blessedness: Unmarried Women in the Urban South, 1800–1865
   Christine Jacobson Carter
Widows and Orphans First: The Family Economy and Social Welfare Policy,
   1865–1939   *S. J. Kleinberg*

Habits of Compassion: Irish Catholic Nuns and the Origins of the Welfare System,
    1830–1920   *Maureen Fitzgerald*
The Women's Joint Congressional Committee and the Politics of Maternalism,
    1920–1930   *Jan Doolittle Wilson*
"Swing the Sickle for the Harvest Is Ripe": Gender and Slavery in
    Antebellum Georgia   *Daina Ramey Berry*
Christian Sisterhood, Race Relations, and the YWCA, 1906–46
    Nancy Marie Robertson
Reading, Writing, and Segregation: A Century of Black Women Teachers
    in Nashville   *Sonya Ramsey*
Radical Sisters: Second-Wave Feminism and Black Liberation in
    Washington, D.C.   *Anne M. Valk*
Feminist Coalitions: Historical Perspectives on Second-Wave Feminism in
    the United States   *Edited by Stephanie Gilmore*
Breadwinners: Working Women and Economic Independence, 1865–1920
    Lara Vapnek
Beauty Shop Politics: African American Women's Activism in the Beauty Industry
    Tiffany M. Gill
Demanding Child Care: Women's Activism and the Politics of Welfare, 1940–1971
    Natalie M. Fousekis
Rape in Chicago: Race, Myth, and the Courts   *Dawn Rae Flood*
Black Women and Politics in New York City   *Julie A. Gallagher*
Cold War Progressives: Women's Interracial Organizing for Peace and Freedom
    Jacqueline Castledine
No Votes for Women: The New York State Anti-Suffrage Movement
    Susan Goodier
Anna Howard Shaw: The Work of Woman Suffrage   *Trisha Franzen*
Nursing Civil Rights: Gender and Race in the Army Nurse Corps
    Charissa J. Threat
Reverend Addie Wyatt: Faith and the Fight for Labor, Gender,
    and Racial Equality   *Marcia Walker-McWilliams*
Lucretia Mott Speaks: The Essential Speeches   *Edited by Christopher Densmore,
    Carol Faulkner, Nancy Hewitt, and Beverly Wilson Palmer*
Lost in the USA: American Identity from the Promise Keepers to the Million
    Mom March   *Deborah Gray White*
Women against Abortion: Inside the Largest Moral Reform Movement of
    the Twentieth Century   *Karissa Haugeberg*
Colored No More: Reinventing Black Womanhood in Washington, D.C.
    Treva B. Lindsey
Beyond Respectability: The Intellectual Thought of Race Women
    Brittney C. Cooper

Leaders of Their Race: Educating Black and White Women in the New South
Sarah H. Case

Glory in Their Spirit: How Four Black Women Took On the Army during World War II *Sandy* Bolzenius

Big Sister: Feminism, Conservatism, and Conspiracy in the Heartland
Erin M. Kempker

Reshaping Women's History: Voices of Nontraditional Women Historians
Edited by Julie Gallagher and Barbara Winslow

All Our Trials: Prisons, Policing, and the Feminist Fight to End Violence
Emily L. Thuma

Sophonisba Breckinridge: Championing Women's Activism in Modern America *Anya Jabour*

Starring Women: Celebrity, Patriarchy, and American Theater, 1790–1850
Sara E. Lampert

Surviving Southampton: African American Women and Resistance in Nat Turner's Community *Vanessa M. Holden*

Dressed for Freedom: The Fashionable Politics of American Feminism
Einav Rabinovitch-Fox

The University of Illinois Press
is a founding member of the
Association of University Presses.

University of Illinois Press
1325 South Oak Street
Champaign, IL 61820-6903
www.press.uillinois.edu